Stylistic and narrative structures
in the Middle English romances

Stylistic and narrative structures in the Middle English romances

by Susan Wittig

University of Texas Press / Austin and London

Library of Congress Cataloging in Publication Data

Wittig, Susan.
Stylistic and narrative structures in the Middle English romances.

Bibliography: p.
Includes index.
1. Romances, English—History and criticism. 2. English poetry—
Middle English, 1100–1500—History and criticism. I. Title.
PR321.W5   821'.1'09   77-8907
ISBN 0-292-77541-5

To my parents

Contents

Acknowledgments   viii
Note to the reader   ix
Introduction   3
1. Problems of stylistic analysis in the Middle English romance   11
2. Larger structural units: the motifeme   47
3. Larger structural units: the type-scene   103
4. Larger structural units: the type-episode   135
5. Speculations and conclusions   179
Notes   191
Bibliography   209
Index   217

Acknowledgments

So many thanks are due to so many people for their help in the preparation of this study. To Seymour Chatman and Philip Damon, then, thanks for the many hours of discussion and commentary: you have been more helpful in the formulating of these ideas than you can know. To Barbara Babcock, who will find no frogs here, thanks for the dialogue that has taken me beyond these pages.

To my children, Robert, Robin, Michael (and you, too, Tran), my gratitude for your patience and kindness; to Jack Bogan and to my husband, James Blake, each of whom came with me through a different part of this work, my gratitude for your unfailing support.

S.W.

Note to the reader

This study is based primarily on the following group of Middle English narratives. These tales were chosen after a full survey of the poems catalogued in Severs's *A Manual of Writings in Middle English* because of their structural affinities. Not included are the "cycle" tales—Arthur legends, Troy stories, Alexander tales, and so on; these narratives are built on a different structural framework. For editions of these and other romances cited in the text, see the first section of the bibliography.

Amis and Amiloun
Bevis of Hampton
Earl of Toulous
Eger and Grime
Emare
Floris and Blancheflur
Havelok
Horn Child and Maiden Rimenhild
Ipomedon
King Horn
Lai le freine
Libeaus Desconus
Octavian
Roswall and Lillian

Sir Amadace
Sir Degare
Sir Degrevant
Sir Eglamour of Artois
Sir Isumbras
Sir Landeval
Sir Launfal
Sir Perceval of Galles
Sir Torrent of Portyngale
Sir Triamour
Squyr of Lowe Degre
William of Palerne
Ywayn and Gawayn

I have slightly modernized the orthography of quotations in this study by printing *th* for þ and ð and *gh* for ȝ.

Stylistic and narrative structures
in the Middle English romances

Introduction

Linguistics and literary critics

For the last dozen years, there has been a growing interest in the development of linguistic models of analysis and their application to both stylistic and narrative study. This approach to literature began with the Russian formalists and was deepened and broadened by the work of such American critics as Louis Milic, Seymour Chatman, Richard Ohmann, and William Hendricks, and by the French structuralists Claude Lévi-Strauss, A. J. Greimas, Tzvetan Todorov, Claude Bremond, and Roland Barthes.

However, the promise of linguistic theory—that it will provide literary critics with objective descriptions of all levels of the verbal text and that it will expand our knowledge of the text-generating process—has not been fully realized. In almost all discussions of linguistic-based analysis the reasons cited for this failure are the same: the lack of a unified conceptual framework within which a variety of approaches at a variety of levels can be brought together; the lack of a widely accepted descriptive lexicon of common terms; and the lack of broadly based applications of the growing number of theories.

In spite of several notable areas of success—in quantitative stylistics, for example—attempts to apply linguistic models to works of verbal art have not been well accepted by the critic who is unaffiliated with any particular linguistic school and generally not trained in methods of linguistic analysis. There are, I think, three major reasons for this lack of acceptance. One is the fact that most linguistic approaches to literature are still plagued by major unresolved theoretical issues. For example, as John Lipski has pointed out,[1] there is a tendency to apply models designed for sentence analysis directly to larger and less clearly defined units of narrative; as a result, the units under analysis are badly distorted by the model. More specifically, linguistic explanations designed to describe the finer stylistic characteristics of the surface level of the work (syntax, metrics, acoustic features, and so on) generally cannot tell us anything about the shape or function of deeper narrative structures, which do not depend on verbal expression. If we are to develop a whole, unfragmented linguistic approach that will take us from the surface of the text to its deeper structures, we will first have to choose or develop a linguistic theory with a focus sufficiently ample to meet the need for intrasentence and intersentence analysis and for the analysis of larger narrative structures.

Linguistic analyses also fail to influence large audiences because many critics find it difficult to cope with the highly schematized abstractions (often represented in algebraic terms) offered in these arguments. One recent example may suffice:

$$T \rightarrow (\#S\#)^n/TDS$$
$$T \rightarrow TQL\ PROP$$
$$\cdot\ \cdot\ \cdot\ \cdot\ \cdot$$
$$\cdot\ \cdot\ \cdot\ \cdot\ \cdot$$
$$S_i \rightarrow TQL\ PROP$$
$$\cdot\ \cdot\ \cdot\ \cdot\ \cdot$$

etc.[2]

Unfortunately, even the accompanying prose explanation of this description of micro- and macrostructural rules does not help most of us to decode this equation. Confronted by arguments about literature presented in these terms, most readers simply abandon the task, feeling that there is little in this difficult and highly specialized discourse that they can apply to their own studies of the text.

Finally, in almost all of the discussions of linguistic approaches to literature, the actual application—if there is one—to a literary work seems almost to be an afterthought.[3] This arises, I believe, from a tendency on the part of most linguistically oriented critics to work deductively: to develop or borrow a model and then to apply it to (or to impose it upon) an exemplary literary work—one specially chosen to meet the requirements of the model. As a result, the application seems to be incidental to the development of the theory; it frequently appears, indeed, that the writer is more interested in the theory than in its proof. Many readers, unused to lengthy abstract discussions, resent the fact that the literary work is diminished in importance beside the theory that is used to explain it. Further, they may instinctively distrust overtly deductive models and accept more readily those models that appear to have been derived inductively from the texts themselves.

It is clear, I think, that any linguistic-based theory of literature which does not attempt to confront these issues—to resolve its own internal theoretical problems, to use a language and mode of discourse clearly accessible to its audience, and to derive (or at least appear to derive) its explanations inductively from the texts themselves—will not be acceptable to the general literary critic, although it may find a limited readership among specialists.

The Middle English romance

The present study is an attempt to provide a linguistic-based explanation—one which meets the requirements outlined above—for the production and reception of a large group of Middle English narratives, the noncyclical verse romances. These tales, which are presented in a variety of Middle English dialects in manuscripts and early prints dating from the thirteenth to the fifteenth centuries, occur in a number of metrical forms (the four-stress couplet, the tail-rhyme stanza, and the alliterative line). They present us with a number of puzzling questions primarily arising out of the stylistic and structural redundance that pervades every level of these works. This characteristic redundance, in fact, is largely responsible for the modern lack of interest in the narratives and for the current tendency to treat them as unfortunate examples of literary hackwork. More seriously, it has also obscured some central issues in generic study, so that, as one critic has observed, it has begun to seem impossible to build a workable generic definition of this "random and heterogeneous collection" of poems.[4] Although we know that these Middle English narratives conform to a very rigid set of literary and social conventions, we have not yet defined those conventions or described their functions in the compositional process and in the audience's perception of the works.

Genre study, the task of placing a work together with its fellows and searching out the shared qualities and common factors, is clearly a necessary and rewarding prologue to an appreciation of the work's uniqueness. Our modern emphasis on the innovation and individuality of a literary work is often unfortunate, because such an emphasis screens out the relationship of the work to other works and obscures our necessary perception of the fundamental systems of narrative laws which operate across an expanse of time. As Northrop Frye has pointed out, the aim of generic classification is not the sterile pleasure of categorization for its own sake, but rather the clarification of felt "traditions and affinities" so that we can see the work in its proper context and learn to understand it within a larger frame than the one it itself presents.[5] The need to discover the generic principles that order these Middle English narratives has become increasingly clear, because we have begun to be aware that we cannot read the tales properly until we know precisely the degree of their conventionality and what that means in terms of the audience's reception. What we need now, I am going to argue in this study, is a generic description based on linguistic and structural analysis which will not only clarify the formal and stylistic affiliations of this group of narratives, but will also attend to the problem of why this form came into being and what cultural needs it satisfied.

But these Middle English tales and the problems they present are not unique. In recent oral-formulaic analyses of myth, Old Testament historical narrative, ancient Greek epic, and Anglo-Saxon poetry, it has become evident that we do not yet fully understand the processes by which traditional, highly stereotypic narratives were created. Moreover, we have not yet even begun to consider the implications for literary analysis of the fact that many modern forms (the gothic novel, the Western, the soap opera, and so on) are created out of formulaic patterns of speech and formulaic structures of narrative in the same way that the forms we shall examine here have been created. The larger question I hope to open, then, lies beyond the bounds of this study and its focus on one particular narrative form. If the theoretical model I propose here is valid, it can be used to describe a large variety of similar literary phenomena from the earliest epic to the latest soap opera. And further, it can serve as a point of departure for discussions of literary works that intentionally violate or call into question the generic patterns of more conventional forms.

Linguistic and structural analysis: a methodological statement

What I hope to do in this study, quite simply, is to provide a linguistic-based model for the analysis of a narrative genre, a model which derives from two sources—from a careful study of the texts themselves and from an adaptation and combination of two structural models: Kenneth Pike's tagmemic linguistics and Lévi-Strauss's analysis of the deep structural patterns of myth.

The tagmemic model,[6] an infinitely flexible model of analysis adaptable to both small-scale textural or surface forms and large-scale plot forms, is particularly useful because it enables us to bridge the distance between the stylistic surface of the text and the mid-level narrative units of stanza, motif, and scene. Because it is based on the concept of selection from a paradigm of choices and substitution within an established matrix, it has strong affinities with such apparently far-removed literary theories as Vladimir Propp's morphological analysis, Milman

Parry's and Albert Lord's oral-formulaic studies, and Roman Jakobson's description of style as recurrence or convergence of pattern.

Lévi-Strauss's mode of structural analysis,[7] which provides the conceptual foundations for this study, is equally well-suited to my purposes, because it provides us with a means to move from the text—that is, from the deep-structural patterns which underlie the narratives—to the social, political, and cultural contexts that produced them. Unlike formalist or New Critical approaches, then, we are not confined in our analysis to the text itself, and we are free to speculate on the forces that impelled these narratives into being. Although these speculations frequently are difficult to substantiate, they surely bring us closer to the establishment of a series of contexts within which the works can take on a larger significance.

Regardless of whether we are working through tagmemic analysis at the superficial level of style, or whether we are exploring the deepest, most elemental structures of these works, we will be viewing the narrative as a system of relations, the individual elements of which, as John Lyons points out, "have no validity independent of the relations of equivalence and contrast which hold between them."[8] Literary structuralists and tagmemicists alike view works of verbal art as componential systems of opposing elements which depend for their meaning and effect upon the interrelated functions of other elements in the same system. These elements are subject to certain fundamental structural laws in terms of which the whole system is defined. The system is not static but dynamic—that is, a shift in the formal relationships of components constitutes a change in the entire system. No part of it can be isolated and viewed without consideration of its relationship to other parts, because a single element has meaning only in its relationships to other elements, only as part of a whole. Depending on the level of focus, that whole may be a sentence, a stanza, a scene—or even a single work, the work of a single author, the works of a group of related authors, or works that share a generic likeness. We can see that in this perspective the whole is viewed as a set of systems of systems, a group of hierarchies in which even the smallest element is functional and necessary on some level.

There has been no firm agreement among literary structuralists about procedures, but there is in general something that can be described as structural methodology. In structural analysis—including tagmemic analysis—the first requirement is the choice and definition of the basic and minimal unit which is defined as being functionally necessary to the existence of the object. In linguistic analysis that basic element may be the phoneme, the morpheme, or the tagmeme (a syntactic unit), depending on the "level of focus" of the study.[9] In any case the basic unit should be a measure of one quantity that remains standard throughout the study. Furthermore, as Kenneth Pike has shown in his distinction between *etic* and *emic* units, the basic unit of measurement must be internal to the system, based on criteria obtained within it rather than imposed from some other system.[10]

The second requirement in structural analysis is a close examination of the linear sequence in which the basic units are combined and in which they are functionally related to one another.[11] This procedure entails a careful description of the internal rules that appear to govern the particular arrangement of items in a series. In literary analysis this kind of study can be carried out at the level of the work's style or surface structure (as we shall see in Chapters 1 and 2) or at the level of deep structure (as we shall see in Chapters 3 and 4); in either case it is essentially a syntagmatic reconstruction of the elemental units following the sequential order established by the work itself. Rigorously applied, such a syntagmatic analysis can reveal unrecognized patterns of narrative organization and structural coherences and can provide effective guidelines for generic classifications.

But syntagmatic study allows us to look at only one axis of a system of dual coordinates. The final step in building a structural model of any set of phenomena, Lévi-Strauss argues, must be paradigmatic; that is, it must go beyond the simple linearity of the surface order to a deeper structural examination in which the infrastructure of formal oppositions is revealed in synchronic organization. To accomplish this, formally recurrent elements of the system are removed from their diachronic or linear order and restored within a grid of synchronic paradigms that demonstrates the latent similarities and associations obscured in the linear sequence. These restored unities, Lévi-Strauss suggests, are based upon pairs of binary oppositions and are mediated by a third force which contains elements of both. In the narrow sense of the term, this binary structural pattern is a generative structure. As both Lévi-Strauss and Edmund Leach have shown in their studies of myth, the substructural binary pattern (or complex of patterns) is a remarkable source of energy, capable of generating an infinite set of mythic variations, whose surface structures may possess amazing diversity but whose underlying structures are the same. If Lévi-Strauss is right, we should be able to find such underlying generative structures at the deep-structural level of any generically related group of works.

Since the literary work in the structuralist view is considered to be a hierarchy of functional systems, it is possible to begin at any one of several different levels: the textural level of small-scale stylistic forms; the patterned groups of lines organized as stanzaic units; the level of formulaic plot structures. Because the style of the Middle English romance has so often proved to be a stumbling block in the path of prospective readers, and because there I can demonstrate more easily some notions that are crucial to the description of narrative structure, I will begin on the level of surface texture or style. Having examined the syntagmatic patterns of the formulaic style, I will move to an analysis of the linearly ordered patterns of motif, scene, and linked scenes. Finally, I will view the romances as variants of a single mythic structure and attempt to provide some speculations and suggestions about the nature and the source of the generative energy found there as well as its relations to the aristocratic world of late medieval England.

I Problems of stylistic analysis in the Middle English romance

Discussions of style in the Middle English romances have always presented a number of perplexing and fundamental problems. The formulation of critical theories which might help to account for the style of these poems has unfortunately been hampered by a complex of issues surrounding the question of their conventionality, and until that question is satisfactorily resolved, our efforts to appreciate or even understand their style are likely to go unrewarded. As a result of this unsettled state of affairs, the stylistic characteristics of the romance have been considered only slightingly at the very best, and they have always suffered in comparison in one way or another to other literary kinds.

If we measure the style of these romances according to criteria based on the style of such writers as Chaucer and Gower, as we are accustomed to do, it is immediately obvious that the romances display a very different set of stylistic features. These lines from *Amis and Amiloun*, typical of the diction and prosodic patterns of most of the romances, would call down from Chaucer only the tongue-in-cheek wrath of the parodist. In fact, there are no established criteria, medieval or modern, which will help us describe and analyze passages like this one accurately:

> "Thou art," sche seyd, "a gentil knight,
> & icham a bird in bour bright,
> Of wel heighe kin ycorn,
> & bothe bi day & bi night,
> Mine hert so hard is on the light,
> Mi ioie is al forlorn;
> Plight me thi trewthe thou schalt be trewe
> & chaunge me for no newe
> That in this world is born,
> & y plight the mi treuthe al-so,
> Til god & deth dele ous ato,
> Y schal neuer be forsworn." (577–588)

Using the most readily available descriptive tools, we can say that these three- and four-stress lines are repetitive and familiar in the context of this poem and others like it. The style is marked by its redundance in the use of highly formalized patterns of expression, such as stereotyped imagery, common idioms, and conventional rhythmic patterns. It is small wonder that most readers have dismissed the style of the romance as being less worthy of attention than other aspects of the narrative. Even Laura Hibbard Loomis, a sensitive and careful reader, is led to remark that the romances are "pedestrian" in style.[1]

But we dismiss serious consideration of style at our own risk, as recent studies in stylistics have taught us, for in so doing we ignore one of the most psychologically effective levels of communication and inevitably fail to recognize the essential unity of all of the structures of any given work. Style is not a superficial facade tacked to the surface in some absentminded attempt at decoration; it is an intrinsically functional element of the work and of any utterance, a unified product of the author's intention, the author's sense of the audience and their expectations, and the author's attitude toward the subject (making allowance, necessarily, for occasional inattentiveness and confusion about purpose). In its general configurations and relationships, stylistic form mirrors on a smaller scale the larger structural aspects of the work; these stylistic or small-scale characteristics must be taken into account, together with other, macroscopic structural elements of the narrative, before we can understand the structure of meaning of the whole. In this view, the stylistic units revealed in these Middle English poems are seen as the smallest formal units within the larger system of patterned narrative units, the selection and arrangement of which come about in answer to the same formal imperatives which dictate larger patterns of narrative structures. These stylistic patterns, then, can be used to illuminate and explicate other levels of the narrative, and in addition they can provide a clearer understanding of the poet's perceptual mode, both the poet's individual and unconscious structuring of the world and the cultural constitution of experience that the poet shares with other poets of the time and the genre.[2] For these reasons we can no longer afford to overlook or lightly disparage such an important part of such a large number of narrative poems.

Redundance

To even the casual reader, the most striking feature of the style of the Middle English romance is its redundance. As we have already noticed, the two hemistiches which comprise the mostly four-stress lines are patterned, repetitive, and often alliterative, with an added acoustical repetition. They are composed primarily of common idioms which vary only slightly from poem to poem and which may occur within a single poem as many as a hundred times. This redundance serves a vital purpose in the poems. The repetition of patterns insures that the message contained will be preserved and communicated through its many oral performances, each of which provides an opportunity for distortion; and the predictability which is the product of such repetition increases the audience's agreement with the ideas offered in the narrative. Whether this redundance is a product of the requirements of oral composition or whether it is retained in written tradition both because it is habitual and because it is felt to be necessary for one or another reason is not of great importance to us now, although that question will ultimately have to be resolved. The most important and most immediate task is to recognize the functionality of the stylistic redundance of the narratives in our study, to attempt to ascertain in some fashion its level of efficiency among the other levels of narrative discourse, and to understand the reasons for its occurrence in these popular tales.

There are several currently accepted approaches to the redundance of the romance or to its stereotyped style, all of which go beyond the narratives themselves for an explanation of their stylistic characteristics. The prevailing approach is a theory of bookshop composition and extensive textual borrowing, limited by Laura Loomis to a discussion of the Auchinleck manuscript but informally applied by other critics to the whole body of Middle English romances. Under the influence of Loomis's authoritative essay, the romances as a group have come to be accepted as narratives designed to please a newly literate and uncritical popular audience (a reading audience), pieced together in lay scriptoria by literary hacks (or, in A. C. Gibbs's more charitable view, "professional commercial writers") who roughly translated and versified Old French texts in collaboration with their "unoriginal and ungifted" coworkers.[3] The stereotyped language of the poems treated in Loomis's study is the natural result of the collaboration between copiers and versifiers in this medieval stationer's-shop-turned-book-factory, she believes. But while the Auchinleck bookshop theory can account for only a small number of extant poems, it has been generalized to apply to a much larger number of narratives; other manuscript collections (notably the Cotton Caligula A.ii) are considered to have been produced under the same conditions in monastic communities, and still others made for the same purpose by "amateurs of literature."[4] The texts, most of which demonstrate a surprisingly large number of verbal parallels, some extending to whole groups of repeated lines, seem to support the theory that their authors had access to other manuscripts from which they copied great amounts of material while consulting among themselves, as Loomis proposes. This unfortunate inclination to approach all of the preserved poems as mass commercial productions or as compositions which belong to a recognizable manuscript tradition has led us to accept the belief that the stereotyped phrases and verbal parallels, the pedestrian qualities of the style, indicate the influence of one written text upon another and demonstrate that these poets either were afflicted with an epidemic laziness or were lamentably wanting in originality and imagination.

There are serious problems involved here, however. For one thing, while Loomis may very well be right in her supposition that the few romances in the Auchinleck collection were gathered together in the collaborative setting of a commercial scriptorium, there is almost no evidence to support any extension of her theory to the majority of the Middle English romances. Since she has used stylistic criteria to support her argument, it will be necessary to explain why those same features she has noticed in these poems can be found with regularity among most of the other romances, a fact which casts serious doubt on the validity of her suggestion that the stereotyped style is a product of consultation and collaboration. Second, the bookshop theory, while it does offer us some interesting speculations about the history of these narratives and about the probable circumstances of their composition, provides no adequate explanation or analysis of the style itself. It simply employs characteristic features of the style to support an argument which is ultimately extraneous to the narratives themselves. In this view, the redundant style is seen as a kind of accidental and undesirable by-product of a collaboration, a highly disfunctional aspect of the narrative form, which impedes the audience's understanding and appreciation rather than furthers it.

Another proposal, that the poems were composed in writing for oral performance by minstrels who needed convenient copies of these long productions (that is, that the poems were composed for a listening audience) has found relatively little favor, even though the romance has long been casually considered an oral genre. Ruth Crosby, an advocate of the oral-transmission theory, argues that the stereotyped diction which seems to be "common property" among the romance writers "bears evidence of the intention of oral delivery," and in support of her proposal she makes reference to the large body of reliable evidence (both textual and contemporary testimony) that the romances were delivered orally.[5] A. C. Baugh, remarking that there was no fourteenth-century reading audience, notes that the poets "wrote with oral presentation in mind, adopting a style, so far as they were capable of it, natural to live presentation."[6] In this approach the stylistic redundance is seen as a functional element in the poems through its provision of easy mnemonic patterns, both for the performer, who perhaps memorized the narratives, and for the audience, who listened to them under some degree of environmental handicap. Although Crosby and Baugh do not stress functionality, their theory at least allows us to incorporate function in our understanding of the style; for this reason it provides a more adequate explanation than the theory of collaborative composition. But it can be objected that almost all of the literature of the Middle Ages was published by oral delivery, including much stylistically complex and nonredundant poetry.[7] Chaucer's poems were certainly written for oral presentation, we are told; yet they are relatively free of padding and stereotyped language and contain a large number of artfully rhetorical manipulations designed to be understood by what must have been a sophisticated listening audience. Why should the romances be so consistently redundant when other poems, also written for oral publication, are not? The theory of oral transmission of written narratives to explain the stylistic characteristics that we have observed is not fully adequate, although it is more satisfactory than the theory of textual borrowing and authorial collaboration.

Redundance and formulaic composition

There is yet another approach which accounts much more adequately for the dominant features that have so far been remarked. From this viewpoint the redundance is seen not as stereotyped diction and pedestrian style but as evidence of formulaic composition, either oral or written. The repeated phrases and stock vocabulary and metrical patterns fit the definition of *formula* proposed by Milman Parry and used with much success in the study of oral formulaic works. A formula is "a group of words which is regularly employed under the same metrical conditions to express a given essential idea."[8] Parry's approach is structurally oriented; in his view the work is composed of a patterned series of recurring verbal-metrical forms, used by the oral poet to facilitate the extempore construction of a story and demonstrating great internal coherence on all levels of the work. Most formulaic studies have followed his lead, even though the definition of the term *formula* has been modified and refined, and several different critical hypotheses have provided new methods and new assumptions about the nature of the formula.

According to Parry's analysis, and that of Albert B. Lord,[9] the formulaic unit, a composite verbal-grammatical structure which affects both diction and metrical structure, is the basic unit of the oral-formulaic line, and its presence in greater or lesser degree is an indication of the possibility of the oral composition of the poem. As we noted earlier, the question of oral composition is not one which we can entertain at this time; although the formulaic evidence we compile here may strongly indicate that the Middle English romances either were composed orally or were direct descendants of orally composed verse, the present state of knowledge about the link between formulaicness and orality (as Larry Benson has argued)[10] does not justify such a judgment in regard to medieval works. The problem of formulaic composition, aside from the problem of orality, is an important one in respect to our texts, however, for its implications can help to lay the lingering ghost of our misconceptions about the style of these narratives.

At least one critic has already attempted to apply Parry's and Lord's formulaic methods to Middle English materials with significant results. As long ago as 1957, Ronald Waldron opened the question with his examination of sixteen Middle English poems of the alliterative tradition (only one of which, unfortunately, belongs to that group considered here).[11] Although Waldron's results were based on a random sampling and were thus only sketchy, he found enough evidence to enable him to suggest that the alliterative style, as late as the thirteenth and fourteenth centuries, is still essentially an oral style in so far as it manifests a clearly formulaic redundance. While Waldron wisely does not commit himself on the question of whether these alliterative poems were orally composed, he suggests that the poets were at least familiar with oral formulas and that their audiences still enjoyed the conventions of oral style. Since Waldron's article, unfortunately, only a few other attempts have been made to discover the extent to which formulaic habits have influenced the style of Middle English poetry.[12] A formal approach, organized around the methods of formulaic analysis and focused on stylistic patterns, would provide us with the necessary background for a structurally oriented study of style. Such a study, of course, could not resolve the much more problematical questions of oral origin.

Formulaic distribution in the romances

At this point in our discussion a definitive analysis of the formulaic nature of the romances would be useful. In the preparation of this study, however, it quickly became obvious that a computer count, the only reliable catalogue of formulaic phrases, was not possible at this time. Although the computer concordance programs developed for such studies as Joseph Duggan's formulaic index of the *Chanson de Roland* are now widely available for modification and use in similar computer-aided formulaic assessments, the task of readying for the computer such a large number of lines of Middle English verse is a formidable one. In order that the computer may catalogue the formulaic phrases in such a way that the reader has convenient access to them, the orthography of the texts that we possess must be normalized. Since we are dealing not with the inconsistencies of one scribe but with the inconsistencies of dozens from all dialect regions of England, the task seems almost insurmountably difficult.

But the necessity for such a formulaic count still remains, and an estimation of formulaic density based on a hand count, even though it is only a temporary expedient, is certainly better than none at all. In order to estimate the degree of formulaicness along the lines laid down by Parry, without the aid of the computer, I have carefully read each narrative a number of times, noting those phrases which I recognized as having appeared at least twice in the course of a single poem. In order to fulfill Parry's requirement that the word group reproduce a given essential idea, I have counted as formulaic only those phrases which convey the same idea in essentially the same words. The only variations allowed in the phrases are variations in word order (for example, both *"Dame," he seyed* and *he seyed, "Dame"* were counted as belonging to the same formula, even though the order is inverted); variations in person, number, and tense of verbs; and variations in function words: pronouns, prepositions, conjunctions, demonstrative adjectives, articles, interjections. I have not counted as formulaic those phrases which fall into the category of the substitution system, a formulaic system of verbal-metrical patterns into which the poet substitutes alternative words in order to serve various semantic and acoustical purposes. Although these other verbal and metrical correspondences must be considered in a larger analysis of formulaic material and do indeed provide the basis for our later extension of Parry's definition, they do not lend themselves readily to statistical verification, which is our purpose at the moment. It is necessary to stress, too, that the single poem has been used as a referent, both because of the unreliability of random sampling and because of the cumbersome statistical adjustments which must necessarily be made between the size of the sample and the size of the referent.[13] If we were to enlarge the referent—that is, if we were to use several poems or the whole group of poems as the referent for the count (as those who have worked with the smaller corpus of Anglo-Saxon poetry have been able to do), the count would be a great deal higher, because, as we shall see, all of the narratives utilize the same formulaic systems with very few and very minute deviations from the metrical and verbal norm. Because of the limitations of the hand-count method, such a level of formulaic correspondences cannot statistically be demonstrated. It should be

Table 1

Narrative	Length	Stanza-form	Percentage of lines which contain formulas
Lai le freine	340	couplet	10
Sir Landeval	500	couplet	11
Sir Launfal	1,044	tail-rhyme	16
King Horn	1,644	couplet	18
Sir Degare	1,076	couplet	21
Havelok	2,822	couplet	21
Sir Isumbras	804	tail-rhyme	22
Sir Amadace	864	tail-rhyme	22
Sir Perceval	2,288	tail-rhyme	22
Horn Child	1,138	tail-rhyme	24
Roswall and Lillian	885	couplet	25
Octavian (southern)	1,962	tail-rhyme	25
Sir Triamour	1,719	tail-rhyme	25
Earl of Toulous	1,224	tail-rhyme	26
Ywayn and Gawayn	4,032	couplet	27
Sir Eglamour	1,377	tail-rhyme	29
Squyr of Lowe Degre	1,131	couplet	30
Libeaus Desconus	2,131	tail-rhyme	30
Sir Torrent	2,669	tail-rhyme	31
Bevis of Hampton	4,332	couplet	34
Eger and Grime	1,474	couplet	35
Sir Degrevant	1,920	tail-rhyme	38
Octavian (northern)	1,731	tail-rhyme	39
Floris and Blancheflur	1,083	couplet	41
Emare	1,030	tail-rhyme	42

kept in mind, however, that the formulaic count would increase markedly if the referent were enlarged to include all the narratives.

Table 1 represents this formulaic hand count, based on a conservative interpretation and application of Parry's definition of the formula. A number of interesting observations can be made immediately. First, it is clear that the majority of the poems contain surprisingly large numbers of formulas (60 percent of the poems are at least one-quarter formulaic by conservative measurement; 24 percent of the poems are at least one-third formulaic). We should notice, however, that the distribution of formulas in the group is not uniform and that we cannot group *Lai le freine* and *Emare*, for example, in the same stylistic categories. The distribution of formulas ranges from 10 to 42 percent, with four poems in the 10–19 percent category, twelve in the 20–29 percent category, and nine in the 30–42 percent category. The two poems which have the lowest number of formulas, it may be noticed, are also the shortest; in these cases we can suggest that the referent is really too small to provide an accurate measure of the poems' formulaic quality. The gap between these first two poems and the third (5 percent) provides the largest discontinuity in the group; otherwise, the rise in formulaic quantity is gradual, and there are no clusters.

We can now agree that the statistical evidence does indeed support the intuitive observation that the style of the poems is fundamentally stereotyped—or, to put it less pejoratively, the style of the poems is marked to an unusual degree by redundant, formalized patterns of speech, which are the dominant feature of the romance style. A formulaic count, however, in spite of its intrinsic statistical interest and the possibility of its usefulness in comparative study, will not provide more than a general outline of the problem unless a more specific attempt is made to discover the use of the formula and the affiliations of formulaic discourse with other structural levels of the work.

The use of formulaic patterns in the Middle English romance

Duggan, in his examination of the formulas of the *Chanson de Roland*, finds that the fixed phrases that occur in the poem can be divided into two groups: those formulas which furnish essential actions of the plot and are usually appropriate only to certain *motifs* (what Parry and Lord call *themes*) or to repeated specific actions, and those formulas, substantival, adjectival, or adverbial, which can be used without restriction as to the narrative context.[14]

Predicate formulas. Formulas of the first group, what Duggan calls "predicate formulas," are an important formal element of the romances because they are the medium through which most of the narrative action is conveyed. The presence of numerous predicate formulas implies a highly formalized, formulaic plot structure based on repeated action.

Among the predicate formulas, perhaps the most useful is the introduction of speech. It is certainly one of the most frequently used formulaic types (in the *Chanson* it accounts for one out of twelve formulas). Here is a sampling of the speech formulas from *Bevis of Hampton* illustrating how a simple half-line pattern may be variously employed. These formulas occur many times in the narrative, although only two occurrences of each formula are noted here: *"Madame," he said* (97, 135); *"Dame," he said* (153, 157); *"Traytour," he said* (187,

3091); *"Nay," said Bevis* (1011, 1105); *Sche said, "Sabere"* (261, 357); *"Lord," he said* (297, 657); *"But Bevis," he said* (431, 1007); *Bevis answerd* (449, 467); *"Go," she said* (100, 554); *"Sir," said the palmer* (1103, 1115); *She sayde, "Mercy"* (2820, 2921); *"Lordynges," he sayde* (3009, 3051); *And sayde "Felawe"* (3136, 3407) (all these lines were taken from the Chetham manuscript). *Amis and Amiloun* also demonstrates an elementary half-line pattern very similar to that of *Bevis* (and to most of the other romances): *"Sir Amis," he seyed* (352, 361); *"Certes," he seyed* (1027, 1084); *"Brother," he seyd* (1066, 1069); *Than seyd the knight* (1807, 1867). A number of formula patterns are always used at the beginning of the line: *& wepe & seyd* (2171, 2332); *than seyd the douke* (841, 862). Others appear only at the end of the line: *he gan to say* (2083, 1781). But, in addition to these simple patterns, the poet has a stock of more complex, whole-line speech formulas:

& seyd, "So god me spede" (231, 450)

& swore, "Bi Ihesu, ful of might" (662, 878)

"Mi lord, the douke," he seyd anon (784, 1228)

Eft his song was, "Waileway!" (1852, 2130)

The Middle English romances differ markedly from contemporary French *romans courtois* (considered by Duggan to be literary works—that is, composed in writing) in that almost all speeches in the romances, even half-line responses, are introduced by some variant of the verb *to say*, while the rapid-fire exchange of dialogue in the *romans* is achieved without the use of formulaic introductions. The difference seems likely to be related to the fact that the Middle English narratives were produced, orally or in writing, for a listening audience; a reading audience can follow the fast-moving dialogue without difficulty, while a listening audience requires some clue to the identity of the speakers. Compare these corresponding exchanges, for example, from *Guillaume de Palerne*, a twelfth-century French narrative, and *William of Palerne*, an English redaction of about 1350:

—Sire Guillaumes, vo merci.
Tot si com vos avés oi
Et j'ai ci dit et raconté
Et cist baron l'ont escouté,
Ai je souffert et fait por toi;

Del guerredon me fai l'otroi.
—Certes, amis, ainc n'oi tel joie,
Comme se riens avoir pooie
Que vos pleust. —Oil, biau sire.
—Amis, or le vos plaise a dire.
—Arai le dont?—Oil sans doute.
Se ce estoit ma terre toute,
Ja n'en iert riens mise defors,
Fors seul m'amie Meliors. (8273–8286)

"Sertes, sire, that is soth," seide Alphouns thanne,
"Me thinketh ye might be hold to quite me mi mede;
& so I desire that thou [do] yif you dere thinkes."
"Ya! wold god," seide William, "that I wist nouthe
In what maner that I might mest with the plece,
Or that I walt worldes god that thou woldest yerne."
"Yis, sire," seide Alphouns, "so me crist help,
Ther nis gode vnder god that I gretli willne,
As o thing that thou woldest wilfulli me graunt."
"Yis, i wisse," seide William, "wilne what the likes,
Theigh thou in hast woldest haue holli al mi reaume;
I wold nowt wilne a mite worth but Meliors allone." (4725–4736)

The alterations felt to be necessary by the English poet are obvious.
Each change of speaker is indicated formulaicly (and this in a narrative
that the poet claims to be translating, presumably in writing); each
speech begins with a phrase that even in this limited context we can
perceive as formulaic in nature. The speeches framed by these stylized
introductions begin to seem almost ritualistic, part of the larger code of
social response. The language of the *roman* characters is lively and
intensely emotional; by contrast, the language of the Middle English
speakers is carefully measured, stately, ceremonial.

Floris and Blancheflur provides several examples of this effect in
two- to five-line formulaic passages that are typically formalized, the
emotion carefully restrained within the language of social exchange:

Than spake the Quene, that good lady,
"For goddes love, sir, mercy" (143–144, 299–300)

Thus they spoken, and thus they seide:
"Here lyth swete Blaunchefloure,
That Florys louyd Paramoure." (216–218, 264–266)

In this narrative, which is highly formulaic (41 percent of the lines contain formulas), whole groups of lines may be repeated several times. A striking example of this is the formulaic report of a conversation:

> Now euery word he hath him tolde—
> How the mayde was fro him sholde
> And how he was of Spayn a kynges soon,
> For grete loue theder ycoom
> To fonden, with some gynne,
> That feire mayde for to wynne. (713–718, 1044–1049)

The ceremonial quality that we have noticed is due in part to the persistence of such speech habits as the formulaic oath, of which we could collect numerous examples. In its more complex form it occurs as a whole-line formula, usually with an introductory formula. These examples are from the Cotton manuscript of *Sir Eglamour of Artois*, a tail-rhyme romance, 29 percent of whose lines contain formulas:

> The kyng seyde, "So God me saue" (217, 1132)

> He sayd "God yelde you, lady gent" (271, 622)

> The Kyng swore, "Be Christis myghte" (442, 1156)

Another important ritualistic speech phenomenon is the expression of grief. These formulas often extend to three-line verbatim systems and obviously were of great utility to the poet. These single-line formulas, from the northern version of *Octavian* (the Cambridge manuscript), illustrate the poet's narrative omniscience and occasional formulaic intrusion into the story:

> What wonder was hyt, thogh she were woo (255, 343)

> Grete dele hyt ys to telle (205, 1560)

> For sorowe ther hertys can blede (288, 345)

The *Emare* poet has created a fairly complex group of verbatim formulas to handle the many descriptions of grief required by the plot—from single-line formulas:

> Sore he wepte and sayde, Alas (290, 646)

to two- and three-line formula systems:

> Sore he grette and sayde, Alas!
> That ever born y was (772–773)

> Sore he grette and sayde, Alas!
> That y ever man born was (556–557)

> And as he stode yn redyng,
> Downe he fell yn sowenyng,
> For sorow his herte gan blede (550–552, 607–609)

> There was nother olde ny yynge
> That kowthe stynte of wepynge,
> For that comely unther kelle (301–303)

> There was nother olde ny yynge
> That myghte forberte of wepynge,
> For that worthy unther wede. (610–612)

The author of *Sir Isumbras* provides a two-line formulaic expression of grief:

> Thay wepede sare and gaffe tham ill;
> The knyghte bad, thay solde be styll. (91–92, 109–110)

and a single-line variation upon it:

> The lady grette and gafe hir ill (187, 196, 304)

Some verbatim formulas occur in several narratives. This example, which is found twice in *Floris* (255–256, 269–270) and once each in the Auchinleck *Bevis* (1311–1312) and *Guy of Warwick* (293), is very persistent:

> When he awoke and speke myght
> Sore he wept and sore he syght.

Another occurs twice in *Isumbras* (385–386, 769–770) and once in *The Squyr of Lowe Degre* (113–114):

> And oft he was in wele and wo
> But neuer so wele als he was tho

A thorough search of the narratives would certainly reveal a large number of correspondences of the same order.

Just as the preceding examples have to do with formalized speech patterns, other formulas which appear frequently have to do with habits of social activity and ritual. The act of kneeling, for instance, becomes another important action, and every poet has at least one formulaic description, all of which are basically alike: *He kneeled down upon his knee* (*Eger and Grime* 774, 1430); *When he kneeled on his knee* (*Eglamour* 1307, 1315); *Torrent on kne knelyd he* (*Sir Torrent of Portyngale* 133, 205); *he knelde yn the halle* (*Libeaus Desconus* 37, 145). The *Ipomedon* poet has a two-line formula which varies in only one word in the second line (these lines are from the Harley manuscript):

> Vppon his knees he hym sette
> And the kyng full feyre he grette (187–188)

> Vppon his knees he hym sette
> And the quene feyre he grette (903–904)

Kneeling is an act often associated with thanksgiving, another important formulaic action. The most basic of these formulas is a two-verse pattern which occurs in virtually the same form in almost all of the narratives:

> The king thar of was glad & blithe
> And thankede hem mani a sithe (*Bevis* Auch. 529–530, 905–906)

> Than were thai al glad & blithe
> & thonked god a thousand sithe
> (*Amis* 1402–1403, 1438–1439; cf. 1783–1784)

> Tho was Havelok swithe blithe
> And thankede God ful fele sithe (*Havelok* 2188–2189, 2842–2843)

Other systems, although they do not provide verbatim correspondences, are very similar:

> The lord was glad and blythe
> And thonketh fele syde
> God and Seynt Mychell *(Libeaus* 1216–1218)

> King Ardus was nevyr so blythe
> He kyssyd Tryamowre twenty sythe *(Sir Triamour* 1684–1685)

> The emperour felle on kne fulle swythe
> And kyste the chylde an C. sythe
> And worschyppyd God fulle ryght! *(Octavian* Camb. 1168–1170)

While only the first of these two groups is formulaic by Parry's strict
standards, the other passages demonstrate a considerable degree of correspondence. In this instance and in the following examples the rhyme
pattern appears to be formulaic. Here the act of greeting, another
stylized social gesture, becomes a significant action in poems which
invariably end in the dramatic reunion of long-separated lovers or
family members:

> Twenty tymys he dud hur kysse
> Then made they game and blysse *(Triamour* 160–161)

> Either other gan to kisse
> And made meche ioie & blisse *(Bevis* Auch. 3057–3058)

> & gonne cleppen and to kisse
> And made meche ioie & blisse *(Bevis* Auch. 3943–3944)

> Then was there yoye and blys
> To see them togedur kysse *(Triamour* 1681–1682)

> There was moche yoye and game
> With clyppyng and wyth kyssyng same *(Octavian* Camb. 1684–1685)

> Thare was joye to see tham mete
> Wyth clypping and with kyssyng swete
> *(Octavian* Camb. 1390–1391, *Isumbras* 337–338, 697–698)

He klypped her ond kyssed her swete (*Emare* 212)

And klippt and kyst wonder swete (*Floris* 806)

The same kind of ritualization is evident in another series of descriptions, the christening of a child:

And cristned the child with gret honour (*Sir Degare* 252)

They crystenyd the chylde with grete honowre
And callyd hyt Tryamowre (*Triamour* 451–452)

They hit crystened with grete honour
And called him Segramour (*Emare* 505–506)

The battle scenes, as it has been pointed out a number of times, contain a good many predicate formulas. E. Kölbing offers a fair sampling of the many repeated lines and phrases in the introduction to his edition of *Bevis*; I will not duplicate his work here, although many of the correspondences will be noticed in a later discussion of larger narrative patterns. It will be sufficient at this point to say that, because the battle scenes comprise such a large part of the action of the narrative, all of the poets developed a repertoire of formulas to describe these scenes. There are, in addition, a number of other action formulas—leave-taking, riding, arriving, moving into the hall, and so forth—which will not be classified here. A complete discussion of the function of these small-scale units is obviously in order, however, and there is much new and interesting ground to be explored here.

Descriptive formulas. The second large category of formulas, those which can be used without reference to narrative context, are those most often criticized in discussions of style in the Middle English romance. Their usefulness to the poet is beyond question, however, and their presence in the poetry of the formulaic tradition should raise interesting questions about narrative technique, characterization, and scene-setting. Names (often linked with an adjective to fill out the meter of the formula), common nouns, and noun-adjective couples are very frequent in this group. These half-line examples from *Amis and Amiloun*, common to almost all of the narratives, serve to demonstrate the substantival formula (again only two occurrences of each phrase are cited): *that frely foode* (57, 557); *that miri maide* (448, 565); *that riche douke* (97, 229); *that hendi knight* (290, 511); *the gentil knight* (368, 436). And these from *Torrent: that ryche londe* (13, 1991); *kyng and knyght* (21, 947); *bothe knyght and squyerre* (386, 2586); *my*

doughter dere (55, 801); *bone and blod* (113, 1714); *men of armes*
(1706, 1455); *and dragons II or thre* (2300, 2325); *dewell of hell* (740,
1012); *lytyll and mykyll* (750, 402); *less and more* (750, 2585). *William
of Palerne*, the single alliterative narrative of the present study, offers a
number of formulas: *& that menskful Meliors* (3965, 3972); *& William
that worthi child* (409, 656); *& that witty werewolf* (2212, 2239); *what
man vpon molde* (2251, 2490); *the kud king of spayne* (2637, 2642);
with grete bobaunce & bost (1071, 3358); *the realest rinkes of the reaume* (3944, 4321); *and a real roughte* (4276, 4289). It may be objected
that these half-line formulas are too small to be considered. However,
they are complete units repeated often in many different contexts;
usually the accompanying half-line unit is also formulaic.

Purely adjectival phrases do not seem to be quite as common as substantival formulas, partly because the poets do not usually linger on
descriptions. The phrases frequently consist of a pair of adjectives
linked by a coordinating conjunction: *feyer and bryght* (*Torrent* 202,
1145); *styff and strong* (*Torrent* 322, 1491); *feyre and free* (*Octavian*
Camb. 511, 783); *wyde and longe* (*Octavian* Camb. 634, 494); *gent and
fre* (*Degare* 115, 771); *gret and long* (*Degare* 374, 565). Frequently a
whole-verse formula is used adjectivally:

with the white syde (*Floris* 362, 835)

and semely in hys syght (*Octavian* Camb. 42, 234)

and whythe as lylye flowre
(*Emare* 66, 205; *Torrent* 1639; *Octavian* Camb. 1363)

the fayrest oon that evyr bare lyfe
(*Earl of Toulous* 38, 188; *Octavian* 26; *Amis* 1535)

Perhaps the most complex of all the adjectival formulas is this whole-
line formula from *William of Palerne*, which occurs at least four times
in the poem:

How faire & how fetis it was & freliche schapen (126, 225, 393, 1447)

Dependent clauses are often used adjectivally, like these examples
from the Cambridge *Octavian*:

that was so swete a wyght (159, 549)

that ys so moche of myght (1242, 1518)

Much more work needs to be done on the adjectival formulas, since those phrases are very often the only vehicle for whatever limited character analysis the poet engages in. It is obvious through these examples, however, that the characters cannot be other than extremely stylized and typical; the language itself does not allow for individualization.

Adverbial formulas of time, place, and manner are among the most-used phrases in all the poems. In spite of the fact that the narratives demonstrate a bewildering variety of scenes and setting, the artistic devices used for setting the stage are all very similar, so that the settings themselves become part of a formalized chronology and landscape. These formulaic phrases depicting the passing of time are shared by almost all the narratives: *upon a nyght* (*Eger* 53, 970); *upon a day* (*Eglamour* 49, 937); *that same time* (*Eger* 19, 364); *in that time* or *in that tyde* (*Eglamour* 283, 318). The most frequent time phrases, however, are the whole-verse formulas:

Sone on the morne when hyt was day (*Triamour* 43, 709)

On the morne, when hyt was day lyght (*Octavian* Camb. 1309, 1336)

So it byfelle appon a day (*Sir Perceval of Galles* 2141, 1781)

Tyll on the morrow the day spronge (*Torrent* 362; *Havelok* 1131)

Adverbial phrases of place abound: *in that land* (*Amis* 26, 62); *on yche a side* (*Eglamour* 284, 312); *into the toure* (*Floris* 844, 849); *in the halle* (*Octavian* Camb. 740, 1269); *in toun and tour* (*Amis* 9, 63); *in his cuntre* (*Amis* 338, 1723); *ouer mures & muntaynes* (*William* 2619, 3507); *over dales & downes* (*William* 2715, 2903). Adverbial phrases of manner are also common: *with gret honour* (*Emare* 145, 179); *with gret pryde* (*Octavian* Camb. 560, 737); *withouten duelling* (*Amis* 496, 673); *fulle hastyly* (*Octavian* Camb. 362, 850).

In addition, there are the numerous minstrel tags, phrases which are directed by the minstrel to the audience. These formulas from *Amis and Amiloun* are typical: *y understond* (25, 62); *as y yow hyght* (37, 901); *without lesyng* (42, 649); *as y yow tel in mi talking* (39, 484); *now hende herkeneth* (280, 1189).

This brief review, of course, represents only a sampling of the formulas available to the composer of romance. The figures in Table 1 and the discussion here are meant to suggest a set of criteria relevant to the style of these particular poems rather than to provide a definitive analysis of them. There are, however, a number of difficulties in the methodology I have followed here and in the assumptions on which it is based; before we can undertake any further discussion of the implications of formulaic style, we need to view the whole issue in light of more recent studies of the formula as a kind of mental template in the mind of the poet, a pattern-making device which generates a series of derivative forms.

Formulaic pattern: a broader interpretation

As we observed earlier, the formula is a composite structural unit, a verbal pattern which fulfills a metrical requirement. A strict interpretation of Parry's original definition insists on the actual verbatim coincidence of both verbal and metrical patterns (like that in most of the phrases listed in the preceding section) and relies on the literal repetition of the phrase as the indication of formulaic diction. James Russo argues, however, that this requirement for the definition of formula is "unnecessarily strict"[15] and points out that it is one which Parry himself found severely limiting. Parry writes: "We are taking up the problem of the Homeric formulas from the side of the repetitions, but only because it is easier to recognize a formula if we find it used a second or third time . . . but there are more general types of formulas, and one could make no greater mistake than to limit the formulaic element to what is underlined [to indicate its verbatim repetition]."[16] Critics other than Russo are concerned with the difficulty of determining the differences between formulaic correspondence and other kinds of verbal-metrical correspondences, many of which demonstrate an impressive degree of formulaic repetitions without being formulaic by the strict *ipsissima verba* requirement. "In an array of phrases which are progressively different from one another in various ways," Michael Nagler asks, "which is a formula, which a modification of the formula, and which no formula at all?"[17]

Lexical substitution systems. The redefinition of more general types of formulas, as Parry has suggested, attempts to remedy this inadequacy by providing for greater variation in the verbal component of the verbal-metrical unit and by establishing formal requirements (metrical requirements) which alone constitute the formula. In this view, a much wider range of alternative verbal-metrical correspondences are seen to fulfill the formulaic requirement. This second, more comprehensive structuring of the formulaic system can be shown to add greatly to our knowledge of formulaic construction in the romances; at the same time, it enables us to account much more adequately for those verbal and metrical correspondences which do not fit into the strict interpretation of the formula but which may be even more important as a compositional device than the fixed formula.

Parry himself devised a system of alternate (rather than identical) choices made by the poet, all of which fit the same metrical structure and mean approximately the same thing. This substitution system (which he saw as existing apart from and in addition to the fixed-pattern formulaic system) provides an explanation of many of the verbal-metrical correspondences we find in the romances. For example, these three substitution systems from *Amis and Amiloun*, two simple and one rather more complex, demonstrate the poet's ability to vary the acoustical patterns of a twelve-line stanza by altering elements of the line and yet without altering the felt formulaic meaning of the whole phrase:

1.   with $\left\{\begin{array}{l}\text{lowreand}\\ \text{mornand}\\ \text{reweli}\end{array}\right\}$ cheer

2. $\left.\begin{array}{l}\text{blithe}\\ \text{glad}\\ \text{eger}\end{array}\right\}$ of mode

3. (al thus) in $\left\{\begin{array}{l}\text{romaunce}\\ \text{boke}\\ \text{gest}\end{array}\right.$ $\left\{\begin{array}{l}\text{as we say}\\ \text{as we tell}\\ \text{as it is told}\\ \text{as (so) we rede}\\ \text{as ye may here}\\ \text{rede we}\\ \text{to rede it is gret rewthe}\end{array}\right.$ [18]

In the first two examples the poet substitutes adjectives based on two-syllable and one-syllable requirements; in the third pattern the line becomes extremely versatile and forms one of the more useful patterns of the poem. The scheme can be used as a three-stress line, designed to fit the metrical demand of the *cauda* (*in gest as it is told, in romance as we rede*), where it most frequently appears. And the addition of the phrase *al thus* at the beginning of the line allows the poet to convert the formula into a four-stress line. The variation in rhyme words (*tell, rede, told, here, say, we, rewthe*) offers great acoustical flexibility within the framework of a fairly difficult stanza form and a rather limited sequence of rhymes.

Another system shared by a number of poets provides an example of the possible uses to which a common phrase may be put. These lines are not strictly formulaic by Parry's definition; yet their lexical and metrical correspondences are obvious. This pattern comes from the Cotton *Eglamour*:

yf $\begin{cases} \text{he} \\ \text{she} \\ \text{ye} \\ \text{thou} \end{cases}$ were neuer so $\begin{cases} \text{nobyll a knyght (727)} \\ \text{fayr ne whyte (811)} \\ \text{kene (1125)} \\ \text{prest (666)} \end{cases}$

yf that he rode never so fast (388)

The *Eger* poet duplicates one of the lines from *Eglamour* and also provides a great deal of variation in the system:

giff that he rode never so fast (407)

$\begin{cases} \text{the lady} \\ \text{Grime} \\ \text{Palyas} \end{cases}$ was never $\begin{cases} \text{soe sounde (1196)} \\ \text{so sore in all his day (821)} \\ \text{more glad and blythe (1289)} \end{cases}$

But I heard never so sweet playing (271)

I sleeped never halfe soe soft (262)

The poet even assembles a two-verse series based on this *never . . . so* system, extended by a *nor yet so* phrase:

For that man was never soe well cladd
Nor yett soe doughtye in armes dread (87–88)

That man was never soe wise nor worthye
Nor yett soe cuning proved in clergye (349–350)

The author of the couplet version of *Ipomedon* possesses a very similar system:

They saw never so goodley a man
Ne so light, ne so glad
Ne non that so rich atyre had (306–308)

Examples of the same formulaic pattern can be found in almost all of the narratives:

Ac wer he neuer so strong a man

And he were neuer so blythe of mode

Sir Isumbras was neuer so fayne

But neuer so wele, als he was tho

Me ne fil neuer swich a cas

The abbot was never so gladd

The knyght was never so sore aferd[19]

In these examples, which are relatively close to Parry's definition of the formula, the artificiality of the distinction between the substitution system and a fixed formula becomes readily apparent. The only requirement necessary to convert a member of one of these substitution sets into a formula, under the strict Parryian definition, is that it be found to occur verbatim twice in the same poem. But both systems operate under the same set of requirements, and, more important, can be shown to have the same genesis in the poet's mind. While we may find the distinction useful in tabulating formulaic material and in establishing a statistical survey (like the limited one presented earlier) to provide guidelines for study, we should not rely heavily upon it for a complete assessment of the formulaic quality of a narrative.

Syntactical-metrical systems. There are a number of verbal-metrical correspondences which do not fall even into the wider category of Parry's substitution system, and some other account must be made of them. These are the syntactical-metrical correspondences which do not depend on lexical repetition. In one sense, the test of syntactical correspondence is much more revealing than that of lexical correspondence, because the line structure is firm enough to maintain the pattern (both metrical and syntactical) while there is a great deal of variation permitted in the choice of terms which are seen to fill out the structure. It is the syntactical-metrical pattern here which is formulaic, and each individual occurrence is only a single manifestation of that basic pattern. We will consider a few examples taken from *Earl of Toulous* out of the many in other narratives.

First, there are the usual simple patterns like the following one, syntactically balanced on either side of a conjunction (*he was a* ADJECTIVE + NOUN *and a* ADJECTIVE):

He was a bolde man and a stowt (16)

He was an hardy man and a stronge (31)

He was a fayre man and an hye (994)

He was a feyre chylde and a bolde (709)

Compare these lines from *Isumbras*:

He was mekill man and lange (13)

He was large man and hegh (16)

He was bothe fayre man and heghe (616)

For he es bothe large and heghe (244)

Although the lexical items display some variation (*man* and *childe* are substitutable; other options would have been available if the line had been used in other contexts), the syntactical-metrical form remains constant. A more complex pattern, a two-stress subject-object-verb arrangement introduced by another two-stress prepositional or adverbial phrase and fulfilling a metrical pattern that requires a masculine ending to the line, is common in *Toulous*:

At a brygge they hym met
Wyth harde strokes they hym besett (436–440)

Thorow the body he can hym bere (773)

The object in the second half of the line may be reflexive:

To soper they can them dyght (695)

On the morne he can hym dyght (317)

In other patterns in the poem, the second half of the line is often filled out by a prepositional phrase which functions adverbially, modifying the verb in the first half of the line (often a *to say* verb):

He spake to them wyth sterne stevyn (73)

When sche spake wyth mylde stevyn (349)

The erl answeryd wyth wordys hende (229)

The marchand seyd wordys hende (955)

The earl answeryd wyth wordys hende (229)

To brynge the wyth mylde mod (1112)

And armyd hym wyth mekill pride (1106)

Another common phrase, based upon a stable comparative-adverb pattern but with considerable verbal variation, occurs only in the three-stress *cauda* of this tail-rhyme poem:

So boldely they can abyde (129)

So gretly can he grylle (165)

So lovely sche was of chere (363)

So feyre sche was of blee (351)

So wyght he was yn were (96)

So stronge he was yn fyght (18)

So grete was ther raunsome (174)

Perhaps the most common pattern in *Toulous*, however, the one which displays the most lexical divergence within an unvarying syntactic-metric pattern, is the two-stress relative clause dependent on a noun in the first half of the line:

The fayrest oon that evyr bare lyfe (38)

The fayrest woman that is on lyfe (188)

Fourty floranse, that ben bryght (386)

Wyth swerdys and axes that were gode (91)

Betwene the erlys that were stowte (347)

He chose two knyghtys that were hym dere (481)

In alle thinge that thou can (461)

And thankyd god that syttyth in trone (458)

For the love of god that sytteth above (644)

A closely related pattern demonstrates added complexity, with a second pattern (*all the* NOUN *that ever* NOUN/PRONOUN + VERB) embedded in the first:

Of all the syghtys that ever he sye (331)

For all the gode that evyr was wroght (389)

All the golde that evyr god made (386)

The same form is often expanded to encompass a two-verse sequence in which the relative clause occupies a whole line to itself (invariably the *cauda*) and modifies a noun in the preceding line:

For to make the lady glade
That was bothe gentyll and small (768–769)

Many a doghty knyght there was levyd
That was wylde and wode (107–108)

Many a wyfe may sytt and wepe
That was wonte softe to slepe (103–104)

He longyd hys feyre lady to see
That was so swete a wyght (839–840)

Then schalt thou see hur at thy wylle,
That ys so worthyly wrought (308–309)

And askyd gode for god allmyght
That dyed on the tree (383–384)

And sithen he thanked god of hys grace
That syttyth in trynyte (119–120)

For sche wolde not do oure wyll
That worthy ys in wonnys (1137–1138)

The examples of these three related relative-clause systems, varying in complexity from a half-line to a whole line to a two-line pattern, with one or more additional embedded patterns, suggest that it is not verbatim lexical and metrical correspondence which constitutes formulaic language but syntactical and metrical correspondence (which may or may not involve verbal correspondence as well).

This approach in its general outline has already been adopted by several critics who have urged that Parry's definition of the formula and his concept of the substitution system be revised to admit a less rigid set of criteria; in their view, the syntactical-metrical patterns are seen as forms into which the poet inserts content. For example, Ronald Waldron notes: "The grammatical or syntactical structure of a formulaic system is, naturally, always fairly constant. [These systems] consist of 'empty' rhythmical-syntactical 'moulds' ready to be filled with meaning."[20] Unfortunately, this attempt to resolve the difficulty has only erected an uncomfortable and unnecessary partition between form and content (and meaning), and has established a dichotomous unit in which constant form and variable content are separable and separated. But as I have already noted, the formula must be viewed as a composite unit that embraces both form and content, neither aspect of which can exist without the other. We can here use Ferdinand de Saussure's famous comparison of sound and sense to a sheet of paper whose two sides are two aspects of an inseparable whole: "Language can also be compared with a sheet of paper: thought is the front and the sound is the back; one cannot cut the front without cutting the back at the same time; likewise in language, one can neither divide sound from thought nor thought from sound; the division could be accomplished only abstractly."[21] The same thing is true in regard to the formulaic pattern which exists only in the state of the realized formula. We can separate its form from its content only abstractly when we discuss pattern types, which are seen in the works only as individual, actual formulas. The form itself may be a kind of pre-existent, preverbal gestalt, as Michael Nagler has suggested,[22] but it can only be defined in terms of its manifested content. The lexical element, then, is what is known as the *manifestation* of the formal pattern; the formula itself exists as the actualization of one of a fairly limited number of potential variant forms.

Tagmemic grammar offers an interesting and valuable contribution to the investigation of this and related problems, a solution which is to a surprising degree anticipated by the work of Parry and Lord. In *The Singer of Tales* Lord argues that formulaic language depends on the substitution of variable elements within a common frame.[23] This approach is also implicit in Parry's early recognition of the substitution system and in the work of all of those who have investigated patterns of substitution in formulaic language. In the Middle English examples I have just reviewed, particularly in the more elementary systems, we can see that the substituted phrases can be viewed as variables—all of which belong to a paradigm or class, and any of which may be inserted into its proper position (or *slot*) in the formulaic pattern. The slot-class pattern is an essential feature of the tagmemic grammar advanced by Pike and others.[24] But before we can try out some of the methods of tagmemic grammar in an application to the corpus of material here, we need to review briefly the premises on which such an application might rest.

Formulas and formulaic grammar: a tagmemic approach

The idea that formulas and formula systems make up a language which operates, like any other language, according to a set of discoverable principles is fundamental to the structurally oriented work of Lord and Parry. Lord writes:

> The method of language is like that of oral poetry, substitution in the framework of the grammar. Without the metrical restrictions of the verse, language substitutes one subject for another in the nominative case, keeping the same verb, or keeping the same noun, it substitutes one verb for another. In studying the patterns and systems of oral narrative verse, we are in reality observing the "grammar" of the poetry, a grammar superimposed, as it were, on the grammar of the language concerned. Or, to alter the image, we find a special grammar within the grammar of the language, necessitated by the versification. The formulas are the phrases and clauses and sentences of the specialized poetic grammar.[25]

From the structural point of view I have adopted in this study, tagmemic grammar may provide some important insights into the way formulaic systems work—both at the level of style and at the level of incident and plot. Tagmemic analysis is a linguistic theory which attempts to take into account the hierarchically patterned features of language structure. Briefly, tagmemics assumes that language is built by a series of grammatical hierarchies of *emic* units, units which have particular and distinctive significance within a given system.[26] (One of these hierarchical patterns might be the five-level group of stem, word, phrase, clause, and sentence, to which may be added the extrasentence structures of paragraph and discourse.)[27] On any given structural level the distribution of *emic* units takes place in a pattern of *slots*. The individual item (word, phrase, clause) is a member of a set or class which includes a number of related words, phrases, or clauses. For instance, in the sentence *Ann and Tom are friends*, the words *Ann* and *Tom* belong to the subject class; in the same paradigm there may be any number of proper names, either male or female (*Richard, Lee, Sara*, etc.) or a limited number of pronouns in the nominative case (*he, she, we, they*). From these paradigms, and depending on the meaning, the speaker can select any one of the single items, all of which are homologous, and then can substitute it into its appropriate position, or slot, in the sentence.[28] The *slot*, then, is one functional position in a syntagmatically ordered sequence of such positions, while the individual set members are paradigmatically related by virtue of the fact that any one of the members could be substituted for any other without altering the functional nature of the slot itself.

The tagmemic assumption that language is generated by means of the substitution of variables within a stable framework is easily demonstrated in formulaic analysis. For example, the simple two-stress system that we saw earlier:

blithe
glad } of mode
eger

consists of two slots, an adjective slot which may be filled by any one of three variants (or more—the poet *manifests* only these three),[29] and the *of mode* slot, which is constant in all the occurrences of this formulaic pattern. In the following whole line pattern from *Ipomedon*, there are again two slots: the fixed *both . . . and* and the variable prepositional phrase:

Bothe of more and of lesse (37)

Bothe to singe and to rede (55)

Bothe to grete and to smalle (58)

Bothe in chambre and in halle (132)

Bothe in chambre and in boure (135)

The more complicated four-stress patterns may work in basically the same fashion, as our earlier example from *Eglamour* shows:

$$yf \begin{cases} he \\ she \\ ye \\ thou \end{cases} \text{were neuer so} \begin{cases} \text{nobyll a knyght (727)} \\ \text{fayre ne whyte (811)} \\ \text{kene (1125)} \\ \text{prest (666)} \end{cases}$$

The constant frame is the unvarying sequence *yf* PRONOUN *were never so* ADJECTIVE/ADJECTIVE PHRASE. The poet selects from the available class the most appropriate item and inserts it into the slot; the filled slots become the manifested formula. Here, the syntactical and metrical slot pattern is firmly fixed, but there is variation permitted in the choice of individual items which may be used to fill out the slot. All of these variants, however, are homologous, because they are substitutable and therefore structurally identical.[30] This element of marked and frequent homology is one of the distinguishing features of formulaic language, and it will be examined more carefully later in terms of larger structural patterns.

Even the complex two-verse systems may be approached in this way, although, as we can see, the verbal variations admitted into the fixed metrical-syntactical pattern are much greater, and the possibilities for homologous embedded systems within the larger pattern complicate the formula to a great degree. For example, the primary slot pattern in the lines below is a sequence which contains a noun in one line and a relative clause dependent on that noun in the second line. These examples are again from *Toulous*:

Many a doghty knyght there was levyd
That was wylde and wode (107–108)

For to make the lady glade
That was bothe gentyll and small (768–769)

And askyd gode for god allmyght
That dyed on the tree (383–384)

And sithen he thanked god of hys grace
That syttyth in trynyte (119–120)

This primary slot pattern, however, is complicated by the fact that the second of these lines is always a three-stress pattern (four-stress relative clauses are automatically excluded from this paradigm because of the metrical pattern), and by the fact that the end rhymes must conform to an already established rhyme scheme, an imperative which is present in every line and which considerably restricts the paradigm.[31] But even within the variants we can see some recurring embedded patterns. The first of the two-line patterns, for example, demonstrates a fixed, homologous pattern in the relative clause (*that was* ADJECTIVE *and* ADJECTIVE) within the larger two-line pattern of NOUN + RELATIVE CLAUSE:

> Many a doghty knyght there was levyd
> That was wylde and wode (107–108)

> For to make the lady glade
> That was bothe gentyll and small (768–769)

In the following two-line slot patterns from *Toulous* a different kind of homologous, embedded pattern is evident (*that* VERB + ADVERBIAL/ PREPOSITIONAL PHRASE):

> And asked gode for god allmyght
> That dyed on the tree (383–384)

> And sithen he thanked god of hys grace
> That syttyth in trynyte (119–120)

We could go on collecting examples of slot patterns in which the metrical-syntactical patterns are manifested by variable form-content composites, but it seems from the examples presented here and earlier in the chapter that the slot-pattern notion of formula does provide a useful approach to some of the problems of formulaic analysis.

A slot pattern, regardless of its length or complexity, can be called a *syntagmeme*, which is an isolatable *emic* syntactical construction. The syntagmeme is an abstract unit; it is manifested on the level of the individual text by the *syntagm*, the individual formulaic expression. All languages are made up of syntagmemes, which may occur on the level of the hypermorpheme, the phrase, or the clause. What seems to set formulaic language apart from most other uses of language, however, is the small number of syntagmemes; that is, a few identical slot-pattern formations account for the identical, synonymous, and homologous surface structures in any given poem; in addition, these same slot patterns recur with a high degree of frequency in all the poems.

It is obvious at the outset that these syntagmemes are not surface structures but rather generate surface structures by certain elementary processes of transformation. Nor are they deep structures (in the sense of the deep structures of transformational grammar), because their constituents can be further reduced; they are, rather, intermediate between deep and surface structures.[32] It is beyond the scope of this study to undertake an examination of the deep structures which through a series of transformations generate surface-structure syntagmemes. All of the results to this point, however, justify the hypothesis that these deep structures are relatively few in number compared to the more various deep structures of literary language, and that they produce a limited number of syntagmeme types[33] which in turn produce a limited number of highly homologous surface structures. The homology of these structures accounts for the redundance that so many readers have noted; it is clear now, however, that these redundant surface phenomena are the product of a much deeper homology, and that this feature is perhaps the single most important structural principle of the narratives. These hypotheses, although they can be tested out here only in a very limited way, raise a number of questions that require more complete answers and which will surely advance our knowledge about the creation of formulaic narratives in general—not just about the Middle English romances.

The formulaic *langue*: cognitive systems and value systems

Ferdinand de Saussure, who recognized in his linguistic studies a formulaic construction which he called a *fixed syntagm*, suggests that phrases like the ones described in the preceding sections (particularly the verbatim lexical formulas) do not belong to the individual speech or utterance (the *parole*) of the speaker, but to the shared language patterns (the *langue*). That is, they are not composed by the speaker but belong to the systematized, highly codified set of language conventions which make communication possible. These fixed patterns, according to Saussure, are pat phrases which cannot be significantly altered by a single individual because they are furnished whole and complete by tradition. "There are probably a whole series of sentences," he says, "which belong to the *langue* and which the individual no longer has to combine for himself."[34] Saussure offers as examples verbatim, cliché-like repetitions ("what's the use," "force his hand"), but, as I have attempted to demonstrate, the correspondences in formulaic language (and Saussure is talking about the formulas of everyday speech) need not be limited to verbal repetition. The important point here is to recognize that in a highly formulaic, ritualized *langue* which is characterized by a small number of syntagmeme types and a high degree of homology among surface structures, the individual poet can display relatively little idiosyncrasy; the choice of syntactical patterns, even of vocabulary, is limited by the limitations of the *langue* itself (although the poet has a great deal more choice than has hitherto been recognized in filling the syntagmemic slot patterns with variant verbal combinations). We cannot say, nor would we wish to, that the composer of the Middle English romance cannot control the choice of words or phrases. It is true, however, that the language of these poems is stereotyped to a degree that is unparalleled in any other English genre; it is true, as well, that as a mode of language becomes more strongly stereotyped, less individual choice can be exerted and the surface features become less idiosyncratic. At that point (and because so little change is allowed to seep into the system) the language tends to become ossified, as it has in these poems.

Roland Barthes has observed, in regard to Saussure's description of the fixed syntagm: "If these stereotypes belong to the *langue* and no longer to the *parole*, and if it proves true that numerous semiological systems use them to a great extent, then it is a real linguistics of the syntagm that we must expect, which will be used for all strongly stereotyped modes of discourse."[35] It is to Barthes's proposal for a "linguistics of the syntagm" that I would like to turn now and to the particular cognitive system and set of values that is imposed by the presence of a great number of fixed syntagmemic forms in the poetic *langue* of the romances. The homologous phrases, as we have seen, function in the line and the stanza almost like conditioned reflexes appropriate to a given linguistic situation. In orally composed poems the phrases are chosen quickly and unreflectingly under the pressure of the oral performance; once they have been learned, they are retained as habitual patterns, both for the poet and (equally important) for the audience, who must, because of the requirements of the oral performance, share completely in the *langue*. In poems which grow out of the oral tradition and in transition texts, the phrases continue to be used because they belong to the genre itself; they are associated with certain narrative patterns which would appear to be almost incongruous— certainly unconventional—in any other style. In any case, the language of the poems we have here is a collection of habitual and redundant phrases and learned linguistic patterns that function almost automatically in the verse, whether they were orally composed or are habitual responses which continue to take place even outside the process of oral composition.

In one sense, redundance in language (that is, either synonymous or homologous redundance) provides greater efficiency in the listener's response, because highly probable phenomena are immediately and easily recognized while less probable phenomena require some time to assimilate.[36] In addition, a high degree of redundance makes it easier for the listeners to correct their errors of perception and results in an even greater efficiency on their part. The many homologous surface and intermediate structures in these narratives enable them to predict accurately the formulaic phrases which will occur next. This expectancy has as its corollary a tendency toward preconditioned response and consent on the part of the listeners, who, if they can accurately predict what is to follow, will be more likely to accept it.[37] All of these facts suggest that formulaic language is psychologically a highly efficient means of conveying a message—at least as long as the members of the audience participate in the *langue* that generates the message and as long as they are not unsympathetic to formulaic discourse per se. (Neither of these conditions, of course, fits the modern reader of the romances.)

But all of this is certainly not consciously perceived by either poet or audience. Because of the habitual quality of the language, it seems to have communicated on a level below that of conscious attention— quite unlike the close conscious attention that must be paid to literary language. The phrases of the romance must seldom have been attended to closely, because they contain nothing new, nothing that has not been heard before, nothing that cannot be predicted. They must have been accepted without question as truth, and their veracity attested by their wide use and acceptance, even in a time when England was undergoing immense linguistic upheaval and we might naturally expect the language of these poems—over the several centuries of their popular existence—to reflect those changes. But the language of the romances does not demonstrate change; instead, it is very like the language of ritual. And, although it lacks the solemnity of ritual, it still embodies a kind of residual incantatory magic that is more important perhaps than factual communication. Perhaps we could most accurately describe the language of these narratives as ritual which has declined in significance, which is no longer self-consciously aware of its own importance, but which is still highly effective as a means of conveying and teaching the values held by the community.

Beside the efficiency and utility of this kind of ritualistic language, it has a very real beauty as well. The stateliness, the dignity of it are perhaps difficult for us to perceive, used as we are to the imaginative and logical intricacies of written literatures. But within the repeated patterns of formulaic language there is a kind of psychological comfort, an assurance that the social institutions in which the audience has invested itself are stable and secure, that the traditions have been preserved, that the future is safe. C. M. Bowra, in his study of the formulaic qualities of heroic poetry, remarks:

> Most formulae are traditional and familiar, and their very familiarity makes the audience feel at home and know in what world of the imagination it is moving. When we consider how conservative most primitive peoples are in their tastes and how much they dislike innovation on any substantial scale, we can see that they will like to be comforted in this way. If they know where they are, they will enjoy all the more the slight novelties which the bard may introduce into his telling of an old tale. For this reason the formulae come to be liked for their own sake as old friends, and the omission of them would leave the audience uneasy and unsatisfied, as if they had not had their proper poetical fare.[38]

Of course, it is not just primitive peoples who find aid and comfort in the repetitions of highly socialized patterns of language: witness the numbers of formulas that occur in our own culture—in any religious service or Western movie or soap opera. But the point that formulas function on the level of group familiarity is well taken. To the audiences of the romance, the great number of fixed phrases and formulaic patterns which belong to the *langue*, to that *wordhord* of communal speech patterns, reinforces a strong sense of fraternity and fellow-feeling which integrates their single selves into a social group that is more powerful, more effective than the sum of its parts.

It is an easily recognized feature of formulaic language that its redundance leads to a sharply decreased level of information.[39] In ordinary language (in this sentence, for example) each word as it appears adds some new amount of information to the statement that is being made. In formulaic language the fact that the listener can predict from the phrase *sone on the morn* that the next phrase will be *when it was day* is a function of *decreased* information. Because the second phrase is really unnecessary (the audience knows what it will be) and because the poet's freedom of choice narrows sharply here, the second phrase adds no information to the statement. Of course, many of the formulas do serve to convey urgent narrative information, as we noticed earlier in the categorization of action formulas. But the narrative structures themselves seem to be highly formulaic as well (as we will see later), and probably most of the audience could predict with great accuracy what scene would occur next—just as we could probably produce on demand a typical Western plot.

If the language does not serve to carry information, what then is its primary function? In addition to carrying a minimal amount of narrative information, the language carries at least one other level of social meaning as well. That is, it carries the additional messages which are encoded within the semiology of social gestures, the language of social ritual: leave-takings, greetings, meals and banquets, marriages and knightings and tournaments. Each one of the highly ritualized events to which the formulas themselves refer is also a kind of formulaic language, a complex system of significations which is as thoroughly understood and articulated in its own culture as that culture's natural language and which is indeed a language even though it may not be a verbal one. In the romances the language of the verse refers much of the time to this second-order system, and its message-bearing function is then doubled. The language of these narratives functions not only as a medium of narrative, but as a powerful social force which supports, reinforces, and perpetuates the social beliefs and customs held by the culture, perhaps long past their normal time of decline.

On a cognitive level this style, frozen into its particular manifestation and largely immobile, presents the world as completely recognized and achieved. As ritualistic language spoken and accepted without hesitation as truth, it provides a declarative, definitive statement about the nature of the social universe, and therein lay its beauty and utility for its audience. But, if it is true that formulaic diction depends upon a store of already developed and understood responses (which is why we are not the poems' best audience), then it is equally true that this same language cannot be a vehicle for new discoveries either about itself or about the nature of the world that it defines and describes. What we see revealed in the stylistic patterns of these poems is an implicit faith in the already established workings of the world on the social, the political, and the natural levels, an unquestioning assumption of regularity and stability and unfailing order that provides a structure of understanding and order in life but at the same time reduces the opportunities for innovation and change. It is a language which does not, *cannot* allow change, for change would destroy the very foundation on which it is built and violate the social contract in which the poems find their energy and authority.[40] The style as it stands here is not a medium of exploration or of inquiry, and we should not expect it to be; it is the style of reiterated answer, the questions having been formulated once, when the form was itself new, and now forgotten. It is a cognitive system which, when it looks at the world, is obliged to see only its own mirror image.

The same observation could very likely be made about all formulaic styles from heroic epic to the lyrics of popular song. The style of the romance is different from most other narrative styles, however, in that its referent does not exist in the real world but in a second-order world of social gesture, a carefully appointed and systematic language in its own right, which is constructed not to approach reality directly but to manipulate it from behind a screen, to make social sense of the relations between human beings as well as between the human world and the natural world. The heroic epic depends to some extent on social phenomena, but the immediately perceivable difference is that the language of epic is a language of direct and forceful action while the language of romance is a language of stance. The formulas, as I pointed out earlier, largely depict social gestures which in themselves are a complex code of communication. What we have in these narratives, then, is a "mythic language," to use Barthes's phrase, a kind of third-order linguistic phenomenon, a closed referential system twice removed from reality and confined to the social conventions and codes of etiquette of a highly ritualized society. From a twentieth-century point of view, the language is imprisoned within its own artistic and cognitive forms without the motivation necessary to provide for its own release, and it is this criticism that we have in mind when we say that the poets are helpless under the force of the formula, and that the language of their poems is pedestrian and cliché-ridden.

The mode of perception and system of values demonstrated in these narratives is remote from us, and the insistence on the preservation of tradition which is the source of the power and vitality that initially inspired them has little hold on the twentieth-century literary imagination. As Morris Croll says at the close of his essay on baroque style,[41] this is not the place to consider what we have gained or lost in this change in perceptual habits; what we must insist on is that we do not attempt to judge these medieval narratives according to the tenets of our modern sensibilities.

2 Larger structural units: the motifeme

From formula to stanza: larger syntactical units

In the preceding chapter we looked at the formula as a stylistic or textural structure, both at the surface level of lexical correspondence and at the deeper level of syntactic and metric correspondence. Our discussion focused on the choice and arrangement of the fixed syntagms (the verbatim formulas) and substitution systems which manifest the syntagmeme or formulaic slot pattern, but we did not consider these formulaic patterns as part of the larger stanzaic system. We cannot talk about the formulaic line, however, without considering its immediate context, the formulaic stanza, a unit which is related both to the small-scale formulaic units of language and to the larger units of narrative structure.

The tail-rhyme romances provide a compositional context in which the stanzaic unit plays an important developmental role. Groups of formulaic lines, in ensembles of three and six and four and eight lines, make up formulaic stanzas which serve as definitive components in the development of scene and episode. These twelve- and sixteen-line groups, bound together within a strict rhyming sequence, function as complete, integral units with a high degree of internal coherence. Usually the stanza is dominated by a single narrative concern. In the following example from *Amis and Amiloun*, for instance, the entire stanza narrates the duke's reward of high office for the services of the two friends. (I have underlined the verbatim formulas.)

> That riche douke hadde of hem pris,
> For that thai were so war & wiis
> & holden of gret bounte.
>
> Sir Amiloun and Sir Amis
> He sett hem both in gret office
> In his court for to be;

> Sir Amis, as ye may here,
> He made his chef botelere,
> For he was hend and fre,
>
> & Sir Amiloun of hem alle
> He made chef steward in halle
> To dight al his meine. (181–192)[1]

The stanza develops the narrative with marked singleness of purpose and a great deal of lexical and syntactic redundancy. Each of the four tercets (divided here for easy reading) pursues the stanza's central story: the duke is pleased with the service of Amis and Amiloun; he promotes both of them, one to the position of chief butler and the other to chief steward.

In addition to the tight narrative organization, there is a repeated syntagmemic pattern that adds to the felt formulaic qualities of the stanza. We can see the similarities of these lines more clearly if we reorder them slightly (see Table 2). The first lines of the second, third, and fourth tercets are noun phrases which name the object of the action that appears in the second lines, while the third lines are used adverbially. The pattern is a three-line slot pattern of *naming*, *action*, and *modification* that is formulaic in the same way that repeated lexical combinations or syntactical patterns are formulaic.

Table 2

Naming	Action
Sir Amiloun and Sir Amis	He sett hem both in gret office
Sir Amis, as ye may here	He made his chief botelere,
& Sir Amiloun of hem alle	He made chef steward in halle

Table 3

Scene-setting	Action
When they were of yeres fyue	Alle her kyn was of hem blythe
When they were seuyn yere olde	Grete ioy euery man of hem tolde
When they were twelue yere olde	In al the londe were noon so bolde

The same formulaic patterning of tercets appears in another stanza, which opens with three lines of formulaic praise of the boys' beauty:

> The children gon then thryue
> Fairer were neuer noon on lyue,
> Curtaise, hende, and good.
>
> When they were of yeres fyue
> Alle her kyn was of hem blythe,
> So mylde they were of mood.
>
> When they were seuyn yere olde,
> Grete ioy euery man of hem tolde
> To beholde that frely foode.
>
> When they were twelue yere olde
> In al the londe were noon so bolde
> So faire of boon and blood. (49–60)[2]

The formulaic quality of the whole stanza, however, extends beyond the verbatim correspondences and the substitution patterns marked here. The formula pattern of the tercets, which is similar to the preceding pattern, can be seen in Table 3.

Modification

In his court for to be
For he was hend and fre
To dight al his meine

Modification

So mylde they were of mood
To beholde that frely foode
So faire of boon and blood

The syntagmeme with its three manifested variants

$$\text{When they were} \begin{cases} \text{of yeres fyue} \\ \text{seuen yere olde} \\ \text{twelue yere olde} \end{cases}$$

serves as the first line of each of the three tercets; the second line is the action line, and the third line is again adverbial and twice syntactically formulaic:

To behold that frely foode

So mylde they were of mood
So faire of boon and blood

In the stanza we have just examined, the tercet pattern is repeated in three of the four tercets, lending a great deal of coherence to the stanza unit; in other stanzas, while there may be less lexical repetition, a high degree of syntactic correspondence holds the stanza together. In the following stanza, for instance, the age formula appears, together with the syntagmemic tercet pattern of naming, action, and modification:

That riche douke, that y of told,
He hadde a douhter fair & bold,
Curteise, hende & fre.

When sche was fiften winter old,
In al that lond nas ther non yhold
So semly on to se,

For sche was gentil & auenaunt,
Hir name was cleped Belisaunt,
As ye may lithe at me.

With leuedis & maidens bright in bour
Kept sche was with honour
& gret solempnite. (421–432)[3]

The first half of another stanza exhibits the same tercet pattern:

That child, that was so fair & bold
Owaines was his name ytold,
Wel fair he was of blode.

When he was of tvelue yere old,
Amoraunt than was he cald,
Wel curteys, hend & gode. (1633–1638)[4]

The correspondences of these stanzas (which also contain similar rhymes) strongly indicate that the poet possesses a formulaic pattern which may be manifested by any number of variants—variants which may or may not offer lexical correspondence, but which certainly reveal other kinds of formulaic patterning.

In some stanzas the tercet pattern, while still apparent, is much more loosely executed. In this passage from *The Earl of Toulous* the pattern is manipulated from tercet to tercet:

There were slayne in that batayle,
Syxty thousand wythowte fayle,
   On the emperours syde,

There was takyn thre hundurd and fyfty
Of grete lordys, sekyrly,
   Wyth woundys grymly wyde;

On the erlys syde ther were slayne,
But twenty, sothely to sayne,
   So boldely they can abyde! (121–129)

The basic tercet pattern—

There were $\left\{ \begin{array}{l} taken \\ slain \end{array} \right\}$ NUMBER + MODIFICATION—

may require either one or two lines, and its order may be slightly different; the remainder is filled in with modifying phrases.

The tail-rhyme stanza seems very well suited to this kind of formulaic development, and it may be argued that these configurations are simply a feature of this particular stanzaic form. Similar patterns can be found in the couplet narratives as well, however, binding together groups of lines. This passage from *Havelok* falls into three sections: the first six lines describe the spread of Havelok's reputation and the extent of his prowess; the two following sections repeat the pattern with greater particularity and refrain-like regularity:

> This selkouth mithe nouth ben hyd,
> Ful sone it was ful loude kid
> Of hauelok, hw he warp the ston
> Ouer the laddes euerilkon;
> Hw he was fayr, hw he was long,
> Hw he was with, hw he was strong;
> Thoruth england yede the speke,
> Hw he was strong, and ek meke;
> In the castel, up in the hall,
> The knithes speken ther-of alle,
> So that Godrich it herde wel
> The speken of hauelok, eueri del,
> Hw he was strong man and hey,
> Hw he was strong and ek fri (1059–1072)

This configuration of stanzaic development occurs at least three more times in the poem:

> Quanne the Erl godrich him herde
> Of that mayden, hw wel she ferde;
> Hw wis sho was, hw chaste, hw fayr,
> And that sho was the rithe eyr
> Of engelond, of al the rike:— (286–90)

> Alle him loueden that him sowen,
> Bothen heyemen and lowe.
> Of him ful wide the word sprong,
> Hw he was mike, hw he was strong,
> Hw fayr man god him hauede maked (957–961)

> Nu haue ye herd the gest al thoru
> Of hauelok and of goldeborw.
> Hw he weren born, and hw fedde,
> And hwou he woren with wronge ledde
> In here youthe, with trecherie,

With tresoun, and with felounye,
And hwou the swikes haueden thit
Reuen hem that was here rith
And hwou he weren wreken wel,
Haue ich sey you euerildel (2984–2993)

These patterned repetitions indicate that formulaic composition operates on a much larger scale than we had hitherto known: the poets
seem to have possessed a formulaic pattern or template which may be
manifested by any number of variants. These variants, which may or
may not demonstrate lexical correspondence, are patterned upon a
common syntactical-metrical form. It is always easier to perceive lexical correspondences, and those are the ones likely to attract our attention; the basic syntactic pattern, however, precisely because it is less
obvious and probably unconscious (both for the audience and almost
certainly for the poet) may well be the most important of the formulaic
qualities of this kind of verse.

While the marked degree of formulaicness that we have seen here
does not extend to all of the stanzas of all of the poems, there are
enough correspondences to warrant the hypothesis that larger syntagmemic patterns exist within the framework of the stanzaic unit and
the formulaic slot patterns of tercets, quatrains, and multi-line groups
that subsume smaller units of phrase and single-line syntagms. The
possibilities for combining patterns are obviously very complex, and
the limitations imposed on the composition by the rhymes are considerable. Stanza composition is a topic which requires a full-length study
of its own, and the discussion here is meant only to indicate the feasi-
bility of such a detailed study. It is clear, however, that these conclusions have important implications for structural analysis.

When we view formulaic language in this way, we avoid the narrow-
ness implicit in confining formular composition to simple phrases or
to one- and two-line patterns, and we are able to see more clearly the
degree to which formulaic structures organize the poem. In this view of
the stanzaic sequence, individual lexical items are seen as the variants
which fill out the slots in the half-line or whole-line formulaic patterns; single lines as the variants which fill out the slots in the tercet
pattern (or whatever line group is appropriate to the length and organization of the stanza); and the tercet (or quatrain) as the variant which
fills out slots in the largest unit, the stanza (which in turn serves as an
element in the development of scene and episode, as we will see). This
hierarchical view allows us to see the poem as a highly integrated system of patterns that in orally composed poetry enables the poets to

create rapidly according to patterns which they have already mastered and are able to manipulate with great skill. In transition poetry and in written texts, this technique is probably habitual but the same in structure and esthetic effect. In either case there is a limited number of these patterns; with further study they can be isolated and discussed in relationship to other structural levels of the poems.

The motifeme

There are a number of stanzas and groups of lines common to most of the narratives which present a semantic coincidence that is broader and farther-reaching than the lexical and syntactic similarities we have been working with in individual poems. This larger kind of correspondence is a function of narrative discourse as well as of language, and belongs to the level of semantically formulaic narrative structures. The examples below will indicate the range of such semantic and formal resemblances. Here the entire stanza (or twelve- to twenty-line group of couplets) functions as a formulaic unit of composition. These are the opening passages from eight poems:

> Ihesu Christ, of heuen Kyng,
> Graunt vs all good endyng
>   And beld vs in hys bowre;
> And yef hem ioye that loue to here
> Of eldres that before vs were
>   And lyued in grett antowre.
> I woll you tell of a knyght
> That was both hardy and wyght,
>   And stronge in ylke a stowre;
> Of dedys of armys that he myght here
> He wan degre with iurnay clere,
>   And in felde the floure. (*Eglamour* 1–12)

> Lord God in Trynite,
> Yeff home hevene for to see
> That louethe gamen and gle
>   And gestus to fede.
> Ther folke sitis in fere
> Shullde men herken and here
> Off gode that be-fore [hem] were
>   That leuede in arthede.
> That Y schall karppe off a knyght
> That was both hardy and wyght;

Sir Degreuaunt that hend hyght,
  That dowghty was of dede;
Was never knygh that he fond
In Fraunce ne in Englond
Myght sette a schafft of hys hond
  On a stythe stede. (*Sir Degrevant* 1–16)

Hende in haule, and ye will here
Of eldirs, that byfore vs were,
  That lyffede in arethede
(Jesu Christ, heuen kynge
Graunte vs alle his blyssynge
  And heuen to oure mede):
I will yow telle of a knyghte,
That was bothe hardy and wyghte
  And doghty man of dede.
His name was called sir Ysumbras:
Swilke a knyghte, als he was,
  Now lyffes nane in lede. (*Isumbras* 1–12)

For goddes loue in trinyte
Al that ben hend herkenith to me,
I pray yow, par amoure,
What sum-tyme fel beyond the see
[Of] two barons of grete bounte
And men of grete honoure;
Her faders were barons hende,
Lordinges com of grete kynde
And pris men in toun and tour;
To here of these children two
How they were in wele and woo
Ywys it is grete doloure. (*Amis* 1–12)

Herknet to me, gode men,
Wiues, maydnes, and alle men,
Of a tale that ich you wile tell,
Wo so it wile here, and ther-to duelle.
The tale is of hauelok i-maked;
Wil he was litel he yede ful naked:
Hauelok was a ful god gome,
He was ful god in eueri trome,
He was the wicteste man at nede,
That thurte riden on ani stede.

That ye mowen nou y-here,
And the tale ye mowen y-lere.
At the beginning of vre tale,
Fil me a cuppe of ful god ale;
And y wile drinken her y spell,
That crist vs shilde alle fro helle!
Krist late vs heuere so for to do,
That we moten comen him to,
And wite that it mote ben so!
Benedicamus domino! (*Havelok* 1–20)

Jhesu Cryst, yn trynyte
Oonly god and persons thre,
   Graunt us wele to spede,
And gyf us grace so to do,
That we may come thy blys unto,
   On rode as thou can blede!
Leve lordys, y schall you telle
Of a tale, some tyme befelle,
   Far yn unkowthe lede;
How a lady had grete myschefe,
And how sche covyrd of hur grefe;
   I pray you, take hede! (*Toulous* 1–12)

Jesu, that was with sper ystonnge,
And for vs hard and sore yswonnge,
Glady both old and yonnge
   With wytte honest,
That wylled a whyle ster her tonnge
   And herkeny gest!

But fele men be of swyche manere,
Goodnesse when hy scholden here,
Hy nylled naght lesste with her ere,
   To lerny wyt,
But as a swyn with lowryng cher
   Al gronne he sytte,

And fele of hem casted a cry
Of thyng, that fallyd to rybaudy,
That noon of hem, that sytte hym by,

May haue no lest.
God schylde all thys company
  Fram swych a gest.

And yeve vs grace goodnesse to lere
Of ham, that before vs were,
Crystendom how they goone arere,
  Tho hyt began!
Of oon the best ye mowne ahere,
    That hyght Ottouyan! (*Octavian* Cotton 1–24)

Heven blys that alle schalle wynne,
Schylde us fro dedly synne,
  And graunte us the blys of hevyne!
Yf ye wylle a stounde blynne,
Of a story y wylle begynne,
  That gracyus ys to nevyne;
Of a kyng and of a quene,
What bale and blys was them betwene,
  Y schalle yow telle fulle evyn:
A gode ensaumpulle ye may lere,
Yf ye wylle thys story here
  And herkyn to my stevyne. (*Triamour* 1–12)

Even a very quick reading of these passages reveals that all of the line groups have three common components: the poet prays God's blessing on the endeavor; the poet exhorts the audience to pay attention to the story; the poet provides a short synopsis of events in the tale or offers a formulaic sketch of the main character. The order of these components is variable, and some flexibility is shown in the manifestation of the pattern: some poets include all three of the elements, while some poets omit or double one or another. The emphasis shifts from poem to poem—the emphasis in *Amis* is on the descriptive component, while in the southern *Octavian* the poet spends sixteen lines exhorting what must have been an unruly audience to silence. But while there is some variation among the poems, the exhortation is invariably included somewhere in the first stanza or group of lines. We can designate this component, then, as the constant component, and we can designate the group of lines structured upon this element as the *exhortation* group.[5]

Table 4

Narrative	Slot 1	Slot 2	Slot 3
Eglamour	prayer	exhortation	synopsis
Degrevant	prayer	exhortation	synopsis
Isumbras	exhortation	prayer	synopsis
Amis	exhortation	synopsis	
Havelok	exhortation	synopsis	prayer
Toulous	prayer	synopsis	exhortation
Octavian	prayer	exhortation	
Triamour	prayer	exhortation	synopsis

In terms of the grammar of narrative form that we have been developing, the slot organization for this group of lines consists of three co-occurrent slots variously arranged; one slot, the *exhortation* slot, is always filled; it is the *obligatory nucleus* of this particular pattern and serves to identify it and contrast it to other patterns.[6] We can see this organization more clearly if we schematize it (Table 4). Secondary contrastive features of the organization are the peripheral slots—*prayer* and *synopsis*—either of which may be filled once or more than once. These slots are optional; they do not always occur (although they are present in the majority of passages).

It seems, however, that at least one of these optional elements must occur together with the nuclear component for the structure to be perceived as complete. For example, this phrase from *William of Palerne* (170) is a component of the *exhortation* pattern:

leue lordes, now listenes of this litel barn

In fact, this is the nuclear component. But when this component or any other occurs alone, the structure is incomplete because its other peripheral features are absent. The configuration of elements, to be complete, should contain a nuclear component and at least one of the peripheral components. The phenomenon of the unattached, floating component, occurring singly and outside of the environment in which it usually occurs, raises several important questions that we will turn to later. For now it is sufficient to observe that most structural components are detachable and may occur in other patterns or alone.

In addition to the fact that the pattern must be complete in one way or another before it is recognized,[7] it is probably also true that a pattern which occurred out of its normal context would be difficult to recognize. That is, the poet would not be likely to use the *exhortation* pattern in any other place in the poem but the opening slot. Because one of its functions is to sketch briefly the story to be told, it is unlikely that it would occur out of order; the fact remains, however, that this pattern always occurs in the same slot in the poem, an observation that leads us to speculate that the narrative is composed of a more or less ordered sequence of slots (or at the very least, that some of its slots are ordered) and that this order has to do with the function of the slot in its sequence.

Since this particular organization (as an abstract unit) occurs unchanged with such regularity in all the poems, it can be called a *type-pattern*. On the level of narrative structure, it is a formulaic pattern of composition just as the syntagmeme is a formulaic pattern on the level of language. Like the syntagmeme, the narrative type-pattern is a form-content composite, an element which is manifested through the choice and substitution of individual variants into an unvarying pattern.[8] This type-pattern, as an entity, is an abstract unit, the sum of all of its possible variants simultaneously occurring; it is characterized by all the elements which identify it and contrast it with other type-patterns.[9]

Tagmemic grammar has already provided a term by which this formulaic composite unit of narrative structure may be designated: Kenneth Pike has called it a *motifeme*.[10] Alan Dundes has argued very persuasively that Pike's *emic* unit is a much more useful and appropriate unit for structural and systematic analysis than the atomistic unit of the *motif*, since it defines elements in a functioning, synchronic system rather than in an abstract classification of a number of systems, and because it is a unit of structure rather than of content. In addition, the motif concept, popular in the study of the romances as well, has led to a kind of summative analysis in which the motifs are simply noted and the tale is assumed to be the sum of those single parts.[11] In contrast, the *emic* approach is holistic rather than atomistic and owes much to Gestalt psychology in its attempts to see parts and wholes. Dundes has emphasized Max Wertheimer's remarks about the function of parts in wholes, a statement that is worth repeating here:

> There are wholes, the behavior of which is not determined by that of their individual elements, but where the part-processes are themselves determined by the intrinsic nature of the whole.[12]

The *emic* approach is designed to deal with the whole on any level (a clause, a stanza, an episode, a complete narrative) and its relationship to smaller parts. It is particularly well suited to the study of narrative structures and especially to the investigation of formulaic, stereotypic structures like the ones we have here.

The structural three-slot pattern that we have seen manifested in the opening stanzas of these poems can then be called a *motifeme*. This structural unit is posited as a minimum unit at the level of narrative discourse; it subsumes smaller syntagmemic units in the same hierarchical fashion as the syntagmeme subsumes smaller syntactical units.[13] This particular *exhortation* motifeme can be diagrammatically pictured as an unordered sequence of obligatory and optional slots:

$$+ \text{ exhortation}^n$$
$$\pm \text{ synopsis} \qquad \pm \text{ prayer}^n$$

($+$ represents an obligatory slot; $\pm$ represents an optional slot; n indicates that the slot may be filled any number of times.)

When the motifeme has been established as the viable structural unit on this level, the term *allomotif* can be adopted for those variant manifestations of the motifeme which occur in any given poem; the common term *motif* (understood as an *etic* unit) is useful here as well.[14] In the stanza quoted above from *Isumbras*, for instance, the three-line sequence

> Jesu Crist, heuen kynge,
> Graunte vs alle his blyssynge
> And heuen to oure mede

can be seen as an allomotif of the *prayer* motifeme. Another allomotif of the same type would be these three lines from the *Triamour* passage:

> Heven blys that alle schalle wynne,
> Schylde us fro dedly synne,
> And graunte us the blys of hevyne!

These allomotifs together make up the motifeme itself. I will generally treat this abstract unit in terms of Pike's *feature mode* (that is, the motifeme will be viewed as the sum of all of its possible variants simultaneously occurring).[15] While such a level of generalization tends to direct attention away from individual narratives and individual variations of the pattern, it is important that we recognize the necessity for such abstraction at this stage of study. Because the narratives have for so long been viewed individually, and because their differences have always been emphasized (with the result that we have not been able to see their connections or to treat them as a generic group), we must turn for the moment to the opposite extreme, reading the narratives not as individual poems but as individual manifestations of common patterns.

Motifeme structure: some examples

Motifemes of the discours. The *exhortation* motifeme, which in the stanzaic romance coincides in length with the stanza unit, is one of the more noticeable of the type-patterns which serve as basic compositional units. It is not a unit of plot, since it does not advance the narrative action; it is, rather, one of the conventions of the Middle English romances which are structurally more important in the telling of the tale than in the action of the tale itself—to use the terms of the French structuralists, in the *discours* of the tale, not its *histoire*.[16] The *exhortation* motifeme, then, is a *discours* pattern.

Another of these patterns of the *discours* is the two-slot *now-we-leave-and-turn-to* motifeme which often marks divisions of the story. (This motifeme functions in many other kinds of narratives as well; in some American literatures, we might recognize it as the *meanwhile-back-at-the-ranch* motifeme).

At the emperour now leve we
And of the lady yn the see
  I shall begynne to tell. (*Emare* 310–312)

Leve we at the lady clere of vyce
And spek of the kyng of Galys
  From the sege when he come home. (*Emare* 742–744)

Leve we at the lady whyte as flour
And speke we of her fadur the emperour
  That fyrste the tale of ytolde. (*Emare* 946–948)

Leve we theyme at the justynge
And talke we now of other thynge,
  Off Ipomydon and the lady shene. (*Ipomedon* 749–751)

Leve we stylle at the quene
And of the greyhound we wylle mene
  That we before of tolde. (*Triamour* 472–474)

A similar two-slot pattern is the *fytte* division that the *Eglamour* poet employs as a structural marker. One slot is the imperative exhortation "make merry"; the other gives the number of the *fytte*:

> Make we mery, so have we blysse!
> For thys ys the fyrst fytte iwys. (343–344)

> This ys the secund fytte of this
> Makes mery, so haue y blys!
> For thus ferre haue I red. (634–636)

> Makes mery, for yt ys beste,
> For this ys the laste geste
> That I now take in honde. (904–906)

Other motifemes which belong to this level of the narrative, that is, to the telling rather than to the tale, the *discours* rather than the *histoire*, include those references to minstrel activity which are not part of the plot, the poet's occasional statements of opinion, and the formulaic endings of the poems.

Motifemes of the histoire. In the Middle English romances most motifemes are part of the action and function as compositional units of the plot. Because all of the motifemes of the romances obviously cannot be considered in detail here, a few patterns will have to serve as models. One of these, the *procession* motifeme, is very brief, rarely over six lines. It is found in a large number of tales and ranges in its manifested variants from simple to complex:

> Thai convayd him out of the toun
> With ful faire processiowne. (*Ywayn and Gawayn* 3347–3348)

> And wyth a grete processyowne
> They broght Gye to the towne (*Guy* Camb. 6963–6964)

> He wente ynto the toun
> Wyth fayre processioun
> That fok com hym agayn (*Libeaus* 1396–1398)

> Thai com ogaines him out of toun
> With a fair processioun
> Semliche bi ich a side (*Amis* 1375–1377)

And all that myght ryde or gon
To Sir Eglamour hyed they than:
   With blys they gon hym hom bryng.
They are so fayn the worme ys sleyn
With processyon they come hym agayn;
   Radly the bellys they rynge. (*Eglamour* 763–768)

There they toke Syr Gye
And lad hym forth, sekurlye,
To Wynchestur, the ryche towne,
Wyth songe and wyth precestion
"Te deum laudamus" syngyng
And god almyghty thereof thankyng. (*Guy* Camb. 10373–10378)

Whan they of the cyte sawe Bevys
Come wyth the dragons hede, I-wys
Al the bellys gan they rynge.
Prestes & clerkes agayne hym dyd synge.
They brought Beuys so into the towne
Wyth fayre processyon & great renowne. (*Bevis* Chetham 2543–2548)

Gye wyth yoye and hys meyne
Turned ageyne to the cyte
All wyth pryde and yolytee,
Wyth moche game and more glee,
Then beganne the bellus to rynge,
Prestys and clerkys meryly to synge.
When they sawe the hed than,
Moche yoye made many a man. (*Guy* Camb. 3799–3806)

To the Citie he toke the wey.
Whan thei within the toun it sey,
Bi his armes thei him knew,
For ioye anoon the trompes thei blew;
The Soudon, kinges, Erles, and barouns,
And the bisshops with processiouns,
Old and yong of the Citie that might,
Went ayeinst him, as it was right,
With daunsing, singyng, and al solempnitie,
So was he broght in to the Citie. (*Generides* 6131–6140)

The nucleus, that obligatory component of the motifeme which is present in all of the individual manifestations or allomotifs, is the procession itself: the townspeople escort the hero into town (the rhyme *town-procession* occurs in the samples in four simple allomotifs and one complex one). A number of poets fill several of the optional and peripheral slots as well: *celebration* (bell ringing, singing, and dancing); *display of the trophy* (the head of the slain dragon or Saracen); *naming of distinguished characters* (priests and clerks, the Soudan, kings, earls, barons, bishops); and in one instance *mention of the town* (Winchester).

In this case, as in the *exhortation* motifeme, the slot pattern is composed of the nucleus (the procession) which serves to identify this pattern and to contrast it with other patterns, and may or may not also include additional filled slots (celebration, trophy, distinguished participants). The allomotifs which fill these variable slots are either *freely variant* or *conditioned*; that is, certain allomotifs are a product of their narrative environment and thus conditioned, while others are not.[17] In this instance, the allomotif components of *bell ringing, singing,* and *dancing* are completely free; any one of them could be substituted for any other with little difference, and they depend on no prior narrative condition. The *trophy* component, however, is conditioned upon the nature of the previous battle—if the knight has slain a dragon, the poet has the option of introducing a dragon's head into this scene; if he has slain a Saracen, the trophy may be the Saracen's head. Although the two allomotifs appear different, they are structurally identical (it makes no difference in the function of the trophy component whether the head is a dragon's or a Saracen's), and both are conditioned by previous events. The whole motifeme pattern itself is also conditioned in that the victory procession invariably occurs at the end of a longer battle sequence (in the examples above, a battle with a dragon or with a Saracen, or a trial by battle between two champions), and at the beginning of a short banquet sequence. This observation gives us an interesting glimpse of the larger framework of this sequence. The configuration of the processional motifeme is fairly simple:

$$+ \text{procession} \quad \begin{array}{l} \pm\text{celebration} \\ \pm\text{display of the trophy} \\ \pm\text{naming of participants} \end{array}$$

But this simple motifeme, as I have just pointed out, has its own place in a large-scale system of narrative units; it is one of the motifemes which follow a battle scene and are conditioned on it, most often in the following order:

+ battle scene (composed of a number of motifemes)
± procession
± presentation of the trophy to the lord
± disarming of the hero
± victory banquet

In some narratives the whole sequence of motifemes subsequent to the obligatory battle scene is omitted; in other tales some members of the sequence are retained while others are omitted. But it is important to note the persistence of the structural pattern which is apparent here and to recognize that the motifeme, with its own configuration of constituent parts (in this case, procession, celebration, and so forth) serves as an optional component in a larger sequence of similar units. The poet is free to decide whether or not to include this particular motifeme in the sequence. Having chosen to include it, the poet is compelled by tradition to maintain the familiar configural pattern which is a part of the narrative structure of this particular motifeme.

It may be objected that any one of these sequences is simply a description of ordinary real-life activity and takes its shape from the patterned sequence of social behavior—and hence that it is invalid to posit these configural patterns as purely artistic manipulation of the narrative. I dealt with this objection earlier (in Chapter 1) in the context of language formulas, where I proposed that the linguistic formulas carry additional messages encoded within the patterned rhetoric of social activity—a rhetoric of activity that both reinforces and persuades its participants to an acceptance of certain culturally acceptable beliefs. We should also note that the poet has already made a series of selections out of the world of experience, selections very likely based on a conscious or unconscious perception of the patterns of that social rhetoric. This selection and arrangement sharpens the already ordered outlines of social life and makes them more apparent. In the relative simplicity of narrative structures are to be found configurations of attitudes that are lost in the confused patterns of the real world. Order in narrative emerges from apparently disordered social behaviors.

Next we will consider a motifeme which serves as an introductory slot in the following large battle scene. The nucleus of the motifeme consists of only a single act, the *bidding to battle*, but several optional slots are often filled:

Than Beuys and Sabere sende theyr sonde,
Wyde about in euery londe
After grete chyualry
After stalworth knyghtes and hardy,
That they myght fynde then
Of euery londe the doughtyest men. (*Bevis* Chetham 2945–2950)

He sent abowte every whare,
That all men schulde make them yare,
  Agayne the erl to fyght.

He let cry in every syde
Thorow hys londe ferre and wyde,
  Both in felde and towne,
All that myght wepon bere,
Sworde, alablast, schylde or spere,
  They schulde be redy bowne. (*Toulous* 58–66)

He sent his sond night and day
Al so fast as he may
  His folk to batayl bede.
"Bid hem that thai com to me
Al that hold her lond fre.
  Help now at this nede.
Better manly to be slayn
Than long to live in sowre and pain
  Oyain our londis thede." (*Horn Child and Maiden Rimenhild* 162–170)

He dide sone ferd ut bidde,
That al that euere mouhte o stede
Ride, or helm on heued bere,
Brini on bac, and sheld, and spere,
Or ani other wepne bere,
Hand-ax, sythe, gisarm, or spere,
Or aunlaz, and god long knif,
That als he louede lem or lif,
That they sholden comen him to,
With ful god wepne ye ber so,
To lincolne, there he lay,
Of marz the seuententh day,
So that he couthe hem god thank;
And yif that ani were so rang,

That he thanne ne come anon,
He swor bi crist, and bi seint Iohan,
That he sholde maken him thral,
And al his of-spring forth with-al. (*Havelok* 2548–2565)

His sondes thanne he sente swithe al a-boute
To alle the lordes of his land to lasse & to more
That oughten him omage or ani seute elles
& warned hem werfore he wightly hem of-sent
& het hem alle highe thider as hard as thei might
Wel warnished for the werre with clene hors & armes. (*William* 1078–1083)

Two poets enclose this *bidding-to-battle* pattern within another pattern, the *council meeting*, and in both cases use direct dialogue, an obligatory component of the *council* motifeme:

At that word Lucas vpstert,
"Sir," he seid, "your counsell is goode:
In short space make your somowns
To Erles, Princes, and Barouns,
And al tho that ow you seruice,
That thei you faile not in noo wise
To be here in her best aray
Within twoo moneths fro this day." (*Generides* 3203–3210)

Vp rose then the dewke of Kente
And to the kynge seyde hys entente:
"Sir kynge, thou muste sende thy sonde
Far into vncowthe londe
To euery towne thorow and thorowe
Both in cute and in borowe
All, that may armes bere,
Swyrde, axe, schelde or spere,
To come to the at a day certeyne,
And that they stande not therageyne;
For of the they schall haue
More wageys, then they wyll craue.
Wyth the kynge then we schall fyght
And hym ouercome wyth goddys myght.
I haue now my cowncell sayde:
Yf hyt be wele, y am well payde." (*Guy* Camb. 10047–10062)

And in *Partonope of Blois* the poet introduces a slight variation: the people spontaneously gather to their lord without being summoned:

> Partonope heryth alle thus;
> And to hym comyng sodenly ys
> Moche pepele of Loreyne and of Freslonde,
> Wythe-owte letter of hym or [any] sonde. (3059–3062)

Here we can see a great deal of freedom manifested within the basic configural pattern. While the nucleus of the motifeme (the single-slot component *send his sonde*) is conditioned by preceding narrative events (the quarrel which leads to the battle), there are other optional slots in the motifeme: *reference to feudal allegiance, reference to wages, the listing of weapons required by the lord*. These are free, independent of any narrative action.

There are two other optional slots, however, which are not free, but conditioned. For example, the direct discourse that we find in the passages from *Generides* and *Guy* is conditioned upon the fact that this motifeme is embedded in the *council* motifeme, where direct discourse is obligatory. (The council is a relatively infrequent occurrence in Middle English romances. It occurs only in *Guy, Generides*, and *Partonope*, three poems which are directly related to Anglo-Norman or Old French sources; in the Old French *geste*, on the other hand, the council is frequent.)[18] In *Havelok* the optional slot *threat* (which occurs, so far as I am aware, in none of the other narratives of this study) is dependent upon a previous systematic feature of this narrative: the characterization, through action, of Godrich, the traitorous earl who has stolen the heroine's land and who is shown here attempting to gather his host against the hero. Because he is earlier shown to be a villain of the worst sort, the people would serve him only unwillingly (he is not their "natural" lord). Contrast the willingness with which the people gather to support Partonope, even without being summoned. In both these cases the component is not dependent solely upon its immediate narrative context, but upon a prior set of conditions established by a preceding allomotif.

What is important here is the recognition that the motifemic pattern may be included within another motifemic pattern. We have seen how, on the level of language structures, a syntagmeme may include smaller syntagmemic units; later in our discussion I will show how scenes may be interrupted to include other scenes. This more complicated feature of narrative distribution may be called *embedding*; the more frequent end-to-end distribution (like the narrative sequence of *procession, presentation, disarming,* and *banquet* which follows many battles) may be called *chaining*.[19]

Another example of an optional slot is the *description of the battlefield,* a motifeme which has no fixed position in any sequence in which it occurs but is always somewhat randomly included in the middle. It is found in almost every battle scene (that is, in conflicts between two armies rather than between individuals) and usually consists of a single slot which is filled any number of times. Here are some examples of this pattern:

> Men myght se over al
> Hedys cirlyng as a ball.
> Sarzins meny myght men mete
> With guttes tirlinge in the strete;
> A thousand stedus men myght se than
> Ren withouten any man. (*Bevis* Chetham 799–804)

> In euery strete men myght se
> Lombardys on hepys dede there lye,
> Hedys and quarters lye in pecys
> And leggis cutt of by the knees
> Hedus with helmys strayling aboute,
> Handys and armes cutt oute and oute
> Dede bodyes quarterrid in thre
> That was grett pyte for to see. (*Bevis* Chetham 4233–4240)

> So mony slowe he in that ffeld in sight
> That to his steroppes they lay vp right. (*Bevis* Chetham 3721–3722)

> So many men and hors were dede,
> The ryuers ronne of blod all rede (*Octavian* Cotton 1759–1760)

> There was swilk dreping of the folk
> That on the feld was never a polk
> That it ne stod of blod so full
> That the streme ran intill the hull. (*Havelok* 2684–2687)

> So moche blode there was spylt
> That the felde was ovyr hylt,
> Os hyt were a flode (*Toulous* 100–102)

> So hard they gan to geder mete,
> That the blood ran down in yche strete;

So meny men there were dede,
That Temmus was as blood red (*Bevis* Chetham 4223–4226)

So muche people to dethe yode
That the stedys dud wade yn blode
    That stremyd on the grounde. (*Octavian* Camb. 1342–1344)

We might call this nuclear component *carnage*. It is usually freely
elaborated as the poets focus attention on pieces of bodies or quantities
of blood or dead horses and dead enemies. In the first two examples
above the *Bevis* poet uses the *men might see* syntagmeme with a list of
scenes of carnage; the other six examples are all variants of the *so* AD-
VERB . . . *that* syntagmeme, a comparative pattern that in this context
only contains reference to the blood spilled on the battlefield:

so many men . . . that . . .
so much blood . . . that . . .
so hard they . . . that . . .
so much people . . . that . . .

The metaphoric patterns here are also formulaic: the blood is like a
stream, a flood, the Thames.[20] The formulaic quality of this particular
motifeme pervades both the linguistic level and the level of narrative
structure.

Our final example is more complex, and as a result the outlines of
the pattern are blurred. So far, the narrative units we have discussed
have been limited to a very short sequence of actions (a one- or two-slot
nucleus with optional peripheral slots), or a fixed descriptive pattern.
But a number of motifemic units involve another, more complicated
configuration, and we need to examine briefly at least one example of
this type.

Eight of the narratives of our study contain a sequence in which the
hero or the heroine (or both), having fallen in love, requires the assistance of a servant or friend to gain that love (see Table 5). The motifeme
that depicts this situation may be quite short or may continue for hun-
dreds of lines; its general pattern, however, is relatively fixed. The
lover first confesses his or her love to the helper (*confession*), who then
offers to assist in some way (*promise*) and makes a plan to gain the
loved one's goodwill or affection (*plan*). The most concise example of
this motifemic pattern is the following passage from the northern *Octavian*:

On hur bedde as sche lay,
To hur sche callyd a may
　　Fulle preuely and stylle;
The maydyn hyght Olyvan,
The kyngys doghtur of Sodam,
　　That moost wyste of hur wylle.
Sche seyde: "Olyuan, now yn preuyte
My councelle wylle y schewe the,
　　That greuyth me fulle ylle:
On a chylde ys alle my thoght,
That me to Parys wolde haue broght,
　　And y ne may come hym tylle!"

Olyuan answeryd hur tho:
"Sethyn, lady, ye wylle do so,
　　Dred ye no wyght;
I schalle yow helpe bothe nyght and day,
Lady, alle, that euyr y may,
　　That he yow wynne myght!
Yt may soche aventour be,
Lady, that ye may hym see
　　Or thys fourtenyght;
At Mountmertrous, y wolde, ye were,
The sothe of hym there shulde ye here,
　　Be he squyer or knyght." (1093–1116)

In this allomotif the poet compresses the action to a very brief encounter. In other *confession* allomotifs, however, the action and the
dialogue are expanded in a number of formulaic ways. An optional slot,
a description of the servant (pared down in *Octavian* to the one-line
phrase "the kyngs doghtur of Sodam") may precede the obligatory confession, as it does in *Generides* and *William of Palerne*:

So oon of hir women come at the last
That she most loued of any woman,—
What was hir name wel tel I can,—
Hir right name was Mirabel,
A gentil ladie, as I you tel,
And of gentil bloode samfayle,
(Hir fadre was an Amyrayle) (*Generides* 1606–1612)

Thanne hadde this menskfyl melior maydenes fele
A-segned hire to serue & to seuwe hire a-boute;

Table 5

Narrative	Confession (Lover)
Octavian 1093–1116	Lady tells Olyvan that she loves Florent.
Earl of Toulous 181–240	Earl asks prisoner to describe lady, says he wants to meet her.
Eglamour 49–108	Eglamour tells squire that he loves Christabell.
William of Palerne 580–652	Melior confesses her love for William at Alexandrine's urging.
Ywayn and Gawayn 909–930	Lunette knows the cause of Ywayn's distraction.
Degrevant 520–608	Degrevant tells his squire that he loves Melidor.
803–939	Degrevant tells Melidor's servant that he loves Melidor.
Generides 1600–1684	Clarionas confesses her love for Generides at Mirabel's urging.
1685–1782	Generides confesses his love for Clarionas at Nathanael's urging.
6183–6220	Garynan confesses his love for Clarionas to Jewel.
Floris and Blancheflur 385–424	Floris tells innkeeper that he is searching for Blancheflur.
443–511	Floris tells burgess that he is searching for Blancheflur.

Promise (Helper)	Plan (Helper or Lover and Helper)
Olyvan offers to help her.	They plan to go to Montmartre.
Prisoner offers to conduct him; he is rewarded.	They plan to go to see the lady.
Squire protests, but consents to help him.	Squire asks Christabell to visit Eglamour.
Alexandrine offers to help her.	Alexandrine plans to let William know in a dream that Melior loves him.
Lunette offers to help him.	Lunette brings Ywayn and Laudine together.
Squire protests but consents to help him.	They plan to go to Melidor's castle.
She protests but consents to help him; she is rewarded.	They plan to go to Melidor's chamber.
Mirabel offers to help her.	They plan to speak with Generides.
Nathanael offers to help him.	Nathanael plans to find out Clarionas's feelings.
Jewel offers to help him.	Jewel plans to abduct Clarionas.
Innkeeper tells Floris that she has been taken to Babylon; he is rewarded.	Floris plans to go to Babylon.
Burgess tells Floris that Amiral has bought her for his harem; he is rewarded.	Burgess advises Floris to seek bridge keeper.

Narrative *(cont.)*	Confession (Lover)
512–704	Floris tells bridge keeper that he is searching for Blancheflur.
705–740	——

> But among alle the maidenes most sche loued one
> That was a digne damisele to deme al the sothe
> & komen of hire oune kin h[er]e kosin ful nere,
> Of lumbardie a dukes doughter ful derworth in wede,
> & that amiabul maide alisaundrine a-hight. (*William* 580–586)

In another optional slot, the servant may beg the lover to tell about his or her feelings:

> "Now for marie, madame, the milde quene of heuene,
> & for that loue that ye loue leliest here in erthe,
> Seiyth me al your seknesse & what so sore yow greuis."
> (*William* 591–593)

> And as she durst, with piteous speche,
> Hir ladie she began to seche
> That she wold tel hir cause whi
> That euel hir toke so sodeinlie. (*Generides* 1625–1628)

In yet a third optional slot, the servant may argue with the master or mistress. In *Degrevant*, where the *confession* motifeme occurs twice at widely separated intervals, one servant protests that the object of Degrevant's love, Melidor, is the daughter of his enemy:

> For I dar saffly swere,
> Gyff he take the in werre,
> Alle Englond here
>   Wold spek of this dede,
> And say hyt ys a folly
> For to loue thin enemy
> Gyf thou gett a vylony
>   But maugre to mede. (581–588)

Promise *(cont.)* **(Helper)**	**Plan** **(Helper or Lover and Helper)**
Bridge keeper tells him that she is confined in Amiral's palace.	Bridge keeper advises Floris to seek porter; devises plan to gain porter's help.
Porter is tricked into agreeing to help.	Porter hides Floris in a flower basket.

Another servant, after Degrevant's second confession, discourages him from pressing his suit on the grounds that the knight has slain Melidor's kinsmen, that his rank is too low, and that another, more suitable lover is about to win her hand:

> The mayd answerus ayeyn:
> "Me think thou trauelus in vayn,
> Thou hast our kunred y-slayn,
>   How myght hit so be?
> I swer the by Godus myghth,
> Com thou euer in hur syghth,
> Thou bes honged on hyghth
>   Hyie on a tre!
> Hyr proferrys par amoure
> Both dukes and emperoure,
> Hyt were hyr disonowre
>   For to taken the.
> The Duke of Gerle for hir has sent
> That he wol haue a tornament,
> Hyt ys my lordys assent
>   With-ynne for to be." (849–864)

In *Eglamour* the servant protests that the lady would make fun of him if he were to go on such a fool's errand as the confession of his master's love:

> The sqwyere seyde, "So mote I the,
> Yow haue tolde me your pryuyte;
>   I schall you gyf answere.
> Ye ar a knyght of lytyll lond:

Take not to eyull, I vndirstond,
　For mykyll wolde haue more.
Yif I went to that lady and told her so,
Perauntur on skorn take hit wold scho
　And lyghtly lett me fare.
Syr, a mon that hewyth ouyr hye
Lyghtly the chyppus fallen in his eye—
　Thus happis hyt ofte aywhare." (61–72)

The porter in *Floris and Blancheflur*, after he has been tricked into pledging his support, fears that he will be killed if he tries to help Floris:

Now I woot how it gooth;
For thee shall I suffer deth! (723–724)

And in *Floris* we find a fourth optional slot in the *confession* motifeme, the rewarding of the helper. Floris wins the porter's help after he has intentionally lost forty marks, a hundred pounds, and a gold cup to the man in a game of chess:

The porter ys Floris man bycome
For his gold and his warysone.
. . . .
And seide, "Y am betrayde aryght;
Through thy Catel, y am dismayde;
Therfore y am wel euyl apayde." (707–708, 720–722)

In the *Degrevant confession* motifeme the hero buys the servant's goodwill and assistance by promising to give her in marriage to his squire with a dowry of a hundred pounds worth of land, certainly an attractive incentive:

"And damesel for thi chere,
And for my god sopere,
Thou shalt haue my squiere,
　Lok yf the paye.
Here I gyf yow be band
A c. pownd worth of land;
Do tak hyr by the hond
　And do as Y the saye." (881–888)

In *Toulous* the earl promises freedom and a hundred pounds to a prisoner who will take him to see the lady he loves:

"Thy raunsom here y the forgyve,
My helpe my love whyll y leve,
   Thereto my trowthe y plyght
So that thou wylt brynge me,
Yn safe garde for to bee
   Of hur to have a syght,
An hundurd pownd wyth gret honoure,
To bye the horses and ryche armoure,
   Os y am trewe knyght!" (208–216)

In the second obligatory slot (*promise*) the helper finally agrees to aid the lover in gaining his love:

"Ma dame," she seith, "nov beth in pees;
Rise up nov and make goode chere,
And I shal help, to my power,
So to counsel you in this dede
That of your porpos ye shul spede." (*Generides* 1678–1682)

I shal the faile neuer moo,
The while y may ryde and goo;
Thy forwardes shal y holde alle,
What-so-euer may befalle.
Wynde now hoom to thyr ynne
While y bethenke me of sum gynne (*Floris* 725–730)

The maid seis, "Y take on hand
That Y shal do thyn errand;
Or Y be flemyd out of lond,
   Y lete for no dred" (*Degrevant* 913–916)

The variants which manifest the third obligatory slot (*plan*) are several. In most instances the lover and his or her helper simply plan to see the loved one or to convey a message (*Toulous, Octavian, Degrevant, Generides, Eglamour, Ywayn*). In other allomotifs a more dramatic, imaginative action is planned: the abduction of the lady (*Floris*) or (in *William*) the creation of a dream which causes William to return Melior's love.

When we look at the distribution of the motifeme in the narrative sequence, we can see several interesting manipulations of the structural pattern. In most of the narratives the motifeme slot is filled only once. In *Floris*, however, the *confession-promise-plan* allomotif makes up the whole central part of the story (385–744) through the technique of recursive chaining. The allomotif occurs four times, and each time it is repeated the hero moves closer to regaining his lost love. In the first instance an innkeeper tells Floris that Blancheflur has been taken to Babylon by a gang of slave traders and is rewarded by a gold cup; a second innkeeper, a "burgeise," tells him that the Amiral of Babylon has bought Blancheflur for his harem and earns a silver cup and a scarlet mantle for his services; a bridge keeper, Dares, advises Floris how to approach the porter of the Amiral's palace; the porter smuggles Floris into the palace in a basket of flowers. These narrative repetitions are conveyed by a number of verbatim lexical formulas.

In *Generides* the allomotif is repeated immediately following its first use: Clarionas confesses her love for Generides to Miral, who promises to help and counsel her (1604–1684); Generides' servant and friend Nathanael, finding his master ill, hears Generides' confession and promises to help him by finding out the state of Clarionas's feelings (1685–1782). It occurs a third time much later in the poem (6191–6220) when Garynan confesses his love for Clarionas to Jewel, who conceives and carries out an elaborate plot to kidnap Clarionas that involves much of the rest of the story.

In *Degrevant* this allomotif appears twice: Degrevant first confesses his love for Melidor to his own servant and obtains his aid to get into Melidor's castle (520–608); later he confesses his love to Melidor's servant and obtains her aid to get into Melidor's chamber (804–939). Earlier we noted that the motif may be chained in a sequence of preceding and following motifs; now we see that it may be employed any number of times and may become an important narrative feature occupying a central place in the poem.[21]

The major difference between this motifeme and the others that we have discussed is a difference in the kinds of patterning. While the other motifemes demonstrated short sequences of actions or descriptions or poetic commentary, this motifeme displays a configuration of characters related to one another through specific action. Each slot of the motifeme can be filled only by action which is specific to certain characters: a lover and a helper. Schematically it includes the following sequence of obligatory slots (ordered in a logical and chronological fashion) and unordered optional slots:

OBLIGATORY
lover confesses to helper

helper promises aid
lover and/or helper formulate plan

OPTIONAL
description of helper
helper begs lover to confide troubles
helper argues with lover
helper is rewarded

In order to show something of the narrative organization of the tale components, I have examined them in isolation, out of the narrative context in which they occur. However, none of these small units has any real significance outside of the system in which it functions, and it is in many ways misleading to talk about the unit outside of the sequence of structure to which it is related. Like a syntagm, an allomotif always serves as an element in a larger sequence of narrative structure. The unit which immediately subsumes the motifeme is the type-scene, just as the motifeme immediately subsumes the syntagmeme. However, this segmentation of the narrative process raises a number of important questions which should be attended to before we can continue our discussion of larger structural patterns.

The segmentation of narrative units

In this study, as in other structural studies, we are confronted with the problem of designating a basic unit of structure. From the point of view I have adopted, that unit may be of any size appropriate to the material under consideration and to the purpose of the analysis; we can talk about language-formula units, about narrative units, and so on. When unit size is viewed in this indeterminate way, however, the problem of segmentation arises. How do we mark off the borders between units? How do we know where one unit leaves off and another unit begins?

There are essentially two different ways of approaching this difficulty. We might assume that each segment is a completely identifiable unit with a clearly marked beginning and ending; when it is assembled into any narrative sequence, it is discrete, and its junctions can be established. This view has the virtue of simplicity: we need only consider the unit and its distribution in sequence, and it is clearly appropriate for the construction of lists of separate items, as in a dictionary.[22]

But while this method (which has been called the *item-and-arrangement* approach) may hold promise for less complex semiological systems, it is far too rigorous for the treatment of narrative; it does, in fact, violate our initial assumption that any narrative is a whole of interacting systems. A much more realistic view, and one which is theoretically more appropriate to my argument here, is the dynamic view (or *item-and-process* view)[23] in which the narrative, as process, is seen as an interwoven pattern of units which fuse and interpenetrate. Whatever the method of segmenting units of narrative structure, it must take into account dynamic process as a major characteristic of narrative form, and the units ultimately chosen must be flexible. Either method of segmentation (*item-and-arrangement* or *item-and-process*) is bound to distort narrative patterns to some extent; the important thing is to be clear about the degree and direction of that distortion.

In the preceding section, I presented a number of examples of motifemic units in a rather more schematized way than would ordinarily be desirable in order to clarify their construction. In a manner of speaking, I was creating a "dictionary" of a small number of motifemes, treating each allomotif as a discrete and discontinuous unit constructed of discrete and discontinuous subunits. In the narrative, however, the allomotif is not discontinuous; it is a pattern woven into an uninterrupted tapestry, its borders merging with the borders of other patterns until the elements are no longer separable. Smaller patterns are subsumed into larger and larger ones and are lost in the multiplicity of forms within larger forms.

But in order to perceive these smaller patterns within the field of larger narrative structures, we need to tolerate some degree of artificial schematization and segmentation. The best way to approach this difficult problem in the analysis of individual units in single narratives seems to be first to mark off the nucleus of the pattern and then to attempt to make some rough judgment about the nature of the peripheral material which is included within the unit. When two allomotifs merge (particularly when one is embedded within another), it may be advantageous to treat them together or simply to note the incidence of their co-occurrence (which may itself turn out to be a pattern of some interest). I have adopted here the rough rule of thumb that a motifeme is a repeatable unit smaller than a type-scene; when I have found a relatively small-scale pattern which is repeated in several narratives, I have marked it off and treated it as a motifemic unit. I have also adopted the usable though not precise criterion of closure; a motifeme is ended when the activity ends, or when the characters specific to it change, or when the poet turns to something else. While these are admittedly very loose criteria, they seem to be preferable to a rigid overschematization that cannot deal with narrative process.

From motifeme to scene-pattern: single combat

The scene-pattern has essentially the same formulaic nature as the two
smaller systems (the syntagmeme and the motifeme) which it subsumes. Typical scenes consist of ordered and/or unordered sequences of
a limited number of motifemic slot patterns (usually only four or five)
which are filled by variants of syntagmemic patterns, often in repeated
sequences of twos and threes. But these characteristic features, familiar through their appearance in the other systems I have discussed, will
become clearer after we have examined a scene at length. One of the
most typical of such scenes is the single combat, an armed, mounted
battle (usually in sport but often in earnest) between a pair of knights.
The following seventy-line example from the Chetham *Bevis* is
lengthy, but it usefully demonstrates all of the motif patterns we will
find in the other narratives.

3473 On the morowe, whan it was day clere,
   Than arose bothe knyght and squyer;
   Fayre tokens dyd they on them throwe,
   Wherby the lady shulde them knowe.
   Syr Beuys and sir Terry
   Armed them ful hastely;
   Syr Beuys bare of colour poymant
3480 A rede lyon of golde rampant.
   Than forthe rode Terry and he
   Thyder, where the iustynge shuld be.
   The fayre lady Helyanour
   Ouer the castel lay that houre,
3485 And al the iustynge she behelde,
   What knyght hym bare best in the felde.
   Than these knyghtes began to ryde,
   Eche at other on euery syde.
   The fyrst knyght, that Beuys rode agayne,
3490 Was themperours son of Almayne,
   And Beuys at hym bare so fast,
   That hors and man to grounde he cast.
   The erle Florens forth gan thrynge
   Agaynst Beuys wyth great hastynge;
3495 Beuys met hym in the felde
   And hyt hym in myddes of the shelde,
   That two londe brede and more
   He cast hym from his hors thore.
   Than rode forth the duke Antoyne,

3500 That than was duke of Burgoyne;
　　　He was stronge and great of pryce,
　　　And thus he sayde to syr Beuys:
　　　"Turn the, knyght, and make defence,
　　　For I wol venge the erle Florence!"
3505 Than wolde Beuys no lenger abyde,
　　　But smote Arundel vnder the syde;
　　　So harde eyther to other droue,
　　　That theyr speres al to-roue.
　　　But Beuys so harde to hym thrast,
3510 That his shulder bone al to-brast;
　　　Thereof he was agreued sore,
　　　For that day myght he iust nomore.
　　　Than rode forth syr Terry
　　　To the kynges broder of Hungry
3515 And gaue to hym suche a rebowne,
　　　That both he and his hors fel downe.
　　　Than cam the erle Hamaut
　　　And to Terry made a saute,
　　　And Terry hyt hym in the shelde,
3520 That he bare hym into the felde.
　　　There was no knyght, verely,
　　　That myght wythstande Beuys nor Terry,
　　　But al the khyghtes for great enuy
　　　Them two assayled cruelly,
3525 And ful narowe them sought,
　　　But Beuis of Hampton spared nought;
　　　The stywarde of that same londe
　　　Beuys cast downe in myddys of the sonde.
　　　Than loughe the lady Elyanore
3530 For the boste, that he made before,
　　　And many Beuys bare thoroughout,
　　　That of theyr lyfe they stode in dout.
　　　They stynted neuer, tyl it was night,
　　　That they wanted the day lyght;
3535 Than they left of theyr Iustynge,
　　　And on the morrow they harde tydynge,
　　　That syr Beuys of Hamptowne
　　　Had wonne the laude and the renowne.
　　　Dame Helyanour wolde nat blynne,
3540 Tyl Beuys was brought to hyr Inne;
　　　She sayde: "Syr, it is gyuen me to counsayle,

Thou shalt me wed, wythouten fayle,
Eyther to other terme of lyfe."

The scene seems to fall very naturally into smaller, relatively discrete units of narrative action, all of which fit the motifemic pattern outlined in the preceding paragraph. The allomotifs occur in this order:

1. arming of the knights (3473–3480)
2. description of the lady spectator (3483–3486)
3. Bevis's first tilt (3487–3492)
4. Bevis's second tilt (3493–3498)
5. Bevis's third tilt (3499–3512)
6. Terry's first tilt (3513–3516)
7. Terry's second tilt (3517–3522)
8. Bevis's and Terry's tilt (3523–3528)
9. description of the lady spectator (3529–3530)
10. general battle (3531–3534)
11. Bevis is awarded the prize (3535–3538)
12. Bevis is awarded the lady (3539–3543)

As we can see, the scene contains twelve allomotifs; there are, however, only four motifemes:

1. the arming of the knights
2. the description of the spectator (two allomotifs)
3. the tilt (seven allomotifs)
4. the reward (two allomotifs)

In order to show the continuity of these units throughout all of the poems, I have selected a number of other single-combat scenes which display the same motifemic configuration as the one we have just examined. The first motifeme in all of these single-combat scenes is the *arming of the knights*.[24]

Any whan Syr Launfal was ydyght
Vpon Blaunchard, hys stede lyght,
    Wyth helm & spere & schelde. (*Sir Launfal* 565–567)

And on the morow the Duk hym dyghth
Also fast as he mighth,
The Eorl hardy and wyghth,
    Cruel and kene. (*Degrevant* 1073–1076)

To his in he wente wel son
And let him armi wel-a-fin
In god armes to justi in (*Degare* 494–496)

On the morwe full tymely
On their wey thei dressed theim sikirly. (*Guy* Caius 846–847)

In these examples the allomotif appears very briefly. In other, more complex manifestations of the motifeme, however, it is expanded into a much more significant unit with more than one function. In *Generides* the combat is a real battle, not a tournament, but the structure of the scene is the same, and here the poet elaborates extensively on the champion's armor, a gift from his leader, the Soudan:

> Whan Generides of that wist
> To arme him he had gret list.
> · · · · · · · · · · ·
> Of hors and arms at his pay
> The Soudon yave him the same day,
> A feire swerd he yave him than
> That was the Emperours Julian
> That thurgh treason was sleyn in Rome
> Of his commons without dome;
> Twoo of tho traitoures stole that brond,
> And broght it into Perse lond;
> The Soudon smote of her heides bothe,
> For traitoures was him euer loothe
> The same swerd was good and bright,
> This goode swerd Claret hight;
> Aboute his nek heng his shelde,
> Bright it shoone ouer all the felde;
> The champe of the feld was goules
> Thik y-poudred with smale foules
> Of riche gold, with a broode bourdure
> Purtraied with sable and with asure;
> Thereto he bare a ful grete launce,
> And heng thereon his conyssaunce
> That Clarionas him last sent (5655–5656, 5665–5685)

Here the poet focuses in turn on each item of the knight's armor—his sword Claret, his painted shield, his lance hung with colors—and the narrative action, which usually sweeps through the tournament scene at a fairly rapid pace, pauses here while the poet flourishingly expands this particular motif.[25] The expansion, however, seems to be along purely conventional lines (like the description of the cup in *Floris*, the embroidered cloth in *Emare*, the wall hangings in *Degrevant*, and the heirloom sword in *Eger*); it does not have any of the thematic significance that the same motifeme has in *Sir Gawain and the Green Knight*, where the elaborate description of Gawain's arms, with the Pentangle painted on his shield, is linked to other elements within the poem. The meaning of this variant, then, may depend upon a system outside this particular narrative; it is associated with items like the cup or the cloth or the sword, which give it added authenticity and esthetic importance.[26]

Borrowed armor is an occasion for expansion of this same motifeme in several other poems. In *Triamour* the hero is young and untried and has yet earned no arms (the act of borrowing the armor further characterizes this unknown young man). When a joust is proclaimed for the hand of the daughter of the King of Hungary, Triamour goes to his guardian, Sir Barnard, and requests arms and a horse:

> He hadde nothyr hors nor spere,
> Nor no wepyn hym with to were,
>   That brake hys herte withynne;
> Faste he be-thynkyth hym bothe evyn and morow
> Where hym were beste to borowe,
>   Arste worlde he not blynne;
> To hys lorde he can meene,
> And pryed hym that he wolde hym lenne
>   Wepyn, armowre and stede (676–684)

With some natural misgivings Barnard finally agrees to outfit the boy:

> Barnard seyde also hynde,
> "Tryamowre, syn ye wylle wynde,
>   Ye schalle wante no wede;
> For y schalle lende the alle my gere,
> Hors and harnes, schylde and spere,
>   And helpe the at thy nede." (694–699)

In the northern version of *Octavian* Florent is also young and untested, but, when a heathen giant slays a dozen knights outside the walls of Paris, he wants to try his hand in battle. He goes to his foster father, Clement, and begs the loan of arms:

"Fadur," he seyde, "sadulle my stede
And lende me some dele of your wede
    And helpe, that y were dyght;
Yf that hyt be goddys wylle,
I hope to fynde hym hys fylle,
    Thogh he be stronge and wyght." (865–870)

Clement's response is less than encouraging; a solid, middle-class butcher who values Florent's performance at the auction block far more than his performance in the lists, he cannot understand the aristocratic yearning of the foundling whom he bought for forty pounds from a gang of robbers:

Clement seyde: "And thou oon worde more speke,
Thys day y wylle thy hedde breke,
    I swere be Mary bright!" (871–873)

But Florent at length prevails and Clement finds for him a suit of ancient, rusty armor which earns for the hero only the scorn of the spectators who gather to watch the battle:

For sorowe Clements herte nye braste,
When he on Florent hacton caste,
    The chylde was bolde and kene;
An hawberke aboue let he falle,
Rowsty were the naylys alle
    And hys atyre bedeene.
Clement broght forthe schylde and spere,
That were vncomely for to were,
    Alle sutty, blakk and vnclene;
A swyrde he broght the chylde beforne,
That VII yere afore was not borne
    Ne drawe, and that was seene.
· · · · · · · · · · · ·
For hys atyre, that was vnbryghte
Hym behelde bothe kynge and knyght
    And moche wondur thoght;
Many a skorne there he hent,
As he thorow the cyte went,
    But thereof roght he noght. (877–888, 913–918)

In the passages from *Generides* and *Triamour* the allomotif is free; that is, it is not contingent upon other narrative elements in the immediate context (although, as I suggested, in *Generides* the expansion seems to be dependent upon an extranarrative system). In *Octavian*, however, the comic allomotif is an element in the continuing burlesque that surrounds the character of Clement, the good butcher of Paris; it derives in each instance from the poet's substitution of a bourgeois element for an aristocratic one in the normal motifeme context—in this allomotif, the substitution of rusty, outmoded armor for royal array.[27] Here the development of the allomotif is conditioned not by its immediate plot context but by another regular system of unexpected and comic substitutions.

In the next three instances, all of which precede the three-day tourney,[28] the development of the *arming* motifeme is conditioned by its immediate narrative environment and by some force, not easily explainable, which seems to hold together certain kinds of components in a traditional association. In *Roswall and Lillian, Ipomedon*, and *Sir Gowther* the hero disguises himself for the three-day fight, although the reason for the disguise is not clearly explained; the armor disguise simply seems to belong to the three-day tourney. On each day the hero arms himself in different-colored armour. In *Ipomedon* and *Roswall* he leaves the court each morning and goes out into the woods, where he meets another man (his servant in *Ipomedon*, a passing knight in *Roswall*) and exchanges armor with him; in *Gowther* he prays each morning and receives a new set of different-colored arms, enabling him to take part in the combat incognito. In *Ywayn and Gawayn* the poet also uses the disguise component:

> The armes he bar were noght his owne
> For he wolde noght in court be knowen, (3400–3401)

The *arming* motifeme, which under ordinary circumstances plays a relatively minor role in the single-combat scene, may become essential to the plot development, as it does in the three-day tournament.

The question of identity, always a major concern in these poems, is the central problem in another example of motifeme expansion, where the arms of the knight are crucial to his subsequent identification after the fight. In *Eglamour*, for instance, there is an ingenious instance of double recognition. Eglamour has become separated from his lady, Cristabell, who is now the prize in a tourney in which the leading contender for her hand is their son (whose identity is also unknown). The son wins here, but just before their wedding Cristabell recognizes him

by his arms and thus happily prevents their incestuous marriage
(1150–1170). Eglamour now comes to the tournament bearing arms
which tell the story of his lost wife and child and provide the clue to
both their real identities:

> For Crystabell was don in the see
> Newe armes bare he—
> Lystyn and I wyll you say sykurly:
> He bare a schyp in armes of gold,
> And a lady drownyng as sche schold;
> A chyld lyand hyr by.
> The chyld was butt a nyght old;
> Hys mast was of syluyre and gold
> In euery poynte to the ye;
> Of reed gold was hys fane,
> Fys fales and hys ropes ylkane
> Was purtred varely. (1198–1209)

In this first class of motifemes within the battle scene, the variant
allomotifs exhibit some rather striking differences. Usually, as we
noted, the arming of the knight is a simple affair, handled with dis-
patch so that the narrator can get on with the business of the battle,
and the majority of the allomotifs manifest only the one-slot nucleus.
But there are occasions when the poet may seek a special effect—
pageantry (*Generides*) or comic realism (*Octavian*)—or when the poet
develops the motifeme for purposes which have to do with other plot
requirements. These are the more complex allomotifs, and they may
possess any number of optional slots: *description of arms, armor as a
gift, borrowed armor, antique armor, armor as disguise, armor as a
means to recognition*.

The second motifeme in this scene, the *spectator* motifeme, is also
manifested by a wide-ranging group of variant allomotifs. It may involve either a number of spectators or the lady alone (as it does in the
passage from *Bevis*); it usually occurs at least twice in the course of the
combat, and if the combat is a three-day tourney, it is likely to be repeated at least once for each day. There are so many examples of this
class of motifs that I can present only a sampling here:

> Then was that lady sett
> Hye up in a garett
> To beholde that play (*Triamour* 721–723)

Crystabell, that lady small
Sche was browght to the wall
   There the crye was made (*Eglamour* 1225–1227)

The leuedi lai in o kernel
And biheld the batail oueri del
Sche was neuer er so blithe
Sche thanked God fele sithe. (*Degare* 965–968)

The second occurrence of this allomotif in the single-combat scene is
often longer and more detailed, for, as the battle progresses, the spectators take sides, sympathizing with the hero when things go badly,
rejoicing when he seems to have the upper hand:

And the ladies everilkane,
That war thare forto se that sight,
Praied ful fast ay for the knight. (*Ywayn* 2608–2610)

Many a gentylman
And ladyes whyt as swan
For Lybeauus handes wrong (*Libeaus* 1366–1368)

Bothe lardes and ladyes
Leyn out yn pomet tours
To se that sely syght;
And prayed with good wyll,
Bothe lode and styll,
Helpe Lybeauus the knyght,
And that fyle geaunt
That leuede yn Termagaunt,
That day to deye yn fyght. (*Libeaus* 1294–1302)

The ledy lay on toure on hye,
The rede knyght ful sonne she see;
She wende it were the strange squyere,
That she hopid shuld be hyr fere.
Her purpos was to hym to wende,
Whan the justes come to ende,
And brynge hym with feyre manere,
To hyr was non so leffe ne dere. (*Ipomedon* 1101–1108)

Grete crie was in the Citie than,
Of Generides thei were agast

That he was so to ground cast,
Clarionas also saw that
Out of the toure there she sat;
Of Generides she was in were,
She wept and made ful heuy chere. (*Generides* 5792–5798)

There is at least one other variation in this motifeme. Two scenes
which earlier employ the allomotif *borrowed armor* to fill the *arming*
motifeme now employ an additional allomotif in the *spectator*
motifeme. In *Triamour* Barnard stands on the wall and cries
"Trayamowre! Trayamowre!" so that everyone will know the name of
the victorious (but unknown) knight. In *Octavian* Clement the
butcher, whose earlier bourgeois displeasure has now turned to proud
delight in the aristocratic prowess of his adopted son, watches from the
walls:

Clement on the wallys stode,
Fulle blythe was he yn hys mode
  And mende can hys chere.
"Sone, for that y haue seene
Thy noble stroke, that ys so kene,
  To me art thou fulle dere;
Now me thynkyth yn my mode,
Thou haste welle besett my gode,
  Soche playes for to lere.
Jesu, that syttyth yn trynyte,
Blesse the fadur, that gate the,
  And the modur, that the dud bere!" (949–960)

And when the giant gets in a lucky blow, Clement shouts from Florent's corner:

"Sone, be now of comfort gode
  And venge the, yf thou may!" (971–972)

At least two nuclear components can be noted in all of the instances
of the *spectator* motifeme. The lady, who is always present, is invariably seated in a high place, on the castle wall or in a tower (this component is an important part of the background in medieval drawings of
tournaments);[29] second, the audience always supports the hero (even
when, as in *Octavian*, they begin by making fun of him). The poet may
use the allomotif to punctuate the action, providing a very stylized,
almost cinematic movement from protagonists to spectators.

The third and most complex motifeme in the single-combat scene is the battle itself, the focal point of the scene. First of all, while the other motifemes of this scene have been composed of an obligatory nuclear component and one or two peripheral, optional components, the *combat* motifeme is constructed upon a fairly complicated and yet well-defined pattern, a sequence of actions that normally occur in the same general order. Second, this motifeme is subject to a certain number of repetitions within the scene (usually three but occasionally two or four). These redundant patterns are not contingent upon any other element in the narrative, it seems, but are stylized representations of real medieval tournaments, which, like any other games, were played by a recognized set of rules.[30] In this case, however, it is very difficult to say where realism ends and ritual representation begins. It will be sufficient for now to point out that the development of this motifeme (like the *arming* motifeme in *Generides*) is contingent upon extra-narrative fact. Here, however, the reference is nonliterary rather than literary; the sequence of actions in this motifeme, as far as we can tell, is largely dependent on the sequence of actions in the real game—except for the obvious fictional device: the hero always wins.

The *combat* motifeme has several important components: the naming of the knights (necessary only if the general fight is a large one); their actual encounter; and the result of the encounter, all of which may require no more than four to six lines. These separate elements can be distinguished in the following examples:

> The fyrst knyght, that Beuys rode agayne,
> Was themperours son of Almayne
> And Beuys at hym bare so fast,
> That hors and man to grounde he cast. (*Bevis* 3489–3492)

> The fyrste that rode to hym thon
> Was the kynge of Arragon,
>   He kepeyd hym in that tyde;
> He gaf hys fadur soche a clowte,
> That hors and man felle downe withowt dowte,
>   And sone he was dyscryed. (*Triamour* 778–783)

> The fyrst knyght he gan to ryde,
> With a spere that wold abyde,
> In myddis the sheld he sette his spere,
> That hors and men he gan downe bere (*Ipomedon* 813–816)

The erle Florens forth gan thrynge,
Agaynst Beuys wyth great hastynge;
Beuys met hym in the felde
And hyt hym in myddes of the shelde,
That two londe brede and more
He cast hym from his hors thore. (*Bevis* 3493–3498)

Gayer smote Gye in the felde
With hys spere thorow the schelde,
That hys spere brake in two
Gyes hawberk dud not soo.
Gye smot Gayer wyth myght,
To the erthe he feele down ryght. (*Guy* Caius 583–588)

The rede knyght anone in-rode.
The blake toke a spere in hond,
To just with hym he thoght in londe;
And eyther with other sone they mette.
In mydde the sheld the stroke they sett.
The blak knyght spere was stiffe and stronge,
And therewith he gan fast thronge
The knyght and stede within a stounde,
That they lay bothe vppon the grounde. (*Ipomedon* 1110–1118)

The formulaic pattern here is based on a subordinate clause used adverbially to show result:

bare so fast that . . .
gaf . . . soche a clowte that . . .
sette his spere that . . .
he gan thronge . . . that . . .
smote . . .that . . .

This pattern is a common one in this motifeme (in fact, so far as I have been able to discover, this particular formula is limited to this motifeme).

In a larger battle such as a tournament, where the hero will engage in a number of single combats and win the prize by knocking down as many knights as possible, the combat allomotif must be kept short and simple with little variation in the sequence of actions, as it is in the examples above. In these allomotifs each victory is usually accomplished in a single course; the knight dispatches his opponent with one blow, delivered "in middes the sheld," that sends "hors and man to the grownde," and he is ready to go on to the next opponent, whom he discomfits in exactly the same fashion. The effect of such a rapid-paced narrative account is one of speed and confusion, with horses and men tumbling about the field in a flurry of limbs and broken armor, but hidden within the confusion is a careful patterning which lends structure to the whole.

In scenes where only two knights fight, the poet handles the material in a much more leisurely way, and although the action is just as violent, it seems more ritualistic. The pattern consists of an optional challenge or a boastful threat, delivered either before the fight or during it; the obligatory initial charge of the mounted men (the charge may be missed by both knights, however); a second charge, usually resulting in the shattering of the spears or the death or disablement of one or both of the horses; and an optional third round fought on foot with swords. The two-part sequential pattern is evident in *Triamour* in the fight between the hero and Burlonde:

> Tryamowre to hym berys,
> And they alle to-braste ther sperys,
>   That bothe to the grownde they yede
> . . . .
> They start up bothe withyn a whyle,
> Ther stedys on the grownde lay fulle stylle,
>   On fote they faght in fere. (1492–1494, 1501–1503)

The unhorsing is often the occasion for the challenge or the boastful threat, as it is in *Degare*:

> But anon stirt up the knight
> And drough out his swerd bright.
> "Alight," he saide, "adoun anon!
> To fight thou sschalt a-fote gone.
> For thou has islawe mi stede,
> Dethes dint schal be thi mede.
> Ac thine stede sle I nille;
> Ac on fote fighte ich wille."
> Than on fote thai toke the fight
> And hewe togidere with brondes bright. (941–950)

and in *Generides*:

> The stede arerud and fel bakward
> And ther lay the king of kinges,

He was yuel paied of these tithinges;
Vp he stert; withdraw him he wold;
But Generides seid he ne shold,
"Laugh there," he seid, "now, sir king,
Thou plaidest with me at thi liking,
Nou shal I, Sir, magre thi leue,
Som what ageyn the now greue." (5924–5932)

and in the southern version of *Octavian*:

Tho seyde the Sarsyn: "Krysten knyght,
    Thou art a vyleyn,
To sle my hors, that hath no gylt!"
Seyde Florent chylde: "All, that thou wylt!" (1097–1100)

In *Ywayn* the challenge is a much more significant element of the battle scene, because it grows out of a minor theme of *invasion of territory*, part of the Celtic fairy-tale background of the story. The first challenge is delivered in the frame story when Colgrevance casts a basin of water upon a stone, and an angry knight appears:[31]

That knight to me hied ful fast,
And kene wordes out gan he cast.
He bad that I sold tel him tite,
Whi I did him swilk despite,
With weders wakend him of rest
And did him wrang in his forest.
"Tharfore," he said, "thou sal aby."
And with that come he egerly
And said I had ogayn resowne
Done him grete destrucciowne
And might it never more amend,
Tharfore he bad I sold me fend. (407–418)

In *Libeaus* there is no magic fountain, but the same Celtic *invasion-of-territory* element is involved. Maugys, the black knight and guardian of the bridge to the Dolorous Island, is challenged by Libeaus, the white knight, who wants to cross the bridge:

He cryde to hym yn despyte,
"Say, thou felaw yn whyte,
Tell me what art thou!

Torne hom agayn all-so tyt,
For thy owene profyt,
Yef thow louede thy prow."
Lybeauus seyde anoon ryght,
"Artour made me knyght,
To hym J made avow
That Y ne schulde neuer turne bak;
Ther-fore, thou deuell yn blak,
Make the redy now!" (1279–1290)

As we have seen, in many narratives the challenge may become a
major element, perhaps even more important than the battle which
follows it. When this occurs, we are probably justified in treating the
challenge as a separate motifeme in its own right, manifested by a
number of allomotifs, rather than as one of the components in the
single-combat motifeme of the single-combat scene.[32] In the normal
scene-pattern, however, it is usually of minor importance and, like the
arming motifeme, serves only as prologue to the actual fight.

The description of the battle itself is made up of a number of formulaic descriptions of the blows traded back and forth; and, like the
other components of this motifeme, it is highly redundant. One of the
blows usually strikes the shield out of the combatant's hand or breaks
it in two:

Lybeauus smot Mauugys so
That hys scheld fell hym fro
And yn-to the feld gan flynge. (*Libeaus* 1312–1314)

Al to peces thai hewed thaire shelds,
The culpons flegh out in the feldes. (*Ywayn* 641–642)

A quarter of his sheeled away is gone
The other he clave in tow
That it ffell into the feyld soe far him froe. (*Eger* 1042–1044)

To the chylde smote he so,
That the chyldes shylde broke yn two
    And fell on euery syde. (*Octavian* Camb. 940–942)

Gye smot Rayner on the schelde
That hyt flewe into the felde (*Guy* Caius 619–620)

He smot Generides with egre moode,
That his shelde cleef euen in twoo,
And in twoo peces it fel him froo. (*Generides* 6026–6028)

Spears are shattered by the force of the blows:

Bothe hy smyte togydere tho
That her sperys tobroste at two
The peces tell fer hem fro
  Of tymbres toghe. (*Octavian* Cotton 1081–1084)

Guy turned hym and smote faste:
Bothe ther sperys all tobraste (*Guy* Camb. 617–618)

Another blow cleaves the opponent's armor:

Doun to the shuldre the swerde drofe
And brake both hauberk and Acton
In many stede the male fel doun (*Generides* 5964–5966)

The lord a strok hym sette
Through helm and basnet
That yn the scheld hyt stode. (*Libeaus* 1168–1170)

And swich a strok he yaf the knight
Upon his hed, so hard iset
Thurgh helm and hed and bacinet
That ate breste stod the dent
Ded he fil doun, verraiment. (*Degare* 960–964)

Manly when they togedur mett
They hewe thorow helme and basenet
And martyrd many a mayl. (*Toulous* 1114–1116)

Lybeauus was werrour wyght
And smot a strok of myght
Thorugh gypell, plate, and mayll (*Libeaus* 1381–1383)

Forth through the shield he did him bare,
Through ventale, and through foreshare,
And so again through the actoun:
Through birnie and through herbergeoun.
(*Sir Eger, Sir Grahme, and Sir Gray-steele* Huntington 1523–1526)

or cuts his right arm off at the shoulder:

> Forth wyth the scholder bon
> Maugys arm fyll of anoon
> Jn-to the feld, saunz fayle. (*Libeaus* 1384–1386)

> To the gyaunt he smote so sore,
> That hys ryght arme flye of thore:
>   The blode stremyd wyde. (*Octavian* Camb. 946–948)

> Guy smote hym thorow the schouldur bone;
> The dewke felle of hys hors anon. (*Guy* 603–604)

> Forth to hym he gan go:
> Hys ryghte arme he stroke hym fro
>   Faste by the schulder bone. (*Eglamour* 589–591)

In the *combat* motifeme, then, we have distinguished three components: the naming of the knights (an optional, peripheral element); the challenge (optional and peripheral); and the blows traded by the opponents (nuclear and obligatory). As we have seen, the nuclear component is itself made up of a sequence of smaller formulaic elements: the breaking of the shield in two parts, the shattering of the spears, the cleaving of the armor, the cutting off of the right arm. The *challenge*, an optional component, may also be viewed as a separate motifeme when it is expanded in such a way as to become more functional. In some cases the challenge seems to be linked to a motifeme that is a carry-over from more primitive narratives, the *prohibition*; in others, it may be a part of a larger episode, the accomplishment of a task.[33]

The final motifeme in this scene is *reward*, which is likely to require only a few lines. Often the reward is granted on the field by a kind of general consensus of the spectators:

> But all the men wyth hartys free
> Haue geuyn Gye the maystree. (*Guy* Camb. 655–656)

> And seide with o criing: "Iwis
> Child Degaree hath wonne the pris!" (*Degare* 583–584)

> Ladyes seyden al by-dene
> Bothe contasse and gwene
> "Yond gentyl knyght on grene
>   Hath deseruyed the gre." (*Degrevant* 1145–1148)

There was none so gode as he
Therefore they grauntyed hym the gree. (*Triamour* 845–846)

    The kyng seyde "So God me saue,
Thow art best worthy here to haue!"
Thus seyde they all bydene. (*Eglamour* 1132–1134)

That euery man to other gan say:
"He may wele be kynge of londe,
For the doughtyest man of hond,
That any man saw euer ere!"
And so sayd all that there were.
They gaffe hym the gre of felde,
For the doughtyest undyr shelde. (*Ipomedon* 1162–1168)

The major component of the *reward* motifeme, however, is the offer of the lady's hand in marriage, which occurs in some form or another at the end of almost every single combat.[34] Some heroes are proposed to several times in the course of a single poem. Libeaus, for example, wins two ladies, Violet and Dame d'Amour, before he settles on a third, the Lady of Synadowne. In the first instance of the motifeme in *Libeaus*, the father offers his daughter's hand:

The Erl Antore also blyve
Profrede hys doftyr hym to wyue
Violette that may;
And kasteles ten and fyue
And all after hys lyue
His lond to haue for ay. (688–693)

Later in the poem Dame d'Amour makes an offer herself:

To chambre sche gan hym lede
And dede of all hys wede
And cloded hym yn pell
And profereded hym wyth word
For-to be her lord
Jn cyte and castell. (1405–1410)

Finally the Lady of Synadowne proposes but insists on obtaining the consent of the king:

And for thou sauyest my lyf
Casteles ten and fyf
J yeue the wyth-outen ende,
And Y to be thy wyf
Ay wyth-out stryf,
Yf hyt ys Artours wylle. (2032–2037)

Torrent, hero of *Sir Torrent of Portyngale*, is offered three princesses—Gaul, Provence, and Norway:

The kyng of Gales proferd hym feyer:
"Wed my dowghttyr and myn Eyer
  When so euyr thou may!" (417–419)

"I haue a dowghttyr, that ys me dere
Thou schalt here wed to thy fere,
  And, yf yt thy wyll be,
Two duchyes in londe
I wille geve here in hand."
  "Gramarcy, syr" sayd he. (930–935)

He wolde hym yeue his doughter dere
And halfe Norway ffar and nere (1376–1377)

But he marries Desonell, the princess of Portugal, whom he first wins in battle (having also accomplished a series of assigned tasks), loses, and must win again:

They yave sir Torent, that he wan
Both the Erth and the woman
  And said, well worthy was he. (1322–1324)

Even Ywayn has two offers of marriage before he is reunited with his wife:

Sho said, "Sir, if it be yowre will,
I pray yow forto dwel here still;
And I wil yelde into yowre handes
Myne awyn body and al my landes." (*Ywayn* 1959–1962)

If thou overcome hem in this stour
Than shaltow have al this honour

And my doghter in marriage,
And also al myn heritage. (*Ywayn* 3137–3140)

In at least three narratives, single combat ends in the threat of an incestuous marriage between the knight, whose identity is unknown, and
his mother, who is the prize in the tournament (*Degare, Eglamour,* and
Torrent).[35] In *Degare* the lady is not at all pleased about the outcome of
the tournament, because she must marry a man about whose background and lineage she knows nothing:

Than was the damaisele sori;
For hi wiste wel, forwhi:
That hi scholde ispoused ben
To a knight, sche neuer had sen,
And lede here lif with swich a man,
That sche ne wiste, who him wan
No in what londe he was ibore.
The leuedi was carful therfore. (*Degare* 585–592)

Happily, the relationship is discovered at the last moment, and Degare
goes on to win a second lady, who offers him all that she has after the
battle:

Again him com the dammaisel
And thonked him swithe of that dede.
Into chaumber sche gain him lede
And unarmed him anon
And set him hire bed upon
And saide: "Sire, par charite
I the praie dwel with me;
And al my lond ich wil the give
And mi self, whil that I liue." (970–978)

The *reward* motifeme, then, is made up of three components: the
agreement of the spectators that the hero has won the prize (optional
and peripheral); the awarding of the lady's hand in marriage (the offer is
obligatory, although the hero may not accept it because of a prior en-
gagement); and the awarding of the lady's land (also obligatory—while
some of the heroes are, or may appear to be, landless, the lady is always
her father's only heir and possessed of many properties). This motifeme
is of great importance in understanding the larger structures of the romance; we will return to it in a later discussion.

The scene we have discussed here is relatively tightly constructed according to a pattern that exhibits only a few variations; that is, the motifemes that make up this scene are more or less bound to an order of occurrence that is both logical and chronological (although not necessarily bound in a cause-and-effect sequence). This kind of patterned motifeme ordering on the scene level is not always the case, however; some scenes are constructed much more loosely, and their schematization is not accomplished quite so easily.

The motifemic pattern of four nuclear elements is, of course, only the framework of the scene. The optional and peripheral components which fill out this framework cannot be discarded in our analysis, however, because they in turn function on lower levels as nuclear components of smaller units. This hierarchical pattern has the advantage of allowing us to see the interrelationships of what appear to be only minor elements of the narrative, but which are necessary at one level or another.

The scene is only one component of the syntagmatic order of the narrative. It is the highest level in a patterned hierarchy of syntagmeme, motifeme, and scene; but it is in turn subsumed by the episode, a linear arrangement of several related scenes, all designed to work toward the resolution of a single narrative dilemma.

3 Larger structural units: the type-scene

The scene as an emic unit

As an example of a formulaic scene, the single-combat scene outlined in the preceding chapter offers certain advantages. It is easily shown to be repeatable, both in single narratives (some poets employ it a half-dozen or more times in the course of one poem) and in the larger system of all of the narratives of our study (there is not one poem in which it does not occur). Its motifeme pattern can also be schematized without serious distortion of the narrative evidence. Finally, its construction is stylized to a degree that is hardly matched by any other scene; on the linguistic level, for example, the syntagmemes exhibit frequent verbatim lexical correspondences. We may find it more difficult, however, to see other scenes as formulaic units. In this chapter I will describe several other scenes in an attempt to provide a general overview of scene composition from an *emic* point of view.

Several approaches to scene analysis in traditional narrative have already added to our knowledge of formulaic structures. While scene composition has not been viewed specifically in terms of the structural hierarchies proposed here, it has been recognized that certain types of scenes are formulaically patterned and that their form is comparatively stable. Albert Lord calls this kind of configuration a *theme* ("a group of ideas regularly used in telling a tale in the formulaic style of traditional song"),[1] which is built upon a core of central elements expanded by the addition of one or more extra elements. These themes can be linked together in a linear fashion to form a group, or combined and repeated associatively to form "larger complexes," as Lord says; these complexes often have such a strongly patterned integrity that the poet "avoids violating the group of themes by omitting any of its members." The poet will "even go so far as to substitute something similar if he finds that for one reason or another he cannot use one of the elements in its usual form."[2]

Quite early Walter Arend demonstrated that Homeric narrative is built of recurring actions, related in much the same detail each time they appear.[3] He called these repeated units of narrative "typical scenes"—arrival, sacrifice, eating, journeying, arming, dressing, and so forth. But as Milman Parry has pointed out, while Arend's analysis of such scene-patterns is sound, his understanding of the reasons for the existence of such formalized recurrences is "almost mystic": he believes that the essential nature of the act is that constant form in which it is retained, and that somehow the Greek "comprehension of reality" perceived this form and knew it to be right and good—and so it was preserved.[4]

Departing from this philosophic view, most scholars have seen the repeated narrative patterns as elements of the poet's craft. "Homer relates the same action in more or less the same way because that was the only way he had learned,"[5] Parry says in response to Arend, and other critics have for the most part agreed. Their agreement has ended there, however, and the definition of these larger narrative units is a very confused issue, primarily because of the failure to agree on terminology. Francis Magoun, describing twelve instances of the *beasts-of-battle* element in nine Anglo-Saxon poems, calls the pattern a *theme*;[6] Albert Lord has called units of this size *motifs*; following Dundes (and insisting on their identification as *emic* units) I have called these narrative patterns *motifemes*. In terms of the larger narrative unit, J. Rychner uses both *theme* and *motif* to designate the unit that Arend had called a *type-scene*.[7]

But whatever the term adopted to distinguish these sizable narrative patterns, the general analytical approach has been the same. The boundaries of the repeated passage are marked out in all of the poems in which the unit occurs, the components common to all instances are noted, and some general conclusions are drawn about the nature of formulaic compositional technique. For example, David Crowne, showing that the theme *the hero on the beach* is made up of four basic "motifs" which are preserved in an "approximate pattern," comments that many Anglo-Saxon poems show parallel uses of the same theme and adds that "similar sequences of episodes can be accounted for as examples of a tendency for themes to be used in a particular order."[8] His definition of theme is adopted from Lord; he does not, however, offer any kind of explanation for the pattern that he has observed or for the function of the theme within its narrative context.

More recently Donald Fry has attempted to lay down some needed terminological guidelines and to clarify the issues on which such discussions are based.[9] Distinguishing between *theme* ("a recurrent concatenation of details and ideas, not restricted to a specific event, verbatim repetition, or certain formulas, which forms an underlying structure for an action or description") and *type-scene* ("a recurring stereotyped presentation of conventional details used to describe a certain narrative event, requiring neither verbatim repetition nor a specific formula content"), he seems to find structural differences in the two narrative components. Themes are isolatable and apparently freely movable, and while he acknowledges a "structural function," he believes that they "contribute very little to the basic compositional structure since they only underlie the surface": their main function is "elaborative," allowing and even justifying details "otherwise unnecessary to the plot."[10]

The question of the isolated component which seems to be included only to "enrich the narrative" (as Fry puts it) is related to an issue I raised earlier. In the discussion of the *exhortation* motifeme which appears in various forms at the beginning of each of the Middle English romances, I pointed out that a motifeme component may appear in patterns other than the one with which we are accustomed to identify it.[11] Fry, however, would like to find an essential difference between the isolated, movable components (themes) and the recurring patterns of "conventional details used to describe a certain narrative event" (type-scenes). This distinction, while it usefully calls our attention to the fact that some elements may occur outside of their normal patterned sequence, does not really clarify the issue; in fact, it only adds to what is fast becoming a terminological muddle. The distinction does not seem to be necessary so long as we acknowledge that there are substantial, coherent patterns of narrative development within the framework of the whole narrative, and that occasionally one or more of the components of those patterns may become detached and appear in another context, taking with it the pattern of associations that it has gained in its original context.

We will retain here the term *type-scene* for those larger units of narrative structure, since it is already in use and already possesses something like the *emic* definition I wish to attach to it, and since the term *theme* has literary implications related to other structures of meaning. The type-scene then, as I will use the term, is an abstract unit, an *emic* scene: a patterned, repeated configuration of events and characters, composed of obligatory and optional motifemes which may be either conditioned or free. Scenes (or *alloscenes*) drawn upon these patterns may occur once or more than once in any given narrative; some type-scenes are manifested in all of the narratives (the *single-combat* scene, for instance), while some may occur in only a few (*the wooing of the knight by the lady*).

One other note before we continue our discussion of type-scene identification and construction. Fry remarks that the scene belongs to a type-scene "pool of variants" (a metaphor which he credits to Bronson) from which the poet selects the most appropriate variant and inserts it into the narrative: "We might look upon the thirteen passages as a sample of a pool of variants, whose common denominator is their narrative content, none of which is a norm from which the others represent departures."[12] This view, which is fast becoming widespread among those who study compositional patterns in traditional narrative, has obvious affiliations to the filler-class concept basic to the tagmemic approach I have developed here. In tagmemic terms, the type-scene pattern is composed of a limited number of slots, optional and obligatory; the slots are filled from a class of scene variants which share certain features (also optional and obligatory). As I suggested much earlier, Albert Lord's proposal of a substitution grammar of formulaic narrative units is essentially similar to the substitution systems of tagmemic grammar.

I will view the type-scene, as I viewed the motifeme, within the hierarchical structure of narrative patterns. In order to define the type-scene, then, we must assume a tentative definition of *episode* as the largest of the narrative structures, subsuming (and in part defined by) the type-scene, the motifeme, and the syntagmeme.

The death of the hero's father

As we move from the easily visible formulaic correspondences illustrated by the tournament type-scene into discontinuous, more complex patterns, we find less reliance on heavily formulaic composition. There is, in fact, a fair amount of innovative plot technique and manipulation of conventional units within the confines of formulaic scene patterns, although here as elsewhere we must be able to perceive the pattern before we can perceive the variation—and we must be able to see the whole pattern before we can see its parts.

A good example of a single, rather well-defined pattern manifested by a number of variant forms is the type-scene we might call *the death of the hero's father*.[13] Together with (or in place of) the type-scenes *irregular birth* and *expulsion*, it fills out the first episode-slot in the narrative, the type-episode *separation*. The simplest and most straightforward illustration of this scene-pattern is found in *King Horn*:

Hit was sone someres day,
Also ich nou tellen may,
That moye the gode kinge
Rod on his pleyhinge

Bi the se syde,
Ther he was woned to ryde.
With him riden bote tvo;
Al to fewe ware tho.
He fond bi the stronde,
Ariued on his londe
Schipes xv,
Of sarazines kene.
He acsede wat he sowte
Other to londe broucte.
A peynym it yherde
And sone answerede,
"Thi lond folc we wilen slon
And al that god leuet on;
And the we solen sone anon;
Sal thou neuere henne gon."
The king licte adoun of his stede,
For tho he hauede nede,
And hise gode knictes ij,
But ywis hem was ful wo.
Swerdes the gonne gripe
And to gydere smyte.
He fouten an onder selde
Some of hem he felde.
He weren al to fewe
Ayen so fele srewe.
Sone micten atteth
Bringen thre deth. (31–62)

The nuclear component of this scene[14] is clearly the slaying of the king, for without this motifeme the narrative purpose of the scene would not be realized. But this component cannot exist alone in its skeletal form; it must be filled out by other story elements. In this narrative we have a very brief scene-setting allomotif ("the good king Murray rode for recreation by the seaside with two companions"), which acts as an introduction to the action; this allomotif focuses on one of the participants, the king. The next allomotif turns our attention to the villains—the Saracen pirates. Its central component is their boastful challenge: "We will slay all of the people of your land and all those who love Christ; we will kill you immediately—you won't get away!" The motivation for the depiction of the Saracens as violent heathens does not come from within the plot; it is part of the pattern of details that always accompany Saracens wherever they appear in these tales, and we would have to turn to the cultural attitude toward heathens for a total explanation of its origin and function. The third allomotif is the battle itself ("they began to draw their swords and to smite one another"); and the fourth is the king's death ("so easily might wickedness bring three to death"). The fourth allomotif is not related directly; it appears indirectly as the poet's attitude toward this scene and as an attempt to create sympathy in the audience for the outnumbered king's party. The function of this allomotif is neither informative nor directly narrative; it is instead emotive, and its formulaic, repetitive nature (*Al to fewe ware tho; He weren al to fewe/ Ayen so fele srewe*) adds to the emotional appeal.

This scene is similar to the single-combat scene with its motifemes of challenge and combat, and it seems that the poet has conflated the two, using one to satisfy the requirements of the other (a common practice, as the next example will indicate). Here the two scenes are so thoroughly conflated that they cannot be separated, nor would there be any reason to do so. The most important thing about this scene, as a manifestation of the type-pattern, is the configuration of characters and their associations with certain events or actions (the father is slain by the villain).[15]

The next example, from *Perceval*, displays the same character-event configuration, but it is executed in quite a different way. The story opens with a tourney at Arthur's court in which Perceval, the father of the hero, wins the hand of Arthur's sister. But during the course of the games he thoroughly disgraces his opponent, the Red Knight, who swears that he will avenge himself:

> And therfore gyffes he a gyfte
> That if he euer couere myghte
> Owthir by day or by nyghte,
>   In felde for to stonde,
> That he scholde qwyte hym that dynt
> That he of his handes hynte;
> Sall neuer this trauell be tynt,
>   Ne tolde in the londe
> That Percyuell in the felde
> Schulde hym schende thus vndire schelde,
> But he scholde agayne it yelde,
>   If that he were leueande. (85–96)

The scene shifts to the marriage of Perceval and Arthur's sister; in due course the young Perceval is born, and to celebrate the occasion his father announces a joust. The elder Perceval is at first victorious, but the Red Knight appears ("to keep the promise that he had made, deploring his past disgrace") and slays him in battle.

Most of the motifemes that we noted in *King Horn* are present here, although their linear arrangement is not the same and the pattern is discontinuous. The first allomotif is the Red Knight's boastful *challenge* (85–90), which occurs in the tournament scene preceding the death tournament; the challenge is repeated during the death tournament itself (121–128). The *scene-setting* motifeme appears ("the knight was pleased, and a feast was declared at the birth of a son, and a joust was called," 109–119); the *battle* motifeme is manifested by the tournament (129–136); and the obligatory motifeme, the *slaying of the father*, takes place at the end of the tournament (137–151). The scene ends with a brief account of the *burial* of Perceval and of his widow's *mourning* (152–160), an optional motifeme which the poet uses emotively.

Noteworthy in this variant of the type-scene is the prefixing of the *single-combat* scene to the *death-of-the-father* scene, a more sophisticated narrative arrangement than the straightforward presentation in *Horn*. The two combat scenes, occurring together in sequence as they often do, ordinarily would be considered as simple repetitions of the same scene; in this case, we can see that they are not. Arthur's tournament provides both the occasion for Perceval's tournament (the marriage, which results from Arthur's tourney, makes possible the birth of the child) and its result (the defeat of the Red Knight in the first tournament provides the motivation for his threat and his ultimate revenge). In addition to this skillful narrative interweaving, the focus is considerably altered from that of other narratives: the *birth of the child*, in many tales a separate scene of great importance extending to a hundred or more lines, is here reduced to its barest minimum and embedded as a constituent element into the *scene-setting* allomotif of the death scene. These segments of scenes here are so interwoven, so carefully plaited together, that to segment them thoroughly (if that could be done at all) would only do violence to the narrative. Most scene construction is like this—intricately twisted elements and segments of connected patterns—and it is only when we can view the scene at a fairly high level of abstraction that we can see its configural form and mark out the patterns that compose it.

Bevis of Hampton[16] provides another example of this same scene, expanding it considerably (to 239 lines) by the addition of several other allomotifs. Bevis's father, old Sir Guy, foolishly marries the young daughter (the *January-May* motif) of the King of Scotland. After Bevis's birth the girl becomes dissatisfied with her husband's sexual abilities and decides to do away with him.[17] She bargains with Sir Mordure of Almayne, who agrees to kill Sir Guy in return for her favors.[18] The death scene proper begins with the traitorous wife's request that Guy kill a boar and bring her its head (175–198). Guy rides out alone into the forest (200–210); he is accosted by Mordure and his men, and Mordure announces that he is going to kill the old man:

> "Ayilt the, treitor! thow olde dote!
> Thow shelt ben hanged be the throte,
>   Thin heued thow schelt lese;
> The sone schel an-hanged be
> And the wif, that is so fre,
>   To me lemman i chese!" (*Bevis* Auch. 217–222)

There follows a pitched battle (223–258); Guy yields but is shamefully beheaded and his head sent to his wife,[19] who responds with great pleasure:

> And she seide: "Blessed mot he be!
> To wif a schel wedde me
>   To morwe in the dai.
>
> Sai him, me swete wight,
> That he come yet to night
>   In to me bour!" (Auch. 286–291)

The motifemes that we found in the other tales—the *death of the father*, the *scene-setting* motifeme, the *boastful challenge*—are used as a framework for this scene, but the addition of other optional allomotifs (the *January-May* motifeme and the *bargaining* motifeme) provides a great deal of variation in the basic pattern. Narratively speaking, the execution of the plot pattern here is much simpler than that of *Perceval*. The story events are arranged with much less intricacy; there is little narrative intertwining and a great deal of symmetrical balance within the scene: the wife's request to Sir Guy to bring her a boar's head—which is part of the *scene-setting* motifeme—is balanced, for example, by the return of her dead husband's head, a part of the *bargaining* motifeme. The actual events of the scene, however, seem to be reduced in importance—or rather the action is subordinated to the delineation of the characters. The death of Guy is reduced to only a few lines, but it is preceded by sixteen lines of dialogue, most of which serve to characterize the villain and the victim. The action of the agreement between Guy's wife and Mordure is minimal, but is accompanied by eighty-six lines of dialogue—most of which has to do in one way or another with the motivation of the characters. It is as though, given the action of the scene already established as a well-defined pattern, the poet is concerned to explain that patterned action, to make it seem reasonable in the context of a way of life that the audience might find familiar and meaningful. The poet is obviously interested here in the characters of the two villains, much more interested than, say, the *Horn* poet, whose characterization of the Saracens amounts to the unquestioning acceptance of a preestablished pattern with no felt necessity to motivate the action. There is of course still very little characterization in the modern sense, for the events of the story and the dialogue that they occasion are the only vehicles available to the poet, but the poet here uses these devices effectively for the delineation of character and, more importantly, motivation.[20] In the character-event configuration that provides the basic narrative pattern, this poet is far more concerned about the characters than about the events—or perhaps it would be more accurate to say that the poet is interested in the characters to the extent that they explain the events.

The fourth example of this scene-pattern, *William of Palerne*, is incomplete, and its interest lies in the fact that the narrative pattern is begun but then suddenly interrupted by a variant of another type-scene, *the expulsion of the hero*. It is acephalous and unfortunately lacks three folios (about 290 lines) at the beginning. But since the narrative is a self-acknowledged translation (commissioned in the 1350's by Humphrey de Bohun), the events of the early sections of the story are supplied by the French romance *Guillaume de Palerne* from which it was translated.[21] The scene (or that portion of the scene) in which we are interested is very brief: the brother of King Embrons plots to kill him and his son William and seize the throne (*Guillaume* 51–57); he bribes two of William's nurses to administer poison (58–60). But at this point the scene is truncated; the boy William, playing with his parent in an orchard, is kidnapped by a werewolf (86–94). The poisoning scene is never resumed, the father dies of natural causes, and we learn much later that the werewolf, an enchanted prince, acted to save the boy from the same fate that awaited the father (*William* 4635–4656). In this instance one type-scene (*death of the father*) is interrupted, and a variant of another type-scene (*expulsion of the hero*) is attached to the unfinished scene in order to satisfy the structural requirements of the larger episode-pattern (*separation*) of which it is a part.

Table 6

Narrative	Plan	Scene
Horn	——	Murray and two companions by the sea.
Perceval	——	Joust is called to celebrate birth.
Bevis	Guy's wife and Mordure plot to kill Guy.	Guy rides alone to forest.
William of Palerne	Brother plots to kill Embrons and son William; bribes two nurses to administer poison.	Family goes to orchard.
Generides	Aufreus's wife and steward plot to kill Aufreus.	Aufreus goes hunting with small group.

Table 6 reviews the basic configurations of the *death-of-the-father* scene. In the first three narratives the nucleus of the scene-pattern remains stable; in two narratives where the scene is complicated by other, intervening patterns, the nucleus is altered and the scene is incomplete.[22]

Death of the father and *expulsion of the hero*: type-scene linking

The emerging pattern that we followed in the preceding section does not end with the type-scene *death of the hero's father*. Another scene, the *expulsion of the hero*, is invariably attached to the death scene which precedes it. This type-scene has a number of variants which we can organize into several groups, two of which (*exile* and *kidnapping*) we will discuss in this section. In all of the instances of this particular

Challenge	Battle	Death
Saracens boast they will kill Murray and his people.	Saracens and Murray.	Murray is slain by Saracens.
Red Knight vows revenge for earlier defeat.	Red Knight and Perceval.	Perceval is slain by Red Knight.
Mordure taunts Guy.	Mordure and Guy.	Guy is slain by Mordure.
___	___	___
___	___	___

type-scene, the hero is the passive recipient of the action; the configuration of characters and events, while rather looser than that of other narrative units we have described, is still highly conventionalized.

In *King Horn* the Saracens at first spare Horn's life because of his "farinesse," but they become concerned that Horn will attempt to regain his father's throne when he is grown, and they decide to set Horn and his twelve companions adrift at sea:[23]

> The children hi broghte to stronde,
> Wringinde here honde,
> Into shupes borde
> At the furste worde.
> Ofte hadde horn beo wo,
> Ac neuere wurs than him was tho! (115–120)

After "all the day and all the night" at sea, Horn and his friends find themselves in Westernesse.

In *Perceval*, immediately following the death of her husband at the hands of the Red Knight, Perceval's mother takes a vow no longer to live in a land where her son may see tournaments and deeds of arms and may decide to become a knight like his father:

> And now is Percyuell the wighte
> Slayne in batelle and in fyghte,
> And the lady hase gyffen a gyfte,
>   Holde if scho may,
> That scho schall neuer mare wone
> In stede, with hir yonge sone,
> Ther dedes of armes schall be done,
>   By nyghte ne be daye;
> Bot in the wode schall he be:
> Sall he no thyng see
> Bot the leues of the tree
>   And the greues graye;
> Schall he nowther take tent
> To justes ne to tournament,
> But in the wilde woode went,
>   With bestes to playe. (161–176)

Even though this is an act of voluntary self-exile on the part of Perceval's mother and is in that sense different from Horn's forced exile, its result is exactly the same as far as the young hero is concerned: both Horn and Perceval are denied their right to follow their fathers as rightful heirs to the land which belongs to them; they are both sent out of their own kingdom because of a fear that they will possess both the land and the privilege to which they are entitled; and, for both, family ties are broken and that crucial element of their identity (their lineage, or rather their patrilineage, since identification with the mother is retained) is destroyed.

The similarities in the type-scene patterns here have shifted from the exact correspondences of character and event that we saw in the tournament scene to a structural correspondence. *Setting adrift* and *self-exile* appear to be two different acts; structurally, they are the same act because they have the same function—they are structurally homologous. In a tagmemic grammar of narrative composition these two scenes are variants of the same type-scene (*expulsion of the hero*) and their nuclear, obligatory motifeme (*expulsion*) is the same, while their peripheral and optional motifs may be very different.

Another narrative is related to this same pattern. In *Emare* the heroine's father becomes enamored of her beauty, obtains the consent of the Pope to marry his daughter, and requires her acceptance (220–252). When she refuses, he becomes "ryght wrote" and orders her set adrift (253–336).[24] The affiliations with the type-scene we have been tracing seem tenuous. The *expulsion* scene is easily recognized, but the *death of the father* is absent. There is a crucial connection, however, between Emare's refusal to commit incest with her father and the father's death as it occurs in other narratives. Both actions destroy the kinship pattern; both actions deny the continuation of the father's blood line (analogous, as we shall shortly see, to the alternate type-scene, *irregular birth*, which is an explicit denial of blood line). Both actions, unrelated as their surface structures may appear, have the same result: the expulsion of the hero or heroine—that is, the final denial of the patrilineal relationship. Emare's refusal to commit incest with her father, then, is structurally homologous to the death of the father.

Earlier we discussed the notion of conditioned and free motifemes. As the patterns in these narratives become clearer, we can see that the optional motifemes at this level may be free, or they may be conditioned upon previous optional motifemes. (For example, Perceval's mother's vow of exile is contingent upon the fact that her husband is killed in a tournament rather than, say, by falling off a horse.) The nuclear motifemes, however, seem to be conditioned upon one another. That is, there appears to be an obligatory link between the death of the father and the exile of the hero; we can say, therefore, that exile is conditioned by the father's death: if the death occurs, the exile must follow it.

But this relationship is not a logical cause-and-effect relationship, and to claim, as some structuralists have,[25] that the narrative sequence is built on a chain of logical causality raises several very serious problems. First, because the two events are sequentially related, it does not necessarily follow that their relationship is a causal one. The occurrence of events in a particular order is the product of a number of forces, of which causality may be one, but not necessarily the only one (and, in the case of narrative structure, certainly not the most interesting one). Second, a system of narrative selection and arrangement which bases its definition upon causality, either in part or as a whole, is ultimately forced to acknowledge causality as the controlling agent for the whole system. The logical end of such an argument is the conclusion that the events of the story occur in their order because of a pattern of logic set in motion by the choice of the first unit. This assertion denies the poet's freedom to alter pre-existing patterns at will and postulates a control from within the narrative system itself. Now it may be true that the number of narrative units available to the poet to fill any given slot in the narrative is limited (that is, it appears to be a closed set), and it may be true that the arrangement of those narrative units (the sequence of slots) is predetermined by some force or forces that we have not yet identified. But the argument from cause-and-effect will not help us to answer these other important questions; it may, in fact, prevent us from formulating the questions by presupposing a system which leads us to neglect a very important aspect of the narrative: the establishment within the boundaries of the story itself of a logic peculiar to that story or to a group of generically related stories. The insistence that one narrative unit is the natural outcome of the preceding unit in an organic relationship[26] forces us to ignore the fact that the poet has made a set of fairly arbitrary and artificial selections, both from the world of natural and social events and from a world (or several worlds) of story events. The poet has, in a number of ways and through a number of models, transformed the real world and its natural laws into a fictive world, where other laws prevail.

To return to our immediate subject: there is some evidence already that the entire sequence (*death-expulsion*) is contingent upon some extranarrative pattern which necessitates its development. That the death of the father is followed by the exile of his son is not a logically necessary fact of narrative (death could just as logically be followed by the hero's swearing allegiance to his father's murderers, for instance); some other cultural formula, revealing itself in narrative form, has created this particular set of narrative demands. The question of why these patterns exist as they do is one of the most important issues in the study of the romances or in the study of any popular narrative form, and we will have to explore its implications at some length later.

The second variation that we find in this group of tales is the kidnapping scene. In *William of Palerne*, as I noted earlier, this scene interrupts the death scene (the poisoning never occurs), and the exile of the hero is carried out with a great deal of narrative ingenuity by having him kidnapped by a werewolf who carries the young child off to a den. The child is in turn stolen from the werewolf by a cowherd. The *kidnapping* type-scene is a favorite one in these narratives, and it often appears more than once: in *Octavian* one of the twin sons (the role of the hero is doubled) is stolen from his mother by an ape, then stolen from the ape by a knight, and finally stolen from the knight by outlaws who sell the child to a butcher from Paris; the other twin is stolen from his mother by a tiger and, in swift succession, by a griffin and a lioness.

In *Havelok* an interesting double variant of the *kidnapping* scene occurs. Before Athelwold dies, he gives the wardship of his daughter Goldborough to Godrich, earl of Cornwall. But after Godrich has assumed power, he decides that Goldborough is a threat to his regime and resolves to award her right to the throne to his own son and to imprison the girl in a castle:

> But sone dede hire fete,
> Er he wolde heten ani mete,
> Fro winchestre ther sho was,
> Also a wicke traytur iudas;
> And dede leden hire to doure,
> That standeth on the seis oure;
> And therhinne dede hire fede
> Pourelike in feble wede.
> The castel dede he yemen so,
> That non ne micte comen hire to
> Of hire frend, with hire to speken,
> That heuere micte hire bale wreken. (316–327)

This usurpation and imprisonment is paralled in Havelok's part of the story: after Birkabein's death, Godard shuts up his wards, Havelok and his two sisters, in a castle:

> Hwan birkabeyn was leyd in graue,
> The erl dede sone take the knaue,
> Hauelok, that was the eir,
> Swanborow, his sister, helfled, the tother,
> And in the castel dede he hem do,
> Ther non ne micte hem comen to
> Of here kyn, ther bei sperd wore (408–414)

Godard kills Havelok's sisters and orders Havelok's death, giving him to a fisherman to be drowned. But the fisherman, Grim, recognizes Havelok's royalty and flees to England with his family and the young prince, who is disguised as Grim's son.

In *Bevis* the *kidnapping* scene undergoes yet another variation, that of the hero taken into slavery by a band of pirates. After his father's murder, Bevis is handed over to Sir Saber by his mother to be killed. Like Grim in *Havelok*, Saber takes pity on the child and saves him, disguising him as a sheepherder. The plan succeeds until Bevis, brooding over his father's murder and his own disinheritance, breaks into the court and attacks his mother and Mordure. Enraged, Bevis's mother orders that he be sold immediately to slave traders:

> Fain she wolde, a were of liue,
> Foure knightes she clepede bliue:
> "Wendeth," she seide, "to the stronde:
> Yif ye see schipes of painim londe,
> Selleth to hem this ilche hyne,
> That ye for no gode ne fine,
> Whather ye haue for him mor or lesse,
> Selleth him right in to hethenesse!" (Auch. 493–500)

In the Chetham manuscript the mother commands that her son be drowned; when the would-be murderers come to the shore, however, another solution presents itself:

> They ffound there shippus bothe more and lesse,
> Of payneme lond and of hethenes;
> They sold the childe for god gret plente,
> And with the paynemus wendith he. (383–386)

The same variant occurs in the *Reinbroun* portion of *Guy of Warwick* (which in the Auchinleck manuscript, at least, seems to be a separate poem, with an initial *exhortation* motifeme). After Guy's renunciation of marriage and his departure on his pilgrimage, his son is left to the care of a family retainer. A group of foreign merchants, seeing the pretty child, decide to kidnap him:

> The marchauns hem bethoughte,
> Yif hii that child haue moughte,
>   Hii wolde stele him there;
> &, yif hii hadde that child bolde,
> Richely in-to her londe thai wolde,
>   And selle hit full dere. (91–96)

It can be observed from Table 7 that this particular type-scene is a persistent element, recurring in sixteen poems for a total of thirty times. (In four narratives—*Torrent, Havelok, Eglamour, Octavian*—it appears in both variants.) Speaking in terms of the slot-class theory of

Table 7

Linking pattern: death of the father/expulsion of the hero

William of Palerne	——	William is kidnapped by werewolf; stolen from werewolf by cowherd.
Bevis	——	Bevis is sold to pagan slavetraders.
Horn	Horn is set adrift by Saracen invaders.	——
Havelok	Grim takes Havelok out of Denmark to England.	Goldborough is imprisoned by Godrich; Havelok is imprisoned by Godard.
Perceval	Mother exiles herself, son.	——

Linking pattern: irregular birth/expulsion of the hero

Octavian	Mother and twin sons are exiled into forest.	Florent is stolen by ape; stolen from ape by knight; stolen from knight by outlaws; sold to Clement by outlaws. Octavian is stolen by tiger, griffin, lioness.
Torrent	Desonell and twin sons are exiled into forest.	Antony is stolen by griffin; Leobertus is stolen by leopard.
Eglamour	Christabell and son Degrabell are set adrift.	Degrabell is stolen by griffin.

Linking pattern: irregular birth/expulsion of the hero *(cont.)*

Triamour	Mother exiled; son Triamour is born in wilderness.	——
Libeaus	Mother exiles herself, son.	——
Lai le freine	Daughter is abandoned in ash tree.	——
Degare	Degare is abandoned in forest.	——
Emare	Emare is set adrift; Emare and son are set adrift.	——
Gowther	Gowther exiles himself.	——
Generides	Generides is raised by his mother.	——
Other		
Guy	——	Reinbroun is kidnapped by traders.

formulaic narrative construction, we can say that all thirty of these scenes constitute a class from which the poet may choose one or more to fill the type-scene *expulsion*. The scenes within the class are composed of a single nuclear, obligatory motifeme (*exile*) and any number of peripheral, optional motifemes which may be used to fill out and support the narrative framework. As I indicated earlier, these peripheral motifemes, while they may be optional at this higher level of type-scene construction, are necessary components of smaller units of narrative, and none can be discarded. From this point of view, all of the scene components are functional at one or another level.

The sixteen narratives are organized in Table 7 to demonstrate still another narrative pattern: the linking of type-scenes. Earlier we noticed that *Horn, Perceval, Bevis, William,* and *Havelok* all display a common linking pattern: the *death of the father,* followed by the *expulsion of the hero.* But obviously not all of the sixteen narratives that contain the *expulsion* type-scene manifest this particular linking pattern; there is, in fact, another pattern evident here. In ten narratives in the table (two-thirds of the total) the type-scene *irregular birth* precedes the type-scene *expulsion.* We can see, then, that the linking pattern of *death* and *expulsion* is only one of two possible linking patterns.

Irregular birth and *expulsion*: type-scene linking and scene structure

The ten narratives in which the two type-scenes *irregular birth* and *expulsion* occur as a linked pattern can be divided, for the sake of convenient discussion, into three categories: those narratives in which the hero is born out of wedlock (*Eglamour, Torrent, Libeaus*); those in which the hero is born in wedlock but the mother is accused (or fears an accusation) of adultery (*Octavian, Triamour, Lai le freine*); and those in which the hero is begotten by a supernatural being or is said to be a supernatural being (*Emare, Degare, Generides, Gowther*).[27]

Two examples (*Eglamour* and *Torrent*) of the first category are similar enough to cause suspicion that the stories demonstrate some direct borrowing, either in a manuscript tradition or in an oral tradition.[28] In *Eglamour,* Eglamour and Cristabell are betrothed, but Cristabell's father sends the hero off to perform several tasks before he allows them to marry. While Eglamour is gone, Cristabell is delivered of a son:

> A knaue chylde has Crystabelle,
> As whyte as whalys bon (803–804)

Her father is so irate that he orders both his daughter and his unchristened grandchild to be set adrift:

> The erle gaf to God a vowe:
> "Dowghtyr, into the see schalt thowe
> In a schyp alone;
> And that bastard that ys the dere
> Christundam schall non haue here!"
> Hyr maydens wepte ylkon. (805–810)

In *Torrent* the same situation occurs. While Torrent is off in Norway visiting a princess whom he has saved from a dragon, Desonell is discovered to be pregnant:

> As she sownyd, this lady mylde,
> Men myght se tokenyng of her child,
>   Steryng on her right syde.
> Gret Ruth it was to tell,
> How her maydens on her fell,
>   Her to Couer and hide. (1783–1788)

Her father orders that she and the unborn child be exiled:

> Tho the kyng said: "My doughter, do way!
> By god, thy myrth is gone for aye,
>   Spousage wyll thou none bide!
> Ther fore thou shalt in to the see
> And that Bastard with-in thee
>   To lerne you ffor to ride." (1789–1794)

However, Desonell's mother (an interesting addition to the scene, and a realistic character in her several appearances in the tale) excuses her because the child's father is an "erles sonne" and a rich man, and begs that she at least be allowed to remain at home until the child is born. After the birth, Desonell and her twin sons are exiled:

> The kyng said: "So mut I thee,
> Thou shalte in-to the see
>   With oute wordys moo.
> Every kyngis doughter ffer and nere,
> At the shall they lere,
>   Ayen the law to do." (1813–1818)

The third linked occurrence of these two type-scenes, in *Libeaus*, is interesting in its narrative compactness. In fact, the two components *irregular birth* and *expulsion* are so reduced that we cannot call them scenes at all, for they have been diminished in their narrative scale, reduced to descriptive elements:

> Hys name was called Geynleyn,
> Be-yete he was of Syr Gaweyn,
> Be a forest syde;

. . . .

Thys Gynleyn was fayr of syght,
Gentyll of doy, of face bryght,
All bastard yef he were. (7–9, 13–15)

The nuclear allomotifs, unadorned, are all that remain of these type-scenes. Here the irregular birth is only briefly noticed, as a given of the tale; the exile, too, while it provides the setting for the early part of the story, is buried in the background. We learn only in passing that Libeaus's mother, like Perceval's mother, keeps the hero apart from human society because she does not want him to see an armed man, and because (according to the version in the Lambeth Palace manuscript) he is "full savage/a gladly wold do oute-rage":

His moder hym kepte with hir myght
That he shulde se no knyght
J-armed in no maner (16–18)

And all for dred of wycke loose
His moder alway kepte him close
As dughty childe and dere. (22–24)

This third example is very different in its narrative execution from the other two; it presents only a skeleton of the two type-scenes and consists of only a few lines, while *Torrent*'s embellished pattern requires sixty-one lines and even the *Eglamour* poet uses twenty-five. But in all three instances the basic motifemic structure of the two type-scenes remains the same: the child is a bastard, and he and his mother are exiled. The configurational core of characters and events common to these two scenes remains constant while the optional events and characters are altered.

In the second pattern of irregular birth and expulsion, the nuclear motifemes are retained, but the peripheral motifemes are very different. The hero's birth is not illegitimate but quite regular; shortly thereafter, however, the mother is accused of adultery. In two narratives this scene is quite elaborate.

In *Octavian* the emperor of Rome and his childless wife vow to build and richly endow an abbey, "that we togedur may haue an heyre." Their piety is rewarded by the birth of twin sons,[29] and the emperor rejoices. His mother, however, tells him that Rome is in danger of being "wrong-heyred," because the empress "hath take a cokys knave." She contrives to place a boy in the sleeping lady's bed and tells the emperor that he will find his wife and her lover together.[30] While the lady sleeps, she dreams of a dragon who steals her sons "in hys palmes alle byrnand so," and when she awakes, she finds that the emperor has beheaded the cook's boy in her bed:

> The emperoure to the knaue wente,
> The hede vp by the hare he hente
>   And caste it till hir thare.
> The lady blyschede vp in the bedde,
> Scho saw the clothes alle by-blede;
>   Fulle mekylle was hir care. (Lincoln Cath. 175–181)

The emperor craftily calls a feast in celebration of the birth and asks his wife's father to render a judgment in a hypothetical case of a lady's treason. The father condemns the woman and children to be burned, and then learns that he has judged his own daughter. At the last moment, however, the emperor commutes his wife's sentence to exile and sends her and his children into the wilderness:

> The emperoure gafe hir fowrty pounde
> Of florence, that were riche and rownde,
>   In romance als we rede;
> And he bytaghte hir knyghtes two
> And bad, that thay solde with hir goo
>   Owt of his lande to lede. (Lincoln Cath. 280–285)

There, as I have already pointed out, both children are repeatedly stolen by an assortment of animals.

The *Octavian* poet has skillfully developed these two linked scenes by combining several motifs, some of which appear in other narratives. For example, the false accusation of adultery occurs in *Le Bone Florence of Rome, The Knight of Curtesy, Earl of Toulous, Emare*, and others; burning (or the threat of burning) can be found again in *Octavian* (1711 ff.), in *Amis*, in *Bevis*, in *Ywayn and Gawayn*, in *Chevelere Assigne*—and as a punishment for adultery, in *Le Morte Arthur*; the prophetic dream, as a warning of betrayal, occurs in many narratives. The old wives' belief that the birth of twins is an indication of the wife's unfaithfulness is not evident in the northern manuscript of *Octavian*; in the southern version, however, the charge is made explicit as motivation for the mother-in-law's treachery:

"For thou ne seghe neuer no woman,
Seth the world ferst began,
But she hadde a byleman,
  That myght conceyue
Two chylderen—that ony lyyf telle kan,
  That ys alyue." (Cotton 127–132)

All of these separate allomotifs (the vow to build a monastery, the mother-in-law's accusations, the deception, the prophetic dream, the judgment, the threat of burning) are tied together within the type-scenes *irregular birth* and *exile*, which provide a narrative framework, a constant and unvarying pattern around which the auxiliary patterns have been woven. Most of these additions appear to be designed to provide a reasonable motivation for the central action, or to further delineate the characters, or—in the case of the dream motif—to foreshadow a coming narrative event. The construction of the *expulsion* type-scene, however, raises an interesting question. The central motifeme *exile* is adequately manifested by the exile of the wife and two children; the *Octavian* poet, however, is dissatisfied with this single allomotif and must repeat it eight times in different ways: the mother dreams of kidnapping, the children are in turn stolen by an ape, a tiger, a griffin, a lioness, a knight, and a band of robbers, and one is finally sold to a butcher. The many allomotifs are redundant; they do not offer us any new information, either about the characters or about the plot—and surely they do not function simply to expand the narrative, either to extend the performance of the poem or to show the poet's virtuosity (although these may be part of their functions).

Students of structural patterns of myth have long attempted to find an answer to the problem posed by the fact that in all mythological systems important stories (and pieces of stories) occur over and over. Those who analyze the oral tradition from the viewpoint of the craft of composition relate this tendency to the exigencies of oral composition or oral performance. C. M. Bowra takes the position that repetition is designed to "comfort" the "simple" and conservative minds of the audience, for whom familiar patterns of detail "assume a special significance."[31] Edmund Leach, however, who has adopted some of the techniques of information theory to a study of mythic structures, sees the problem in a much wider perspective:

The redundance of myth is a very reassuring fact. Any particular myth in isolation is like a coded message badly snarled up with noisy interference. Even the most confident devotee might feel a little uncertain as to what precisely is being said. But, as a result of redundancy, the believer can feel that, even when the details vary, each alternative version of a myth confirms his understanding and reinforces the essential meaning of all the others.[32]

Redundant patterns do not offer us new information; they reinforce what we already know—they increase information in the sense that they decrease the uncertainty involved in decoding the message contained within this structural pattern. By repeating this particular motifeme in this single narrative the poet emphasizes its importance and attempts to make sure that the audience does not misunderstand the message. These efforts appear to be largely unconscious, and as such are extremely powerful: unconscious perception of pattern cannot be brought to light, examined, and rejected; it provides a fundamental screen through which the world is viewed, while the screen itself remains invisible and unquestioned.

The patterns seen here are redundant on all levels of structure: the language is formulaic; the narrative components are formulaic (as individual, detachable units appearing in other tales); the functional relationship of the components within the structure of the type-scenes is formulaic; and the linking pattern which holds these two type-scenes together is formulaic. The redundant structures are multiplied past counting.

Sir Triamour, unlike *Octavian*, manifests these type-scenes in a straightforward way without much repetition, but it is quite similar to *Octavian* in both optional and obligatory structures. King Ardus of Aragon and his wife Margaret are childless; hoping they might beget an heir, Ardus vows that he will go on a pilgrimage to the Holy Land, and on the eve of his departure Margaret conceives a son. The king commands Marrok, the "false and fekyll" steward, to care for his lady in his absence, but Marrok desires the queen:

> He wowyd the quene bothe day and nyght,
> To lye hur by he had hyt hyght,
>   He dredyd no peryle (67–69)

The queen refuses him, and Marrok, fearful for his own safety, tells her that his tempting was only a test of her faithfulness to her husband.[33] But when the king returns, Marrok tells him that Margaret has deceived him:

"Ye wene the chylde yourys be,
Hyt ys not so, so mote y the,
  The quene hath done the trayne!
Another knyght, so mote y spede,
Gat the chylde syth thou yede,
  And hath the quene for-layne!" (169–174)

Marrok claims that he himself slew the guilty knight and advises
Ardus to send his wife out of the country:

"Syr," seyde Marrok, "ye schalle not soo,
Ye schalle hur nother brenne nor sloo,
  For dowte of synne;
Bettyr hyt is, syr, be my rede,
Owt of yowre londe sche be flemyd in dede,
  And faste ye schalle hur comawnde to wynne;
But take hur an oolde stede,
And an olde knyght that may hur lede,
  Tylle sche be paste yowre realme,
And gyf them sum spendynge,
That them owt of thy londe may brynge,
  Y can no bettyr deme." (211–222)

Marrok's display of sympathy toward the woman, however, is only a
very clever disguise for his own treacherous plot. At the king's order,
Sir Roger accompanies the queen in her exile; they have gone only a
short way when they are ambushed by Marrok's men. Roger is slain
(his faithful dog later returns to accuse his slayer),[34] but the queen es-
capes and rides alone to Hungary, where she gives birth to Triamour
in the wilderness.

  In all of these variant scenes (*Octavian* and *Triamour* and their
analogues) the configuration of characters and their relational patterns
are identical: the husband is deceived by an accuser, and the wife and
child (or children) are the innocent victims of the treachery. The fact
that the roles of treachery may be filled alternatively by a cruel
mother-in-law or by an envious steward who sexually desires the innocent wife is important only when we focus on the variants of the pattern; functionally, the relationship of the accuser to the other two
characters is the same, no matter who plays the role or how the acts are
motivated.

  The third narrative in this group, *Lai le freine*, is related to the other
two tales only in the structural core of the type-scenes. The wife of a

West Country knight, hearing that her gossip has been delivered of twin sons, declares that the mother of the twins has been unfaithful:

> Wele may ich man wite therfore
> That tvay men hir han hadde in bour (70–71)

When she herself bears twin daughters, she is faced with a predicament: be considered an adulteress, confess that she slandered her neighbor's wife, or slay one of her own children. Upon the advice of the midwife, she decides to abandon one of the little girls, together with tokens of her noble lineage: a gold ring and a brocaded cloth. The midwife is entrusted with the task of abandoning the child:

> The maide toke the child hir mide
> & stale oway in an euentide,
> & passed ouer a wild heth.
> Thurch feld and thurch wode hye geth
> Al the winterlong night,—
> The weder was clere, the mone was light—
> So that hye com bi a forest side;
> Sche wax al weri & gan abide.
> Sone after sche gan herk
> Cokkes crowe & houndes berk.
> Sche arose & thider wold.
> Ner & nere sche gan bihold.
> Walles & hous fele hye seighe,
> A chirche with stepel fair & heigh. (145–158)

The midwife leaves the little girl in a hollow ash tree beside the church, where she is found the next morning by the porter, who takes the child to the convent to be raised.

The nuclear allomotifs in *Lai le freine* (*irregular birth, exile*) have undergone some permutation in comparison with those in *Octavian* and *Triamour*. While the nuclear allomotifs remain essentially stable, alteration of the optional allomotifs have caused some deformation and a subsequent transformation of parts of the pattern. The charge of adultery does not come from a wicked or envious accuser, but from the wife herself; she is, the poet tells us:

> A proude dame and an enveous,
> Hokerfulliche missegging,
> Squeymous and eke scorning. (60–62)

She subsumes both the roles of accuser (she says that her neighbor's wife is an adulteress) and victim (she fears that she will be considered unfaithful, convicted by her own charge), and she takes on characteristics of both roles, the guilty and the innocent. She punishes herself for her own crime.

This combination of elements is not unique to this particular poet, of course; it can be traced to Marie de France's *Lai de Fraisne* and to the account of Countess Margareta of Holland.[35] In a number of other analogues, the accuser is a noblewoman, while the victim is a poor woman. But wherever this scene occurs in this particular configuration, it can be viewed as a variant of the basic type-scene linking pattern: *irregular birth* and *expulsion*.

The variation of the peripheral motifemes of the *irregular-birth* type-scene in *Lai le freine* also involves a transformation in the peripheral motifemes of the linked scene. Instead of the *exile* of mother and child, commanded by an irate father or husband, the child alone is exiled. The modification of the pattern is necessitated by the earlier merging of the roles of accuser and victim, and by the fact that this poet does not focus any attention at all on the father of the child. This omission may indicate that the father's role is expendable in the functioning of this type-scene, and that the only characters important to the successful completion of the pattern are the mother and the child.[36]

Sir Degare bears some resemblance in one of its nuclear allomotifs and in the peripheral allomotifs which surround it to *Lai le freine*. The daughter of the King of Little Britain is forbidden to marry any knight except the one who can defeat her powerful father in battle. Riding through the forest one day, she is separated from her father and her ladies and accosted by a knight, a "gentil, yong, and iolif man," who tells her that he is a fairy knight, and her leman:

> Tho no thing he coude do she
> But wep and criede and wolde fle;
> And he anon gan hire atholde
> And dide his welle, what he wolde.
> He binam hire here maidenhod
> And seththen up toforen hire stod.
> "Lemman," he seide, "gent and fre,
> Mid childe I wot that thou schalt be;
> Siker ich wot, hit worth a knaue.
> Forthi mi swerd thou sschalt haue;
> And, whenne that he is of elde,

That he mai him self biwelde,
Tak him the swerd and bidde him fonde
To sechen his fader in eche londe." (109–122)

The lady is indeed with child and begs her women to help her conceal
her pregnancy, fearing that men will say the child is the product of an
incestuous union. ("Men wolde sai bi sti and strete/That my fader, the
king, hit wan/And I ne was neuere aqueint with man.") When Degare is
born, he is wrapped in a cradle with four pounds of gold and ten pounds
of silver and a pair of gloves which will fit only his mother. The maid
takes the child:

The maiden tok the child here mide
Stille awai in auen-tide;
Alle the winteres longe night
The weder was cler, the mone light.
Than worth she war anon
Of an hermitage in a stone;
An holi man had ther his woniyng.
Thider she wente on heying
And sette the cradel at his dore
And durste abide no lengore
And passede forth anone right. (219–229)

In this variant of the type-scene, as in the previous one, there is no
accuser, and the decision to exile the child is made by the mother herself. But there the similarity ends. The opening situation (the father
who prohibits his daughter's marriage) is a "rationalization" (according
to Laura Hibbard Loomis) of the incestuous father motif-complex that
we noticed in *Emare*.[37] Emare's refusal to marry her father is structurally analogous to the *death-of-the-father* motifeme; here, while the
daughter herself is not expelled, the son of her illegitimate union with
a fairy knight is, because people might think he is the son of her father!
We have here the conflation of two type-scenes not fully realized in
narrative form: the *death of the father* (only very sketchily suggested)
and the *irregular birth*.

The rape of the princess by the fairy knight is quite a different complex of motifs than the description of the shrewish mother in *Lai le
freine*, and our response to the two scenes is different, although structurally, on the level of the type-scene, their functions are similar. The
differences are achieved by the choice of variant allomotifs. The
character-event configuration provides a more sympathetic interpreta-

tion of the act of abandonment (the mother as victim of the rape, the unwilling abandoning of the child, and so forth) than that of the earlier narrative. In this case, we can see how much alteration is achieved in a pattern in which the central motifs remain the same (and the structural function of the whole type-scene is unchanged), but where the peripheral components are systematically altered to produce a particular effect.[38]

In addition, the substitution of this complex organization of allomotifs has structural consequences later in the narrative, for other allomotifs are linked to it—not linearly, but in an associative pattern. In *Degare*, for instance, the tokens (the identifying gloves) make possible the hero's identification of his mother; the sword makes possible the subsequent identification of the father (these are nuclear motifs in the *recognition* type-scene). We are made aware once again of the difficulties involved in the segmentation of narrative structures: the discontinuous nature of linked patterns and the impossibility of ever disentangling them completely is clearly evident here. At best we can only suggest that certain motifemes in one type-scene are connected to, attract, or even require certain subsequent motifemes in other type-scenes, and that this relationship is part of the gestalt of the whole narrative. Certainly in this case, when tokens remain with the hero when he is kidnapped or abandoned, we expect them to function as identifying marks later in the tale.

The last few narratives in the linked type-scene patterns we have marked out here exhibit many shifts in their peripheral allomotifs, but I will treat them here as a group. *Generides* bears some resemblance to *Degare*. King Aufreus, on a magic stag hunt, meets the fairylike Sereyne, and she conceives a son. Sereyne, a princess of Syria, bears the child in secret (Aufreus is already married) with the help of her maid Medean, and they give the boy, Generides, to a laundress. He is raised in the castle of his mother without knowing who his father is (91–798).

In *Gowther* a childless woman prays for a child by any means ("on what maner, scho no roght"). She is visited by a figure which at first appears to be her husband ("as lyke hur lorde, as he myght be") but reveals himself to be a devil:[39]

When he had his wylle all don,
A felturd fende he start up so
    And stode and hur beheld.
He seyd: "y have geyton a chylde on the,
That in is yothe full wylde schall bee
    And weppons wyghtly weld." (73–78)

True to his father's prophecy, the child grows up with such terrible strength that he frightens everyone and finally forces his mother to identify his real father. When he learns that he is the son of a devil, he goes immediately to Rome, where the Pope exiles him from human society:

> "Wher ser thou travellys be northe or soth,
> Thou eyt no meyt, bot of howndus mothe
>   Cum thy body within,
> Ne no worde speke for evyll ne god,
> Or thou reyde tokyn have fro god,
>   That forgyfyn is thi syn." (282–287)

In this narrative the events which compose the *expulsion* type-scene are of a very different order and resemble in some ways the self-exile of *Libeaus* and *Perceval*. Interestingly enough, in all three narratives the child displays supernatural strength.[40]

As I have already pointed out, *Emare* resembles the narratives of the *Octavian* group. There are, however, two exiles in *Emare*, only one of which we have discussed. Later in the narrative Emare, now the wife of the King of Galys, is delivered of a child, Segramour; a letter is sent to her husband, but the wicked mother-in-law, plying the messenger with ale and wine, intercepts the letter and substitutes her own message:

> Another letter she made with evyll,
> And sayde the qwene had born a devyll,
>   Durst no mon come her hende.
> Thre heddes hadde he there
> A lyon, a dragon, and a beere,
>   A fowll feltred fende. (535–540)

Horrified, the king sends a letter in return, commanding merciful treatment for his wife and son; this letter, too, is stolen by the queen, who sends an order that Emare and the child be cast adrift:

> Another letter she lette make,
> That men sholde the lady take,
>   And lede her out of towne.
>
> And putte her ynto the see,
> In that robe of ryche ble,
>   The lytyll chylde her wyth;

And lette her have no spendyng,
For no mete, ny for drynkyng,
But lede her out of that kyth. (586–594)

We remember this structural pattern most likely for its appearance in Chaucer's *Man of Law's Tale*. There and in *Emare* the child is not really a devil; he is, however, treated as though he were one, so that the pattern is structurally analogous to others in this group. The *substituted-letters* motifeme, which also appears in Chaucer's narrative, is common to tales which share this same general narrative pattern: the combination of two motifemes, the *incestuous father* and the *innocent persecuted wife*.[41]

I suggested earlier that the two patterns (*refusal to marry the father* and *death of the father*) seem to be homologous on a structural level; at this point, it would also appear that the *irregular birth*, which is also a denial of patrimony, is analogous to the *refusal to marry the father*. If this is true, then the two motifemes, the *incestuous father* and the *innocent persecuted wife*, are redundant in that they are structurally identical. On that basis *Emare* appears to be the product of the end-to-end chaining of two occurrences of the same structural pattern.

In the two type-scene patterns we have examined in detail in this section—*irregular birth* and *expulsion*—we have seen that the substituted peripheral motifemes usually constitute a complex of systematically associated patterns, in which peripheral allomotifs of one scene have an influence upon the allomotifs in the succeeding scenes (and in other subsequent scenes). These patterns are not a necessary component of the basic narrative structure; some of them, in fact, are redundant structures, small-scale copies of the larger structural patterns. But, while these seemingly inessential complexes may be superfluous in terms of the execution of the nuclear structure, we can by no means discard them, for they contain components necessary to the working out of smaller patterns.

The nuclear motifemes of some type-scenes are associated with those of other type-scenes in characteristic linking patterns. The two linking patterns described here are *death of the father* and *expulsion of the hero*, and *irregular birth* and *expulsion of the hero*. It is important to recognize that these links are causally related only from a retrospective point of view, working backward through the tale (that is, the death of the father, in logical terms, does not necessarily entail the hero's expulsion, nor does his irregular birth, although expulsion may be a consequence of the father's death or of irregular birth).[42] Apart from this retrospective view, the story must be seen to create its own special kind of narrative logic, whether that logic be based on the poet's free choice of narrative components (the selection of peripheral allomotifs which fill out the interstitial spaces of the plot and compose related minor patterns) or upon the cultural formulas reinterpreted in the basic structure of a culture's myths.

In the case of these linked scenes,[43] we can see that the most important concern here in the opening movement of the story is to deny the hero's patrimony, either through the death of the hero's father or through the hero's irregular or apparently irregular birth. The villainy in these scenes is designed to support this denial; in some narratives there is an explicit usurpation of land and birthright and a concomitant loss of identity; in others the loss of birthright and heritage is not explicit and is only assumed in the more immediately important loss of identity. The redundant features of these stories (the repeated kidnappings of *Octavian* and *William of Palerne*, the double imprisonment of Havelok and Goldborough and Havelok's exile, the exiles and kidnappings of *Bevis, Torrent, Eglamour* and *Emare*) constitute within the set of these particular stories a paradigm of importance.

As Leach has observed, this kind of redundancy increases the certainty that the message will be received without error. If this reading of the structural patterning is valid, the message contained in these linked type-scenes seems clear enough—for the culture which designed and listened to these narratives, the issue of patrimony is a very crucial one: any man or woman whose patrimony becomes suspect must be expelled from the community.[44] But more than that, as I shall attempt to show, the loss of the hero's patrimony is restored by the hero's marriage—and I will suggest that a temporary loss of patrilineal identity is a necessary condition to love, marriage, and political success in the romances of thirteenth- and fourteenth-century England.

4 Larger structural units: the type-episode

The episode as an emic unit

Like the motifeme and the type-scene, the *emic* episode (or *type-episode*, as we shall call it here) is a generalized and more or less abstract pattern of large-scale narrative units that are manifested in different ways by different poets. As a type-pattern, it consists of certain contrastive identificational features (nuclear and obligatory type-scenes, some arranged in typical linking patterns); as an actual realization of the form, it exists as a collection of nuclear and peripheral scenes arranged according to the general demands of the formular pattern and according to immediate and specific narrative demands created by preceding optional components. Within the actual narrative, manifestations of *emic* episodes are distributed in formulaic sequences according to a pattern that the poet may or may not consciously recognize as a major governing agent of the poem. These sequences are not all linearly fixed; there is a great deal of freedom in the syntagmatic arrangements of episodes, just as there is considerable freedom within the general confines of the pattern, a freedom demonstrated in the composition and arrangement of syntagms, allomotifs, and alloscenes. However, the primary organizational scheme which holds episodes together is linear. That linearity most often is patterned and formular; it makes sequential sense to the poet and to the audience and is likely to be seen by them as a natural order. I suggested earlier that the meaningful configuration of action and event is not ruled by a causal logic produced within the narrative itself. We must look elsewhere for its origins: if the structure is archetypal, we must look to certain basic psychological contexts which are common to the various cultures in which it appears; if the structure is peculiar to a given society, we must look to the patterns of cultural experience for the origins that created and sustained it.

In the analysis of groups of narratives realized according to these formular patterns, we must often deal with such enormous amounts of material that the only possible method is to work at a high level of abstraction with very large pattern sequences. But these large and general patterns offer the same kinds of problems that have appeared in the analysis of smaller units—primarily the problem of unit definition and segmentation. How do we know whether to call the narrative unit under examination a *scene* or an *episode*? Where do these units begin and end? What are the criteria for segmentation?

In an earlier part of the discussion I raised the problem of segmenting continuous narrative structures and proposed that, given the nature of interwoven narrative structure, rigid segmentation was both undesirable and unlikely to yield useful results, for narrative must be analyzed as a dynamic process. Narrative units are not discrete or discontinuous, nor can they be treated as though they were, and the criteria for segmentation and unit definition must be correspondingly flexible. The type-episode, then, is viewed here as the largest narrative unit in a hierarchical series of smaller narrative constructions—its definition is relative to the system as a whole and has no meaning or validity outside of that system. In other words, it is not an absolute. As an *emic* unit, the type-episode is repeatable (it can be found in other narratives and may occur more than once in the course of the same narrative); in addition, it demonstrates closure (an episode ends when the activity specific to it ends, when old characters disappear or new characters are introduced, when a new problem enters the narrative, or when the poet signals that the episode has been completed). The end of an episode coincides with the end of a scene or with the end of a linked pattern of several scenes, and the poet may recognize its ending and the beginning of a new sequence formally with the *now-we-leave-and-turn-to* formula or with some other ending device. The analytic segmentation of these large structures, then, is based primarily on the poet's actual segmentation in the process of composition—as far we can reconstruct it—rather than on some theoretical system of parts imposed from outside the narratives. Granted, these criteria are very loose, but the nature of the problem demands, at least for the present study, that they remain so.

While these narrative units, as *emic* units, are very stable (a fact which helps to account both for their continued appearance and for their resistance to evolution), their actual execution in the form of the alloscene is flexible. Some poets have favorite scenes which they expand to almost episode-length (tournament and battle scenes, for example, which may continue for thousands of lines) by repeating the obligatory units over and over, while they may use certain other episodes as transitions and contract them to their minimal structure

—to perhaps no more than a few lines. But even in these expansions and contractions of narrative materials (which are themselves of great interest in understanding the process of narrative construction), the basic structural features are retained, containing the essential patterns fundamental to all such units, whether elaborately or barely furnished.

Episode structure: *King Horn*

With these rather flexible criteria in mind, let us turn now to a narrative typical in its adherence to a particular pattern, yet unique as are all narratives in the realization of the pattern. Perhaps the best poem for this kind of examination is *King Horn*: it is one of the better-known Middle English romances, and we have already looked closely at its initial scenes. The whole poem is relatively brief and simply constructed by comparison to the longer poems—and yet even that apparent simplicity is deceptive, for it conceals subtle narrative shapes whose recognition requires a thorough acquaintance with the genre (as its audience must have had).

The popularity of *King Horn* is attested by the fact that even though it is one of the earliest of the Middle English romances, it is extant in multiple versions. The Anglo-Norman version (*Horn et Rimenhild*) gives us three manuscripts and a set of fragments all belonging to the thirteenth century. There is a later prose redaction (*Ponthus et la belle Sidoyne* (ca. 1371–1390), which is reproduced in at least seven manuscripts and in seven French editions, in four English translations (two manuscripts, two prints), a German translation, and an Icelandic translation. In addition, there is the ballad-like *Horn Child and Maiden Rimenhild* (ca. 1320) which differs in many details but is similar in episode-structure; and nine or ten Scottish ballads recorded by Child, most of which retain only Horn's return to rescue Rimenhild from marriage, his revelation of his identity, and their marriage. What we are dealing with, then, is a single variant of a story which is extant in at least thirty-seven versions and which certainly existed in a great many more now lost.

The synopsis of Table 8 outlines the story as it is found in the Laud manuscript. In this narrative the segmentation of scenes and episodes is relatively simple, for there is little interweaving of narrative units, and the construction is for the most part linear. There are two notable exceptions to this general linearity: both occurrences of the prophetic dream (Rimenhild dreams that a fish has broken her net, and Horn dreams that Rimenhild is shipwrecked and threatened by Fikenild) are

Table 8

Separation 31–86	Horn's father is killed by Saracen pirates; they burn churches; his mother flees to cave.
87–144	Horn and 12 friends are set adrift.
Adoption 145–263	Horn is received into court of King Aylmer; his instruction is awarded to Athelbrus.
Love 264–280	Rimenhild falls in love with Horn.
281–495	She summons Horn to her chamber; there is a brief deception involving the substitution of Athulf, but Horn is brought at last and Rimenhild declares her love; Horn says he is low-born and cannot marry her unless he is knighted; Rimenhild agrees to ask her father to knight Horn.
496–554	Horn is knighted by Aylmer, with his 12 friends.
555–618	Rimenhild again summons Horn; she requires that he fulfill his promise; Horn objects that he must "do prowess" first; Rimenhild agrees; she gives him a magic ring.
Service and revenge 619–682	Horn slays Saracen invaders, brings leader's head to Aylmer.
Betrayal 683–746	Fikenild and king go riding.
689–728	Rimenhild tells Horn of her dream that a fish has broken her net; Horn forecasts evil, but they plight troth.

729–746	Fikenild tells king that Horn has seduced Rimenhild.
Separation 747–800	Aylmer exiles Horn; Horn tells Rimenhild not to wait longer than seven years; he gives her to Athulf's care. Horn takes ship to Ireland.
Adoption 813–852	As Cutberd, Horn is taken into court of King Thurston of Ireland.
853–892	At Christmas feast, invading Saracen giant rides into hall and challenges king; Horn accepts challenge.
Service and revenge 893–962	Horn slays giant in battle; he discovers that the giant is the slayer of his father; Horn destroys pagan invaders.
Love, negative 963–988	Thurston offers daughter Reynild as wife and makes Horn his heir; Horn declines, but he remains in the king's service for six more years and enjoys Reynild at his pleasure.
Threatened marriage and rescue 989–1001	Rimenhild is promised to Mody of Reynis; Athulf sends messenger to Horn, who promises to return; messenger is drowned; Horn takes leave of Thurston, gathers a force, sets sail.
1091–1140	Horn arrives in Westnesse after wedding; palmer reports that Rimenhild was married by force; Horn disguises himself as palmer.

1141–1308	Horn comes into hall; Athulf mourns Horn's delay; Horn reveals himself to Rimenhild by jests, reference to dream, ring.
1309–1341	Athulf and Rimenhild let Horn and his men into hall; Horn kills Mody; Fikenild and Aylmer swear fealty to Horn.
Marriage 1343–1352	Horn and Rimenhild are married.
Recognition 1352–1380	Horn reveals his identity as son of king of Sudene; he gives Rimenhild to care of her father and takes his leave.
Revenge 1381–1468	Horn returns to Sudene; he finds Athulf's father, who describes the state of the country.
1469–1480	Horn blows his horn to summon his men; they slay all Saracens.
Restoration 1481–1492	Horn rebuilds churches; restores his mother to her former position.
Threatened marriage and rescue 1493–1520	Fikenild builds castle, decides to marry Rimenhild.
1521–1538	Horn dreams that Rimenhild is shipwrecked and Fikenild threatens her; Horn decides to return to Westnesse with his men.
1539–1584	Horn arrives at Fikenild's castle; Arnoldin reports that Rimenhild was married by force; Horn and his men disguise themselves as harpers.

1585–1602	Horn and his men enter hall; Horn reveals his identity to Rimenhild by making a lay.
1602–1612	Horn slays Fikenhild.
Restoration 1613–1644	Horn makes Arnoldin king of Westnesse, Althelbrous king of Reynis; weds Athulf to Reynild; makes Rimenhild queen of Sudene.

embedded within the scenes which the dreams themselves foretell. With these two exceptions the narrative proceeds straightforwardly,[1] as the outline in the table indicates.

The episode structure of *Horn* is relatively well defined. There are a total of sixteen separate episodes; several of them, however, are repeated more than once: *revenge* occurs three times (the first occurrence, however, is only a foreshadowing of the real act and lacks the actual nuclear element); twice it is concurrent with the episode *service* (the performance of assigned tasks). *Threatened marriage and rescue* occurs twice, both times with an identical sequence of scenes. *Restoration* occurs twice. In addition to the repetition of single episodes, the sequence of linked episodes (*separation-adoption-love*) occurs once in the Westnesse sequence and again in the Ireland sequence (the fact that Horn does not love Reynild does not structurally affect the sequence). As we shall see, this particular sequence of linked episodes occurs in many narratives.

The entire tale, then, consists of only eight separate episodes loosely organized into three discrete episode-patterns: the Westnesse sequence (*separation* through *betrayal*); the Ireland sequence (*separation* through *love*); and the sequence which begins with the first *threatened marriage* and ends with the final *restoration*. The Horn-Rimenhild and Athulf-Reynild marriages unite all of the geographical areas of the poem, and the distribution of lands provides a final political unity.

The poetic economy exhibited in *Horn* is remarkable (although certainly not unique among these narratives) and can only derive from a long tradition of oral composition; the narrative variety (the poet's ability to manipulate motifeme and scene) is also remarkable. Let us look briefly at one of the repeated episodes, *threatened marriage and rescue*, to see how the poet is able to achieve this variety within a compositional structure that is, from the evidence here, fairly fixed.

Table 9

Rimenhild-Mody

Threatened marriage 989–1000	Rimenhild is promised to Mody of Reynis.
Warning 1001–1090	Athulf sends messenger to Horn, who promises to return; messenger is drowned. Horn takes leave of Thurston, gathers force, sets sail.
Arrival and disguise 1091–1140	Horn arrives in Westnesse after wedding; palmer reports that Rimenhild was married by force; Horn disguises himself as palmer.
Revelation of identity 1141–1308	Horn comes into hall; Athulf mourns that Horn has not come; Horn reveals himself to Rimenhild by jests, references to dreams, ring.
Slaying 1309–1341	Athulf and Rimenhild let Horn into hall; Horn kills Mody; Fikenild and Aylmer swear fealty to Horn.

Rimenhild-Fikenild

Threatened marriage 1493–1520	Fikenild builds castle, decides to marry Rimenhild.
Warning 1521–1538	Horn dreams that Rimenhild is shipwrecked and Fikenild threatens her; he decides to return to Westnesse.
Arrival and disguise 1539–1584	Horn arrives at Fikenild's castle; Arnoldin reports that Rimenhild was married by force; Horn and his men disguise themselves as harpers.
Revelation of identity 1585–1602	Horn and his men enter hall; Horn reveals his identity to Rimenhild by making a lay.
Slaying 1603–1612	Horn slays Fikenild.

This episode consists of five type-scene slots, two obligatory (the *threat of a marriage* and the *rescue*) and the remainder optional (see Table 9). The first scene is the threat of the marriage; in both cases Rimenhild's guardian (Athulf in the first, her father in the second) is powerless to stop it. The second scene, the warning of Horn, is accomplished once by a messenger, who fails to return with the assurance that Horn is coming, and once by a prophetic dream—both serve an identical function. In the third scene Horn arrives at his destination and is met by a man (a palmer or Athulf's cousin Arnoldine) who reports on the situation; Horn then disguises himself (as a palmer or as a harper). The fourth scene takes place in the hall where the disguised Horn reveals his identity to Rimenhild; the fifth scene is the slaying of the would-be husband (Mody, Fikenhild). The first occurrence of the type-episode is much more embellished (352 lines against 119 lines for the second occurrence); for example, Athulf's mourning for Horn's failure to return occurs only in the first episode, and Horn reveals his identity there in three different ways rather than only once. But the basic episode-structure, the sequence of slots, is identical in both occurrences of the type-episode. A measure of the poet's success in achieving variety within this pattern is certainly the fact that very few readers have recognized this economical method and have understood that the two episodes are based on the same episode-pattern.

This type-episode, however, is only one component of a larger compositional sequence; while it is complete in itself and can be treated as a whole with regular and ordered parts, it is almost always found (as it is in *Horn*) in a linking pattern with another type-episode, *marriage*.

Threatened marriage and rescue and *marriage*: a two-episode linking pattern

The episode-sequence *threatened marriage and rescue* and *marriage*, which functions as a structural frame for over a third of *Horn*, is one of the most frequent episode-patterns in all of the Middle English romances. The linking pattern does not always occur entirely without interruption—that is, another episode may be embedded within the sequence, often *revenge*, often *service*, occasionally *recognition*. However, both episodes occur together in an uninterrupted sequence often enough to allow us to see them as a common linking pattern. Moreover, the two episodes are almost always causally related in a direct way, unlike most other sequences in the poems; one character (usually the lady's father or her guardian, often the lady herself) attributes the marriage to the fact that the hero has earned the lady by his heroic actions on her behalf.

Although both episodes may not be fully realized, enough of their structure usually remains to identify them. For example, a sequence which begins with the threat of a marriage and proceeds to rescue may not always end in an actual marriage (the Norway episode in *Torrent* or the Ile d'Ore episode in *Libeaus Desconus*), for the hero may be already married or betrothed or may have other pressing commitments. In such cases the marriage episode is often negatively realized, although it remains identifiable; the hero may refuse the offer of the lady's hand and leave (as Ywayn does, after defeating Sir Alers) or he may stay with the lady he has won for a period (enjoying a husband's rights, as do Torrent, Libeaus, and Horn) and then move on to other adventures. In some instances the threat itself may not be explicitly described as a threat of forced marriage (it may appear as a threat of rape); yet the continuation of the sequence (the rescue, the marriage) is explicit, and we can only assume that the *threatened-marriage* episode has been rationalized and its structural core deleted for one or another reason.

Table 10 indicates the persistence of these two episodes in the narratives in which they occur. The rationalized *threatened-marriage* episodes do not appear here, because it is often difficult to prove that these are threats of marriage and not another variant; the negatively realized episodes (chiefly the marriage episodes) do appear on the chart, however, because their relationship to the sequence can more definitely be shown. It will be noticed that not all *threatened-mar-riage-and-rescue* sequences end immediately in marriage; the threat and rescue may be repeated as many as three times before the marriage finally takes place. In *Generides*, for example, Clarionas is threatened once by the King of Egypt and twice by his son before Generides, her rescuer, marries her at last and puts an end to the business. Marriage does not always stop the threats, however, as we see in *Horn*, where Fikenhild marries Rimenhild after she has been married to Horn—who marries her officially (they have been betrothed) after she has already married Mody![2]

Brief mention should be made of the type-episode *love*, which usu-ally occurs before this sequence takes place or may follow the *threat-ened-marriage-and-rescue* episode. It has not been included in this se-quence because, while love or a lover's commitment may motivate a knight to rescue a lady, that is not always the case. In some episode sequences love does not figure at all—in the Norway sequence in *Tor-rent*, the Ireland sequence in *Horn*, the Ile d'Ore sequence in *Libeaus*, the Sir Alers sequence in *Ywayn*. It seems best for this and other rea-sons to handle *love* as a separable type-episode which may belong to a linking pattern but is often separate.

As we can see in Table 10, the scenes which describe the type-episode *threatened marriage* demonstrate much less elaboration and invention than do the scenes which fill the slots of *rescue* and *marriage*. The threat may be offered in one of several ways (often the entire sequence of episodes occurs more than once in a poem, as it does in *Horn* and others). A suitor may simply announce that he desires to marry the lady (*Horn, William, Roswall, Torrent, Degrevant, Guy*); his suit is acceptable to the lady's father or guardian, and although the lady herself may be unwilling (having already pledged herself to the hero), the marriage is scheduled or actually performed. In other instances of the same type-episode an unacceptable suitor (usually a heathen or a giant) besieges the lady's castle (*Perceval, Degare*) or makes war on her father's lands (*Bevis, William, Generides, Triamour, Gowther, Guy*); he may trick the lady or abduct her (*Bevis, Generides, Torrent*) or he may even enchant her (*Libeaus*). In one narrative the heathen Amiral of Babylon plans to make the lady one of his harem; in another the Fairy King carries her off as she sleeps under a tree; in two cases, the marriage threat is incestuous, posed by the lady's own son, who was kidnapped or abandoned as a child and who now appears and wins his mother's hand in a tournament. The hero may rescue the lady before the marriage takes place (*Bevis, William*, and others) or the marriage may actually occur, in which case the hero may obtain a divorce for her (*Torrent*) or she may live with her husband for as long as seven years (*Bevis*), all the while remaining chaste and true to her first love!—or she may even kill her husband (*Bevis*).

The *rescue* type-episode is filled out by a variety of alloscenes. The pattern established in *Horn*, in which the hero appears disguised at the wedding feast, reveals his identity, and makes off with the bride, appears in three other narratives. In *Bevis* the similarity of one of these scenes to the *Horn* sequence is quite marked. On his return to Ermony Bevis meets a knight who tells him that Josian has been married to Ivor against her will for seven years (Auch. 1975–2040); next he meets a palmer with whom he trades clothing and obtains directions to the castle (2041–2068; cf. *Horn* 1091–1140, 1539–1584); at the castle, he hears Josian lament Bevis's loss and reveals his identity by successfully riding the horse which Josian had given him earlier (2069–2180).[3] Josian tells Bevis that she is still a virgin and begs him to take her away with him; together with a steward the two lovers escape. The same sequence of scenes appears in *Generides*, where Generides, disguised as a beggar, appears at the wedding feast of Clarionas, identifies himself by a ring (as Horn does) and takes her away dressed as a laundress. In *Guy* the role of the hero is split between two characters: Guy, the hero

Table 10

Narrative	Threatened Marriage
Horn	Mody marries Rimenhild.
	Fikenild marries Rimenhild.
Bevis	Bradmond wants to marry Josian; he invades land.
	Yvor marries Josian against her will; they live together seven years but she is chaste.
	Earl Myle tricks Josian into marriage; she strangles him and is condemned to burn.
William of Palerne	The prince of Greece wants to marry Melior.
	The prince of Spain wants to marry William's sister; he invades land.
Generides	The king of Egypt demands homage from Sultan of Persia, also demands possession of his daughter Clarionas for twelve days.
	The prince of Egypt abducts Clarionas.
	The prince of Egypt tries again to marry Clarionas; he invades her land.
Roswall and Lillian	A false steward, masquerading as Roswall, attempts to marry Lillian.
Triamour	Helen must choose a husband at three-day tournament.

Rescue	Marriage
Horn comes to wedding feast disguised as a palmer, identifies himself, rescues Rimenhild, slays Mody.	
Horn comes to wedding feast disguised as a harper, identifies himself, rescues Rimenhild, slays Fikenild.	Horn and Rimenhild are married.
Bevis defeats Bradmond in battle.	
Bevis, disguised as palmer, rescues her.	Bevis and Josian are married.
Bevis rescues her from fire.	
William and Melior, disguised as white bears, deer, escape.	William and Melior are married.
William defeats prince of Spain in battle.	
Generides defeats king of Egypt in battle.	
Generides comes to wedding feast disguised as a beggar, identifies himself, rescues Clarionas disguised as a laundress.	
Generides defeats him in battle.	Generides and Clarionas are married.
Roswall defeats steward in three-day tournament.	Roswall and Lillian are married.
Triamour defeats all other candidates.	

Narrative *(cont.)*	**Threatened Marriage**
	Burlonde wants to marry Helen; he invades land.
Torrent	Giant imprisons princess of Gaul.
	The prince of Aragon marries Desonell.
	Giant imprisons princess of Norway.
Eglamour	Giant wants to marry Organata.
	Degrabell wins the hand of his mother Christabell in joust; they are married.
Degare	Degare wins the hand of his mother in a joust by defeating his grandfather; they are married.
	Knight wants to marry lady; he invades her land.
	Degare and father battle incognito.
Perceval	Sultan wants to marry Lufamour; he invades her lands.
Degrevant	Duke of Gherle wants to marry Melidor.

Rescue *(cont.)*	**Marriage**
Triamour defeats him in battle.	Triamour and Helen are married.
Torrent slays giant and rescues her.	Torrent refuses to marry her.
Torrent defeats prince in a joust; defeats Aragon's champion; obtains Desonell's divorce.	
Torrent slays giant and rescues her.	Torrent refuses offer to marry her, but stays with her for 12 months.
	Torrent and Desonell are married.
Eglamour slays giant and rescues her.	Eglamour refuses offer to marry Organata.
Eglamour defeats his son and rescues Christabell from incestuous marriage.	Degrabell marries Organata.
	Eglamour and Christabell are married.
The relationship is recognized at the last moment through a token.	The marriage does not take place.
Degare defeats knight in battle.	Degare marries lady.
Father and son recognize one another by a token.	Degare's mother and father are married.
Perceval defeats Sultan in battle.	Perceval and Lufamour are married.
Degrevant defeats him in battle.	Degrevant and Melidor are married.

Narrative *(cont.)*	**Threatened Marriage**
Libeaus Desconus	Maugys beseiges the lady of Ile d'Ore.
	Irain, a magician, wants to marry the Lady of Synadowne; he and his brother Maboun transform her into a snakelike creature.
Gowther	The sultan wants to marry the emperor's daughter; he invades her lands.
Partonope	Melior must choose a husband at three-day tournament.
Ipomedon	Lady must choose a husband at three-day tournament.
	Duke Geron wants to marry the lady; he invades her land.
Guy	Duke Otoun attempts to marry Ozelle.
	Outon again attempts to marry Ozelle.
	Otoun attempts to marry Ozelle again, having imprisoned Terry.
Ywayn	Sir Alers attempts to marry lady; he beseiges her castle.
Floris	Sultan buys Blancheflur for his harem.
Sir Orfeo	Fairy king abducts Heurodis.

of the poem, and Sir Terry, whose lady, Ozelle, has been twice previously threatened by Duke Otoun and rescued. The third time, Otoun imprisons Terry; Guy, acting for Terry, blackens his face, obtains an appointment as his friend's jailor, reveals his identity at the wedding, and rescues both the imprisoned Sir Terry and Terry's lady.

Rescue *(cont.)*	Marriage
Libeaus defeats him in battle.	
Libeaus defeats the two in battle and transforms the lady with a kiss.	Libeaus and the lady are married.
Gowther, disguised in God-given armor, defeats him in three-day battle.	Gowther and the emperor's daughter are married.
Partonope defeats all other candidates.	Partonope and Melior are married.
Ipomedon, disguised in colored arms, defeats all other candidates.	
Ipomedon, disguised as a fool, defeats Geron in battle.	Ipomedon and lady are married.
Terry rescues her at church door.	
Terry abducts her.	
Guy, disguised, is appointed Terry's jailor; he comes to wedding feast, identifies himself, rescues Terry and Ozelle.	Terry and Ozelle are married.
Ywayn defeats him in battle.	Ywayn refuses to marry lady.
Floris offers his life for Blancheflur's.	Floris and Blancheflur are married.
Orfeo harps for him, is rewarded by promise of any gift he wants; Orfeo asks for Heurodis.	Orfeo and his wife are reunited.

Disguise, a common component of the *rescue* episode, plays an important part in other manifestations of the pattern. In one outstanding example William and Melior (in *William of Palerne*) disguise themselves as white bears and later as deer in order to escape from Melior's impending marriage to a very eligible Greek prince. The chase sequence which takes place while they are disguised constitutes, structurally, the entire *rescue* episode—made up of a number of minor crises and adventures all having to do with their escape and Melior's rescue, aided by Alphonse (who is really a prince of Spain who has been transformed into a werewolf by a wicked stepmother). The split role of the hero here also corresponds to the split in the Guy-Terry sequence of *Guy*.

In the three-day tournament, often employed in these tales to designate a husband for the lady, disguise is coupled with battle. In *Roswall* marriage has been proposed between the lady Lillian and a false steward masquerading as Roswall. Disguised in different arms each day, Roswall enters the tournament, which is held in celebration of the impending marriage; he defeats his rival (thus rescuing the lady from the unwanted marriage) and wins her hand. In *Gowther* a sultan has invaded the land, demanding to marry the emperor's daughter, but Gowther, disguised in miraculous arms sent to him by God, defeats the sultan in three days of battle and wins the emperor's daughter. In *Triamour*, *Ipomedon*, and *Partonope* the sequence involves a marriage threat only indirectly, but still possesses the same structural components: the unwilling lady has been ordered by her council to take a husband, and the three-day tournament is supposed to enable her to select the man. In *Ipomedon* the hero is disguised each day in different arms; in *Partonope*, the hero merely hides his identity, and the interesting sequence which involves the change of armor is omitted; in *Triamour* the unknown hero fights in borrowed arms, as we have already noted. It is interesting to note, in passing, that the repeated sequences of episodes in *Ipomedon* and *Triamour* are quite similar in terms of the scenes used to fill the episode-slots. In both narratives the hero first wins the lady in a three-day tournament; he goes off to other adventures, but returns when he learns that she is besieged by another suitor, whom he defeats in battle; he then marries the lady, having won her twice.

The most common form of the *rescue* episode is the battle. William of Palerne defeats the King of Spain, who wants to marry his son to William's sister and has pressed his unwanted suit by wasting the land and burning the cities; Generides goes to battle on two occasions to rescue Clarionas from forced marriage (once with the King of Persia and once with the Prince of Egypt, who has abducted her quite ingeniously by accusing Generides of having seduced her); Triamour vanquishes Burlonde; Torrent defeats the champion of the King of Aragon to obtain Desonell's divorce; Degare slays a knight who has beseiged a lovely lady; Perceval defeats a sultan who has made war on Lady Lufamour; Degrevant vanquishes the Duke of Gherle in a pitched battle. The battle itself may take the form of a tournament, a war, or single combat, but in any event force is clearly the only way to resolve the situation.

The marriage episode which ends this two-episode sequence is very heavily formulaic throughout the tales, a fact which is probably due to the formulaic quality of the ritual which attends the celebration in real life. The episode may be elaborately formulaic with details of feasts and dances and jousts (as it is in *William of Palerne* and *Generides*), or it may be reported in a few lines. The episode may end the narrative (as it does most often) by resolving all of the structural imbalances, or it may provide a starting point for other adventures. In *Bevis*, for example, the marriage takes place almost in the middle of the poem; in a sense, the narrative begins all over again with the birth of Bevis's sons and ends with their marriage.

A structural phenomenon occurs here which we should notice, for it is prevalent in these narratives and provides most of their structural complexity: the component which fills two or more functions at the same time—a feature that Propp called *assimilation*. Several examples occur in the episodes we have just examined. In *Torrent*, for instance, the hero rescues the Princess of Aragon from a giant who has imprisoned her; he refuses her hand in marriage because earlier (64–96) he had agreed to perform the task of killing the giant in order to prove himself worthy of Desonell. In *Eglamour* the same sequence occurs: Sir Princamour has promised his daughter to Eglamour if he will perform three tasks. In carrying out one of these, the killing of a giant, Eglamour rescues Orgonata, daughter of the King of Sydon, but he refuses to marry her. (Orgonata is later given to Eglamour's son Degrabell as a prize in a tournament.) The slayings of the giants fill two narrative slots at the same time: the rescue of a princess from a threat of forced marriage and the performance of a required task in order to win the hand of a princess. The single structure has a double morphological function.

In *Degare* the sequence is rather more complex, but the structural pattern is still clear. Degare wins his mother in a tournament by defeating his grandfather; the two are married, but, before the marriage can be consummated, the son's identity is discovered through a pair of gloves, tokens left with him when he was abandoned. In this episode, *threatened marriage*, Degare is an altogether unsuitable husband, and the incestuous marriage must be nullified in some way. The same situation occurs in *Eglamour*, and since the two patterns are structurally homologous, we can use one to clarify the other. In *Eglamour* Degrabell wins the hand of his mother Christabell in a tournament. After the wedding the son's identity is discovered through his arms (so far the sequence is exactly parallel to that in *Degare*) and another joust is proclaimed to find a more appropriate husband for Christabell. Eglamour appears incognito, defeats his son, and marries the lady from whom he has been separated for more than fifteen years. Returning to *Degare*, we find an analogous situation later in the poem when the hero encounters his fairy-knight father and they do battle (as do the father and son in *Eglamour*), but, before either of them can win, their identities are made known. The poem ends with the marriage of Degare's father and mother, and with the marriage of Degare to the lady whom he has earlier rescued from a threatened marriage. In both *Degare* and *Eglamour* (and perhaps in *Torrent* as well, although there the narrative situation is rather more confused, owing to the corruption of the manuscript) the father must rescue the mother, who is threatened by an incestuous marriage to her son, by defeating that son in battle; the *threatened marriage* in both cases involves the *recognition* of the lost son (a double morphological structure), and the *rescue* (the defeat of the son by the father) involves the *recognition* of the lost father (another double morphological structure). But as if that complexity were not enough, the situation in *Degare* (and perhaps in *Eglamour* and *Torrent* as well) is even further complicated by the fact that the initial move in the story appears to be a rationalization of the *incestuous-father* story. When Degare defeats his grandfather (his mother's father), he has in effect rescued her from the threat of an incestuous relationship at the same time that his rescue constitutes another (perhaps more serious, because more immediate) threat. Seen from that viewpoint, *Degare* appears as a systematically structured series of *threatened-marriage–rescue–marriage* episodes (the father threatens his daughter, the son threatens his mother, and a knight threatens a lady). Two of these serve additional morphological functions in the tale: the first *rescue* serves as a new *threat*, and *threat* and *rescue* both serve as *recognition*. The double and even triple use of these structural features provides great economy in the poem's composition; it also, however, provides for very great complexity in plotting and often obscures the structural patterning which serves as the poem's framework.

We need to mention here briefly the last two poems in Table 10 which use the type-episode *threatened marriage and rescue* as the structural frame for the narrative: *Floris and Blancheflur* and *Sir Orfeo*. In both of these poems the action begins with the abduction of the heroine. In *Floris* the low-born Blancheflur is sold to merchants and finally to the Amiral of Babylon because, interestingly enough, she poses a threat of an unsuitable marriage to Floris, the son of the king of Spain. In *Orfeo* Heurodis is stolen by the Fairy King and taken away to his castle.[4] In both poems, the body of the narrative is concerned with the search for the lost lady and her final recovery. The very different surface features of the two poems have obscured this common framework, however, and their similarity, so far as I know, has not been pointed out before.

Service and *marriage*

The type-episode *service* appears in a linking pattern with the episode *marriage* in several narratives. In these occurrences it either accompanies or serves as an alternative to the episode-sequence described in the preceding section. In the Middle English romances the hero may earn his bride in one or two different ways: he may save her from marrying someone else, and/or he may perform a task or a series of tasks for her father or for her. Most often, service itself is not enough; only in *Emare* (and perhaps in *Amis*) does the episode appear alone.[5]

As Table 11 indicates, three kinds of service appear in the episodes which fill these slots. The hero may be commanded by his lady to distinguish himself as a knight before she grants her favors (*Guy, Squyr of Lowe Degre*). In both narratives where this occurs, the period of service is seven years, at the end of which the hero returns, and the pair are married. (In *Guy* this episode-sequence coincides with the *threatened-marriage–rescue–marriage* sequence; the threatened lady is not Felice, however, but Terry's lady, Ozelle, whom Guy rescues and Terry marries. The separate stories of Guy and Terry are skillfully brought together by a pattern of substituted heroes in the same way that the *Amis and Amiloun* story is constructed.)

In another variant of the episode-pattern the father may command that a series of tasks be performed before the hero may marry the daughter. In *Torrent* and *Eglamour* the sequences are structurally identical down to the optional motifemes in the scene-patterns and the doubled structure (the *service* episode parallels the *rescue* episode). These two narratives represent the only appearance in Middle English romance of the favorite folktale component *task*, in which the hero is assigned a certain difficult problem.[6] It may be that the trial by combat, seen here in *Earl of Toulous* (the earl serves as a champion to save the lady from the false charges of her betrayers) and in *Amis* (more complicated, because there are two heroes and a substitution is made during this episode),[7] is a survivor of this more primitive component. In any event, both these trial-by-combat episodes also fulfill the type-episode *revenge*, and as such they serve a double function: to win the lady by service and to avenge her betrayal.

In the third group of variants (*Horn, William, Bevis*) the hero simply

Table 11

Narrative	Service	Marriage
Guy	Felice commands that Guy serve as knight in foreign lands for seven years.	Guy and Felice are married.
Squyr of Lowe Degre	Lady commands the squire to serve as knight in foreign lands for seven years.	Squire and lady are married.
Torrent	Torrent performs three tasks for King of Portugal: slays giant, procures falcon, slays second giant; is permitted to marry daughter.	Torrent and Desonell are married.
Eglamour	Eglamour performs three tasks for Sir Princamour: kills deer and boar and giant owners, slays dragon; is permitted to marry daughter.	Eglamour and Christabell are married.
William	William defeats Saxons who have attacked Rome.	William and Melior are betrothed, later married.
Bevis	Bevis defeats Saracens, slays boar.	Bevis and Josian are married.
Horn	Horn defeats Saracens for Aylmer.	Horn and Rimenhild are married.
	Horn defeats Saracens for Thurston.	Horn refuses to marry Thurston's daughter.
Emare	Emare serves at banquet for King of Galys.	King and Emare are married.
Ipomedon	Ipomedon serves as a squire in the lady's court.	Ipomedon and the lady are married.

Narrative	Service *(cont.)*	Marriage
Roswall	Roswall serves as a squire in the lady's court.	Roswall and the lady are married.
Toulous	Earl of Toulous defends the lady in a trial by combat.	The Earl and the lady are married.
Amis	Amiloun (impersonating Amis) defends Belisant in a trial by combat.	Amis and Belisant are married.

performs some deserving feat, a service which justifies his newly gained knighthood and wins the love and admiration of the lady. In both *William* and *Bevis* this scene is followed by the lady's forthright declaration of her love for the unknown knight; in *Horn,* as we have seen, the declaration precedes the performance of the service.

The variant in *Emare, Ipomedon,* and *Roswall* represents the simplest execution of the pattern: the courtly service of the hero (or heroine) as a squire or serving maid. Emare serves at the banquet table dressed in a miraculous blue robe; her service so impresses the King of Galys that he marries her straightaway. Ipomedon and Roswall both cut such dashing figures at court that they are immediately employed in the lady's service. In both of these narratives the episode *service* is coupled with the three-day tournament in the *threatened-marriage–rescue* sequence, which finally allows the squire to marry his mistress.

Love, betrayal, separation: a three-episode linking pattern

One of the more interesting patterns is the three-episode sequence of *love, betrayal,* and *separation,* which demonstrates a great deal of stability in its character-event configuration. In this pattern we find the "forth-putting lady," who unashamedly (and in very uncourtly terms) declares that she must have the hero; the apparently low-born hero who insists that he is too poor and too churlish to marry her (he means this in quite literal terms and not in the elaborately courtly metaphoric sense used by some of the French romancers), but capitulates reluctantly when she promises to reward him (*Horn*) or threatens to tear off her clothes and swear that he has raped her (*Amis*); the villainous betrayer who tells the heroine's father that she has been seduced; and the

Table 12

Narrative	Love
Horn	Rimenhild declares her love to Horn, who is reluctant but agrees if she can arrange his knighthood.
Bevis	Josian declares her love to Bevis, who is reluctant but agrees if she will become Christian.
Amis	Belisant declares her love to Amis, who is reluctant but agrees when she threatens to tell her father he has raped her.
Generides	Clarionas loves Generides; confesses her love to Mirabel; Generides loves Clarionas; he confesses his love to Nathanael; the two servants bring pair together.
Squyr of Lowe Degre	Squire confesses his love to daughter of King of Hungary; she accepts him.

understandably angry father who sees the family's prospects for a more profitable marriage about to slip away. (Table 12 indicates the distribution of this linking pattern in the narratives of our study.) While parts of the configuration (the eager lady and the reluctant groom) are traditional and have apparently gained their stability through long usage,[8] the attachment of *betrayal* to this type-episode may well be a product of some contemporary situation. It is easy to imagine how carefully guarded a young girl's chastity would be if her future chances for an advantageous marriage (advantageous to her family, that is) depended upon it; it is equally easy to imagine her father's anger if he should discover that she had been dallying with one of the unpropertied young

Betrayal	Separation
Fikenild tells Aylmer that Horn has seduced his daughter; Rimenhild's prophetic dream.	Horn is exiled; he goes to Ireland for seven years.
Two knights tell Erymm that Josian has promised to be baptized to win Bevis's love.	Bevis is sent to Bradmond with letter commanding his death; he is imprisoned for seven years.
Steward spies on lovers, tells father that Amis has seduced Belisant.	Duke commands trial by combat between Amis and steward; Amis must leave to find Amiloun to substitute for him.
Malachas spies on lovers; tells father that Generides has seduced Clarionas; Generides' prophetic dream; Jewel tells father that Generides has seduced Clarionas; later tells him that Generides has taken her to a forest lodge.	Generides is imprisoned. Jewel abducts Clarionas.
Steward spies on lovers, tells father that squire has wooed his daughter.	Squire is imprisoned; later released and sent abroad for seven years.

men of the household. The immediate exile of the unfortunate man is probably one of the more humane of the father's punishments.[9]

This concurrence of patterns is much more widespread than Table 12 indicates, however, and the major interest of this linking pattern lies in the fact that there is an evident correspondence between the sequence of episodes and the type-scene linking pattern on a smaller scale (irregular birth and exile) that functions as a structural frame in the first episode (separation). That is, a love relationship is either described or assumed (a man loves his wife, who bears him a child or children); their love is betrayed (the wife is accused of adultery, the children are said to be bastards or supernaturally conceived); and the wife and child are exiled by the angry and sorrowful husband—just as the hero is exiled by the father of his intended bride. The stable configuration of characters and events (lovers, betrayers) is repeated both on the level of small-scale narrative pattern (in the type-scene *separation*) and on a much larger scale (the three-episode linking pattern described here). The patterned sequences are structurally homologous on different levels of the narrative and form a deep-structural paradigm, a fact which supports my earlier suggestion that formular composition, perhaps conscious on the surface levels of syntagm and motifeme construction, permeates the narrative to an extent which is beyond the conscious control of the poet. If this is so, the redundance suspected here is not a simple matter of repetition for emphasis or even an indication of the economic and functional art of oral composition. Instead, redundance on these hidden levels (beyond the immediate, conscious grasp of a listening audience) suggests that these features may in some way represent a basic situation which generates the narrative energy that brings the tale into being. Stated without elaboration, the problem here is that love results almost always in betrayal and separation (fifteen poems manifest this pattern in one way or another either on the scene or the episode level). The narrative cannot end until these imbalances are restored to a more acceptable state: love eventually culminates in the establishment of a state of political, social, and personal equilibrium. More specifically, love arises almost always between apparently unsuited partners; the narrative cannot end until these partners are discovered or proved to be suitable and the imbalances (here observed on a social and economic level, but perhaps derived from an unconsciously felt but more pervasive sense of the kinship imbalances which will be restored by the marriage) are redressed. Love ends in a respectable, acceptable, and happy marriage.

The remarks in the preceding paragraph grow out of a syntagmatic analysis of the linear structure of the poems, but when we begin to work with large episodic units, the analysis inevitably becomes paradigmatic—that is, the reconstruction of large-scale correspondences and the assimilation of apparently unlike surface features to homologous patterns. The units that occur at this level seem to function as intermediate structures like the syntagmemic patterns I proposed on the level of language. These narrative patterns do not exhibit the variety of the surface features or the simplicity of deep-structural features; rather, they are partly realized elements which are generated by deeper structures and in turn generate the surface structures of the individual narrative through a series of operations which are analogous to the *rewriting rules* of grammar.[10] I cannot offer a detailed account of these rules here, although I have described some of them in earlier sections (the doubling of allomotif, alloscene, and episode units, embedding, chaining, the use of direct and indirect discourse, the use of shifts in point of view, the use of some components in a double function, and so forth). It would seem that there are a relatively limited number of these rules for the reconstruction of narrative from a deep structure, and that they are alike in all narrative genres—although it is probably true that some genres do not admit the use of certain rules (the rearrangement of chronological time is not available to these poets, for instance), and that some rules which we are more accustomed to call narrative devices are of a later development than others. Although I cannot provide a complete analysis of all of the intermediate structures of the narratives in this study, at least some speculative observations about lower kinds of organizational configurations will be made now that we are working with basic structures.

Prohibition, violation, and restitution

There is one other linking pattern which merits discussion here because, like the preceding sequences, it is framed in the love-marriage pattern; it is of interest, too, because of its infrequent occurrence in the Middle English romances, while it is one of the primary components of folktale structure. This three-episode sequence, *prohibition*, *violation*, and *restitution*, occurs in only three narratives, although in each of these tales it serves as a major structural frame for much of the story.[11]

In *Partonope* the hero is brought by a magical ship to a beautiful but apparently empty city, where he is served by invisible servants and led to a magnificent bed. In the darkness he becomes the lover of Melior, who forbids him to look at her for two and a half years. Later he returns with a magic lantern (given him by his mother, who urges him to violate the prohibition) and looks at Melior. He nearly goes mad when he loses his lady, is nursed in secret by Melior's sister, and finally makes restitution by defeating all of his rivals in a three-day tourney (which also satisfies the *threatened-marriage–rescue* sequence and thus serves two functions).

The second half of *Ywayn* has many similarities to the Partonope story. The prohibition is cast as a commandment: Ywayn is told to return to Laudine in a year's time—that is, he is prohibited from returning late. His failure to keep the commandment is seen both by Laudine and by Ywayn as a violation. He goes mad, spends a year in the woods, and is nursed by a lady whom he defends from a threatened marriage. The rest of the narrative details his restitution.

In *Launfal* the knight is commanded by his fairy-mistress, Dame Triamour, not to disclose the secret of their relationship. He is prodded by Guinevere into revealing his mistress's identity (here Guinevere has the same function as Partonope's mother), is tried by the court, and suffers the loss of his lady because of his violation. But just as Launfal is about to be exiled, she appears and takes him away with her.[12]

As Alan Dundes and others have pointed out, the prohibition-violation structure is fundamental to most folktales.[13] In the Middle English romances this structure is always connected with the fairy-mistress, a folktale element. Even Laudine, the most rationalized of the three ladies, still bears traces of fairy characteristics; according to R. S. Loomis (*Arthurian Tradition and Chrétien de Troyes*), she is a literary descendant of Morgain, one of whose forms appears to have been that of a fountain nymph. On these grounds it is possible to group the three narratives together as bearing evidence of a shared structural pattern: *prohibition, violation, restitution*. But since no other narratives exhibit this pattern, it remains apart from that of the larger number of our tales, at least for the moment.

The love story: single episodes and linking patterns as a basic story structure

The episode sequences that we have discussed in the last four sections constitute one of the two basic plot structures of the Middle English romance: the love story. Its composition is often quite complex, but its outline is simple and very familiar. The hero and the heroine fall in love, but the equilibrium (however brief) established by that love is destroyed by the introduction of one or more complications: *betrayal* and *separation*; *threatened marriage* and *rescue*; *service*; *prohibition*, *violation*, and *restitution*. All of these one-, two-, or three-episode complicating patterns—doubled, tripled, embedded, and arranged in any number of ingenious patterns—are framed within the simple sequence of *love* and *marriage*.

The pattern can be carried out in many ways. In *Horn*, for instance, the *love-marriage* sequence is complicated by two major intervening episode-structures: *betrayal* and *separation* (Horn and Rimenhild are betrayed by Fikenild; Horn is exiled) as well as *threatened marriage* and *rescue* (the Mody and Fikenild incidents). The same developmental pattern, on a much larger scale, is seen in *Bevis*: Bevis and Josian are betrayed by a pair of knights, and Bevis is exiled and imprisoned; he returns to rescue Josian from an unconsummated seven-year marriage, and they are later married. In *Eglamour* and *Torrent* the major intervening structure is *service*; in *Degare* and *Emare* and *William* it is *threatened marriage*.

Given the many different kinds of variants that are theoretically possible and the changes that might have been made in this formular pattern, it is surprising to see that for the most part the changes were not made and the poets were content to remain within the confines of the plot. The structure itself appears to have great stability—more stability than the surface structures (the syntagms, allomotifs, and alloscenes), which are much more susceptible to change. The poets were able to operate with greater freedom in the delineation of their characters, for instance, and in the manipulation of plot sequences; there is much less apparent freedom in the manipulation of these larger, more stable structures which are characteristic of the genre. The *love-marriage* sequence belongs to the deep-structural level of the genre itself and cannot easily be altered.

The love story, however, is not the sole generating structure of the romance. There is another, equally important structure which is manifested in a formulaic series of episodes and episode linking patterns: the *separation-adoption* sequence.

Separation and *adoption*

In *Horn* the episodes which open the poem belong to a sequence of type-episodes, *separation* and *adoption*. This sequence is a typical linking pattern shared by a great many narratives, as Table 13 shows. In sixteen of the poems this linked sequence opens the action of the narratives. In two poems, *Eglamour* and *Torrent*, it takes place much later and ends the action rather than begins it; in these two instances the hero's wife and son(s) are exiled, not the hero himself. In two more poems, *Emare* and *Bevis*, this episode-sequence occurs twice, once at the beginning of the narrative, once again toward the end. And in *Guy* the sequence is established in the attached romance of *Reinbroun* and constitutes the whole of that separable tale.

In Chapter 3 we discussed in detail the two type-scene linking patterns, one of which constitutes the first episode of a large number of stories: the *death of the hero's father* and the hero's *exile*, and the *irregular birth* of the hero and his *exile*. Taken together as the type-episode *separation* (the larger unit under which these type-scenes are subsumed), the pattern demonstrates that the initial move in these narratives deprives the hero of his patrimony and at the same time destroys his patrilineal identity. In the type-episode *separation* a stable situation (a family) is disrupted and its stability changed to instability by the subtraction (or in Proppian terms, by the *lack*) of a single feature, patrilineal identity.

A second type-episode, *adoption*, is invariably linked to *separation*. In all seventeen of the poems of this group (which together with their

Table 13

Narrative	Separation	Adoption
Horn	Horn and twelve friends set adrift after slaying of his father.	Horn is taken in by King Aylmer of Westnesse.
Bevis	Bevis is sold to pirates after slaying of his father.	Bevis is taken in by King Erymyn of Armony.
Guy	Reinbroun is stolen by merchants.	Reinbroun is adopted by King Argus of Africa.
William	William is kidnapped by werewolf after attempted poisoning of his father.	William is adopted by cowherd. William is adopted by emperor of Rome.
Amis	Amis and Amiloun go with parents to court of duke.	Duke adopts Amis and Amiloun.
Roswall	Roswall is exiled for freeing prisoners.	Roswall is adopted by poor woman. Roswall is adopted by steward.
Generides	Generides is raised away from his father, with his mother.	Generides is cared for by laundress. Generides is taken in by Sultan.
Perceval	Perceval's mother exiles herself and son.	Perceval is taken in by Arthur's court.
Libeaus	Libeaus's mother exiles herself and bastard son of Gawain.	Libeaus is taken in by Arthur's court.

Narrative	Separation *(cont.)*	Adoption
Degare	Degare is abandoned because he is illegitimate.	Degare is adopted by hermit; adopted by hermit's sister; taken in by his mother's court.
Lai le freine	Child is abandoned because she may be thought to be bastard.	Child is adopted by abbess.
Havelok	Goldborough is imprisoned; Havelok is imprisoned, exiled.	Havelok is adopted by Grim the fisher.
Octavian	Mother is exiled with two sons, Florent and Octavian, who are kidnapped by animals.	Florent is adopted by Clement, a butcher; Octavian and mother taken in by King of Jerusalem.
Triamour	Triamour's mother is exiled; Triamour is born in wilderness.	Triamour and mother taken in by Sir Barnard of Hungary.
Emare	Emare is set adrift.	Emare is taken in by steward.
Torrent	Desonell and sons are set adrift; children are kidnapped by animals.	Antony is adopted by St. Antony; Leobertus is adopted by King of Jerusalem; Desonell is taken in by King of Nazareth.
Eglamour	Christabell and son Degrabell are set adrift; son is kidnapped by animals.	Degrabell is adopted by King of Israel; Christabell taken in by uncle, King of Egypt.

conjectured sources and analogues represent a very large body of medieval narrative), the hero, having been separated from his father and having lost with that separation his identity, is forced to assume another identity: he becomes "low-born," a "thrall," a "strange squire" with no identifying lineage or with a very different and not very respectable one. In twelve narratives the hero is adopted by a character who is explicitly a yeoman-class character: a forester (*Bevis*), a fisher (*Bevis, Havelok*) a cowherd (*William*), a poor woman (*Roswall*), a merchant's wife (*Degare*), a laundress (*Generides*), a butcher (*Octavian*), a steward (*Roswall, Emare, Triamour*), a hermit (*Torrent, Degare*), an abbess (*Freine*). In thirteen narratives, although the hero is received at the court of a king or a duke and is admired by all for his fairness and his strength (some may even suspect that he has "gentil blood"), his lineage is unknown, and he is considered to be low-born.[14]

The obligatory type-scene in this episode is the *adoption* of the hero, which may be executed in a number of very different ways and often may occur several times in a single tale. In fact, there seems to be a considerable amount of freedom in the surface development of this type-episode—more freedom than we see in most other episode patterns. In addition to the obligatory *adoption*, the poet is apparently required to observe that the hero is the fairest and strongest of all his comrades and that he demonstrates prowess in all of his endeavors— but aside from these requirements, the episode is quite freely developed. In *Havelok*, for instance, the refugee prince of Denmark is raised in England by Grim the fisherman, carrying baskets and "working for his dinner"; when he is older, he goes off to Lincoln to serve as a cook's knave. His strength is prodigious; he is a man of good will, and everyone loves him:

> Him loueden alle, stille and bolde.
> Knictes, children, yunge and holde;
> Alle him loueden that him sowen,
> Bothen heyemen and lowe. (955–958)

Similarly in *William of Palerne* the young prince grows up as a herdsman, learning to "schote vnder the schawes" and to bring home meat for dinner—"conies and hares, pheasants and other fowl." All his young forest comrades admire him:

> So kynde & so corteys comsed he there,
> That alle ledes him louede that loken on him ones (194–195)

In *Amis*, on the other hand, the two young heroes are adopted by a rich duke who teaches them to joust in tournaments, to hunt, to serve at the table. They are so gentle and generous that the whole land loves them:

> With riche & pouer so wele thai wrought,
> Al that hem seighe with word & thought,
> Hem loued many a man;
> For thai were so blithe of chere,
> Over al the lond fer & nere
> The los of loue thai wan. (196–201)

The episode may be long and rather fully developed, as it is in *Havelok* and *Octavian*, where the poets take advantage of this particular pattern to introduce a sequence of minor scenes built around the lower-class characters typically found in this episode—earthy, comic scenes, rich in realistic, *fabliau*-like detail. In *Octavian* this broad humor centers around the butcher Clement, who boasts to his wife that Florent (a boy he has purchased from a gang of thieves) is his own bastard son, born of some heathen lady during Clement's pilgrimage to the Holy Land. In *Havelok* the comic figure is the hero himself, a country bumpkin who shambles into Lincoln without hose or shoes and, wrapped up in an old sail, takes up service with the Earl's cook. On the other hand, the episode may be very short and undeveloped. In *Triamour* the poet merely observes that Triamour (who, with his mother, has been taken in by Sir Barnard), is "mekyll of boon and lyth":

> Every man lovyd hym aftur ther estate
> They had no chesone hym to hate (469–470)

When the episode is shortened in this way, it seems designed to serve as a transition episode; that is, the poet includes it because it is necessary to the working-out of the given pattern, but the real interest lies in some other episode, probably the preceding or succeeding one or both, which will be developed more fully. In the interests of narrative economy, this scene is trimmed to its barest bones and made to serve as a transition.

However the episode is executed, whether it be long or short, fully developed or left in its skeletal outline, it is clear that it continues the structural pattern of the preceding episode, *separation*, to which it is invariably linked. In the *separation* type-episode, the hero's relationship with his father is destroyed; in the *adoption* type-episode, a substitute father is found who, according to the customs of the social class to which he belongs, teaches and trains the young hero and raises him to be an admirable man, loved by all who know him. With this scene a new stability is achieved—again a kind of familial stability—by the addition of a single feature: a new and different kind of patrilineal identity.

Loss of property: an alternative pattern

A few narratives do not exhibit the two-episode linking pattern of separation and adoption. These narratives begin for the most part not in the childhood but in the adulthood of the hero, and offer as the opening move a different pattern: *loss of property*. Although these tales constitute a relatively minor subgroup within the genre, they are of interest in their adoption of narrative formulas that seem to belong to other episode sequences, and they may use these typical patterns as vehicles for moral commentary.

Loss of property serves as an initial type-episode in five narratives (*The Earl of Toulous*, *Degrevant*, *Launfal*, *Amadace*, and *Isumbras*) and as a sequel-episode in *Amis*. The type-episode is relatively simple in its outline, and the formular pattern and its variants can be summarized in only a few sentences.

In *Toulous* and *Degrevant* a landed knight's property is taken away from him by a richer and stronger neighbor, and the two do battle over the theft.[15] In *Launfal* and *Amadace* a knight known for his largesse is impoverished because he recklessly gives away all his property; he is forced to dismiss his servants and live alone.[16] In *Isumbras* a knight is visited by a bird (an angel in another version) and given a choice between suffering in youth and suffering in old age; he chooses to suffer in youth and, Job-like, loses his lands, his money, his family, and is left alone. The episode in *Amis* is related to an earlier episode in which Amiloun disguises himself as his friend Amis and kills a steward in a trial by combat. For this trick, he is visited with leprosy, and his wife takes all of his property and banishes him to a life of begging. *Amis* represents an interesting combination of the two initial episode-patterns, for the romance proper begins with the more common *separation-adoption* sequence, while its sequel begins with the type-episode *loss of property* as a result of an action undertaken in the earlier part of the story.

There are some interesting differences between this episode and its alternate, *separation*, but for the purposes of our discussion it is more important to understand the fundamental structural similarities between the two type-episodes. Both have to do with the loss of property and social rank; both have to do with the exile of the hero from his home. In fact, the loss of property always entails separation, and, as a consequence, loss of identity (although not always a literal loss of identity).[17] Structurally the two type-episodes are homologous.

The situation is made more complex because this initial episode has in at least two instances been used as an allegorical frame with an explicitly moral content. In *Isumbras* the knight's pride is seen as the flaw which causes him to lose his lands and goods ("In his herte a pride was broghte/Of goddis werkes gafe he righte noghte"), and the narrative is transformed into a polemic against the sin of pride. In *Amis* Amiloun's false-swearing (his disguise proclaims him to be someone else in the sacred moment of the trial by combat) is apparently the cause of his leprosy. Both of these narratives contain a fair amount of outright moral commentary (in *Amis* the second part of the tale is demonstrably more didactic).

Revenge

The type-episode *revenge* is difficult to discuss because it is used so loosely in the Middle English romances. Unlike the episodes which so often occur in the Icelandic sagas, for instance, and which seem to serve as the structural underpinning for that narrative form,[18] revenge in the romances does not appear to be obligatory or essential; it often occurs in answer to certain kinds of villainy, but not always. And when the death of the villain does take place, it usually comes about within the framework of an impartial justice—that is, judgment is often a community verdict upon the guilt of the offender rather than judgment summarily executed by the victim or the victim's kin.[19]

There are two kinds of villainy which prompt the occurrence of the type-episode *revenge*: the slaying of the father and/or the exile of the hero; and the betrayal of the lovers (or of the heroine). In several instances, as has already been mentioned, *revenge* serves a double function, and the episode is conflated with another type-episode (usually *service*)—a compositional device which often obscures the outlines of both episodes and makes the structural identification of either of them more difficult and less certain. The employment of the *revenge* episode in *Horn* provides us with a good example of this structural complexity. In *Horn* the type-episode occurs in three variant versions (the three-part occurrence is unusual and points to *Horn*'s affiliations with the saga; in the romances revenge commonly takes place only once or at least in only one episode). The first use of the episode-pattern (619–682) is only a foreshadowing of the actual event to come; in order to prove that he is worthy of his newly won knighthood and of Rimen-hild, Horn slays a band of Saracen invaders—apparently without re-membering that it was Saracen invaders who killed his father and exiled him. A variant version of the same episode occurs several hun-dred lines later, in the Ireland sequence, when Horn accepts the chal-lenge of the Saracen giant who has invaded Thurston's land (893–962). In the service of Thurston, Horn battles the giant, by chance discover-ing during the combat that his opponent had earlier slain his father; the giant's death constitutes revenge for the death of the hero's father. Both of these enactments of the scene, however, are conflated with the episode *service;* structurally it does not matter whether the opponents in those scenes are Saracens or dragons. In comparison to these two double structures, the final episode of Horn's return to Sudene and his slaughter of the Saracen host (1381–1480) is much simpler and more straightforward; it satisfies only the single episode-pattern. The three repetitions of this type-episode, in three different geographical loca-tions, are arranged in an order of progressive clarifications (although this is almost certainly not a conscious effort on the part of the poet). The account of Horn's first battle with Saracen invaders (in Westnesse) does not identify them as the killers of Horn's father; the second (in Ireland) identifies only one killer; the third (in Sudene) identifies the whole Saracen invading force which killed Murray and destroyed his people. This repetition is probably an indication of the oral-composi-tion origins of the poem and of the poet's craft—beyond that, however, one is tempted to wonder if the poet obscured Horn's several reprisals because personal revenge is no longer easily accepted as a means of dealing with the transgression, which in the romances demands another kind of settlement.

As Table 14 demonstrates, the episode-pattern *revenge* may be filled by several variant scenes: the hero may avenge himself in battle (this scene occurs four times); a council may judge the villain or he may be required to undergo a trial by battle (five times); or the crime may be avenged by accidental or providential means (four times). More than one manifestation of the episode may occur, often one directly follow-ing another. For example, Havelok defeats Godard in battle, but a council judges that he shall be burned to death; in *Octavian* a council decrees that the emperor's mother-in-law shall be burned, but she cuts her throat before the judgment can be executed.

Among these variant scenes the deliberate slaying of the offender occurs only in *Horn* and *Bevis*, where the hero leads a force into battle against the villain. In other cases where the hero kills the villain, re-venge is achieved unintentionally as a consequence of another act with

Table 14

Narrative	Villainy	Revenge
Horn	Saracens slay Horn's father.	Horn kills Saracens in Westnesse, in Ireland, in Sudene.
Perceval	Red Knight slays Perceval's father.	Perceval kills Red Knight.
Bevis	Bevis's mother and Mordure kill Bevis's father.	Bevis defeats Mordure in battle, burns him; Bevis's mother falls down stairs and breaks her neck.
Havelok	Godrich kidnaps Goldborough, shuts her up in tower; Godard kidnaps Havelok, shuts him up in tower.	Godard is judged by a council and executed; Havelok defeats Godrich in battle and he is condemned by a council.
Octavian	King's mother causes Octavian's wife and sons to be exiled.	Council condemns her to burn, but she cuts her throat.
Eglamour	Princamour exiles his daughter and child.	Princamour falls out of a tower and breaks his neck.
Torrent	King of Portugal sets his daughter and her children adrift.	Torrent sets King adrift in a leaky boat.
Triamour	Marrok causes Triamour's mother to be exiled; kills servant.	Servant's faithful dog kills Marrok seven years later.
Amis	Steward betrays Amis and Belisant.	Amiloun kills steward in trial by combat.

Narrative *(cont.)*

| *Toulous* | Two knights betray earl's wife. | Toulous defeats knights in trial by combat. |
| *Squyr of Lowe Degre* | Steward betrays lovers. | Steward is killed in a fight. |

other intentions. In *Perceval* the hero is unaware of the real identity of his opponent, and the punishment of his father's killer is accidental. The death of the Red Knight, like that of the Saracen giant in *Horn*, has a double function in fulfilling both the episode-patterns of *revenge* and *service*. The murder of the steward in *Squyr of Lowe Degre* is not planned as revenge for the man's betrayal but is an act of self-defense when the steward sets up an ambush outside the lady's bower.

Another common form of revenge takes place as the outcome of a trial, where the villain is made to stand to account for his deeds. A council may judge and sentence the offender (in *Havelok* this structure, like the initial *separation* episode, is doubled); or the villain and hero may do battle in a trial by combat. This scene occurs in two poems, in *Earl of Toulous*, where there are *two* villains against whom the hero must do battle, and in *Amis and Amiloun*, where the hero realizes that he is guilty and his friend Amis must substitute for him (instead of two villains, there are two heroes). This judgment, however, is not considered to be the revenge of the hero, but the verdict of God: it is providential justice.

Providential justice may take other forms. A wicked mother-in-law in *Octavian* is sentenced to be burned, but she cuts her own throat. Sir Princamour of *Eglamour* and the wicked mother in *Bevis*, both of whom earlier sentenced their own children to death, fall down stairs and break their necks. A slain servant's faithful dog in *Triamour* kills his master's murderer (and Triamour's betrayer) seven years after the deed. In these variants revenge is successfully achieved, but neither the hero nor the community is responsible for it. Like the trial by combat, such punishment is seen as the verdict of God upon the guilty.

There are a number of other acts which can be categorized as *punishment* and which follow certain predictable patterns, but most of these have been treated in the compositional structures in which they occur and so are not considered here. Speaking generally, *revenge* as a type-episode is almost always handled rather perfunctorily, and that fact, together with the fact that very often the structural patterns of *revenge* and *service* are conflated, seems to indicate that revenge is not a major concern of these narratives, nor is it structurally essential to the re-establishment of equilibrium at the end of the story. In fact, in only five poems is revenge *necessary* to the political, social, or personal restoration which takes place at the end. The villains of *Havelok*, *Horn*, and *Bevis* remain in possession of the land they have wrongfully taken, and in order for the hero to be restored to all of his rights, it is necessary to evict them. In *Amis* and *Toulous*, the villains pose a threat to the continued safety of one or another character and must be removed in both cases by trial by combat. In the other narratives the type-episode *revenge*, while it occurs, is not necessary to the working-out of the plot or to the structural balance achieved at the end of the poem.

In comparison to the Icelandic sagas and other Germanic tales, the Middle English romances seem to be remarkably careless in their handling of villains. There is, of course, a great deal of bloodshed in these poems, and that fact should not be minimized. But the violence is directed toward certain well-defined ends (the rescue of the lady from the threat of a forced marriage, which may require the death of the man who threatens her; the defense of lands and property against invasion; the defeat of marauding giants or dragons). Punishment or revenge, while it occasionally occurs, is not an important structural component. These tales (and the Continental stories which evidence the same structural patterns) are much more concerned with social and personal restitution than with personal retribution, and the structural differences between the saga and the romance can be seen at just this point.

Recognition, restoration, and marriage

In the Middle English romances, where loss of identity plays a major structural role and where the *knight in disguise* is an essential motifeme in many type-scene patterns, *recognition* becomes one of the more important type-episodes. As such, it occurs in almost all of the narratives in some form or another, often expanded and elaborated so that it occupies a focal point in the tale, or is occasionally neglected to accommodate some other closing episode, or (when it is used to resolve only a temporary disguise) is buried midway in the plot-sequence. In the episode linking pattern *recognition-restoration-marriage* it plays a part necessarily previous to the concluding two type-episodes. In many narratives recognition seems to be a prior condition of marriage—that is, marriage to a commoner cannot seriously be considered for the lady, and the knight must be found to be of equal or higher rank before the wedding takes place.

The *recognition* episode itself is executed with great freedom among the narratives, both in the means by which recognition is achieved and in its variant distributions in the tales. Recognition by a token is the category which is most often noted; the tokens themselves are listed independently as motifs in the *Motif-Index*.[20] The lost hero (or heroine) may be identified by a robe (*Freine, Isumbras*), by a pair of gloves (*Degare*), a ring (*Perceval, Horn, Freine*), a cup (*Amis*), a broken weapon (*Degare*), a horse (*Bevis*), a heavenly light and a birthmark (*Havelok*), or armor (*Torrent, Eglamour*). The same structural function (that of an agency in the revelation of the hero's identity) may be performed by another character rather than by a token or identifying mark: he may be identified by a helper (*William, Ywayn, Toulous, Floris*), by a member of his own family who knows his identity (*Roswall, Emare, Octavian, Generides, Triamour*), or by the lady he has rescued (*Gowther, Libeaus, Partonope*). In other narratives the hero may take it upon himself to tell who he is (*Bevis, Reinbroun*).

Categorizing the episodes in this way, however, does not allow us to see the various manipulations which may occur in the scenes which make up the type-episode. Usually, of course, the revelation is carefully prepared for much earlier in the story by the description of some identifying element which is either given to the hero or associated with him. The revelation, however, may be extremely abrupt; it may interrupt or terminate another narrative sequence—a fight or tournament (*Degare, Reinbroun, Ywayn, Partonope*) or a threatened marriage (*Freine, Degare, Eglamour, Roswall, Horn*). The original episode may continue after the recognition, with the substitution of the recognized character for one of the characters in the interrupted sequence. For example, in *Lai le freine, Roswall*, and *Horn* the threatened marriage is turned into a real wedding by the sudden recognition of the identity of the hero or heroine, and the preparations made for one wedding are simply used for another.

Perhaps the most interesting manifestations of the type-episode are those two which include reciprocal transformations. In *William* the werewolf is freed from the spell and returned to his former state as a prince of Spain (a version of *recognition*); immediately thereafter, he reveals William's identity as the true king of Apulia. In *Libeaus* the lady of Synadowne has been transformed into a snake-creature by her wicked captors (one of whom wants to marry her), and only the kiss of a relative of Gawain can set her free. Libeaus's kiss, which breaks the spell, also reveals him as Gawain's son (a fact he had not known until that time). Related to these two tales are two of the three fairy-mistress stories, in which the lover's identification of his mistress violates her commandment. In *Partonope* the hero is induced by his mother to transgress Melior's interdiction and see what she looks like; in *Launfal*, the hero is provoked by Guinevere into revealing the existence of his lady. In each of these two narratives the lady (after a suitable period of penance) makes a subsequent and reciprocal identification of the hero at the end of the story, and he is re-established in her good graces.

In some tales *recognition* scenes are distributed within the plot structure rather than collected in one major episode. In *Horn* the hero identifies himself several times (always at a wedding feast and in conjunction with the threat of a marriage); in *Degare*, the hero is identified by his mother (through a pair of gloves) and much later by his father (by a broken weapon). In two versions of *Octavian* the hero is identified once by his father and once again by his mother—earlier in the narrative he had given indications of his noble birth by his tendency toward aristocratic possessions (a noble charger, a falcon). Havelok is identified three different times, by Grim and Ubbe (who both stand in the role of foster father to him) and by Goldborough, his wife. This repetition and structural redistribution of the components of the type-episode allow the poet to create suspense and occasionally to play with elements of dramatic irony. (In *Octavian* Clement continues to believe that his foster son is low-born, although the audience knows differently.)

The other two type-episodes in this sequence seem to follow more or less formulaicly in accord with the qualities of the type-episode *marriage* that have already been pointed out, and it seems reasonable to suppose that the whole group of three episodes function as a single unit and tie together the two single strands of the narrative chain, the *love-marriage* sequence and the *separation-restoration* sequence.

Separation-restoration and love-marriage

In this chapter we have examined the episode type-pattern, the largest composite structure of the narrative, and its manifestation in individual episodes of individual tales. We have also discussed its occurrence in certain well-defined linking patterns, chains of related episodes which are associated in a linear sequence and make up the syntagmatic structure of the narrative. We are now in a position to clarify the relationship of these linking patterns taken as wholes to see how they function individually as well as within the narrative system.

Essentially the structural configuration of the Middle English romance is based on the conjunction of two separate episode-patterns, which in turn are composed of the smaller linking patterns we discussed earlier:

separation restoration
separation, adoption (revenge), recognition, restoration
loss of property, restoration

love marriage
love, betrayal, separation, marriage
love, threatened marriage, rescue, marriage
love, service, marriage
love, prohibition, violation, restitution, marriage

The first linking pattern, the fairly uncomplicated and uninvolved story of separation and restoration, is usually made up of four type-episodes: *separation, adoption, recognition,* and *restoration.* The young hero's patrilineal identity and his rights as lord of the land are taken away from him by accident or design; he is adopted, either immediately or at some later date, into a court; much later he is recognized as the son of his father and the rightful lord of the lands of his birth; at the end of the narrative he is finally restored to all of the rights earlier denied to him, and he is often reunited with his lost family. While other episodes may occur (the type-episode *revenge* may be found in this cycle) as optional and peripheral components of this linking pattern, these four elements are present in every occurrence of the pattern among the narratives of this study.

That this pattern of linked type-episodes is an important one is evidenced by the number of narratives which are composed according to its design. Sixteen tales open and close with this sequence (*Octavian, Emare, Perceval, Triamour, Horn, Gowther, Libeaus, Havelok, Degare, Freine, Roswall, William, Bevis, Generides, Guy,* and *Reinbroun*). Two more tales (*Torrent* and *Eglamour,* which share so many structural similarities) open with the *love-marriage* sequence, the second linking pattern; but midway through the narrative, when the performance of assigned tasks is complete, the *separation-restoration* sequence is embedded in the tale: the hero's lady and his sons are exiled in a pattern which matches that of *Octavian, Triamour,* and so many others. In *Bevis* this linking sequence occurs not once but twice: the story opens and closes with it (Bevis is sold to pirates, later regains his lands and position; Bevis's sons are born in exile, adopted by a forester and fisher, and later restored to their land and position). In the composite tale of *Guy* and *Reinbroun* (treated here as a single tale made up of two separable parts), the Reinbroun story is composed exclusively of the *separation-restoration* sequence, while the Guy-Felice portion of the story is composed entirely of the *love-marriage* sequence. It is likely that the poet felt some structural requirement for bringing the two stories together, as the authors of *Torrent* and *Eglamour* apparently did.

Amis and Amiloun represents an interesting combination of patterns in the *separation-restoration* sequence (which proves to be an alternative to the one we have just discussed: *loss of property* and *restoration*). The story opens with the separation of Amis and Amiloun from their parents and their adoption by a rich duke; later, Amiloun's father dies, and the son returns to take possession of the family heritage. These four episodes represent a somewhat rationalized version of the *separation-restoration* sequence, complicated by the fact that the love story belongs to Amis, and Amiloun plays only a peripheral (but still important) part in it. However, the tale goes on to describe how Amiloun loses his family lands to an overbearing wife when he is stricken with leprosy (a result of his interference in the *love-marriage* sequence of Amis's story) and how his lands and his health are finally restored to him with the help of his friend. The tale is, then, a composite of the two alternative patterns, only one of which is usually found in a given tale. It is the only narrative in this study which is constructed in such a complex way.

Other occurrences of the *loss-of-property—restoration* sequence are found in five other narratives, where the linking pattern serves as a framework for much of the tale. *Degrevant* and *Toulous* are purely secular tales, and the usurpation of the hero's lands in his absence by a powerful neighbor provides the impetus for the action. As we noticed earlier, however, *Amadace* and *Isumbras* (both of which have thematic as well as structural affinities with the second part of *Amis*) are vehicles for moral commentary, and the reasons for the loss of the land (profligate generosity on the one hand and inordinate pride on the other) point to moral flaws in the heroes' characters.

In the earlier discussion of the *love-marriage* sequence I suggested that the love story acts as one of the generating structures of the romance, capable of creating any number of formular surface structures. It is now apparent that the romance consists of two such generating structures (the love story, the separation and restoration story), and that these deeper structures serve to define and characterize the genre. Their combination, together with the formular surface features that we have noticed, can be taken as the boundaries of a formal definition of the Middle English romance.[21]

The syntagmatic narrative structure of the Middle English romance is the combination of these two linking patterns, either of which could logically and narratively stand by itself as a single story. In the romance, however, one linking pattern is made to require the other (for reasons which are probably not literary, but sociological) in order to be completed. The linking patterns are woven and interwoven very tightly, with episodes embedded within episodes and episodes which belong to one pattern being used in a double function to satisfy the requirements of another episode in the other pattern. But all of this complicated structural manipulation does have a quite serious purpose, for, as we look closely at the structural shapes of the two linking patterns, we see that invariably the complications introduced and then resolved in the *love-marriage* sequence enable the poet to restore imbalances brought about in the initial *separation-restoration* sequence. The two patterns, brought together in a single tale, depend on one another for resolution: marriage cannot be brought about without recognition of the hero's identity, for the princess cannot, after all, really marry an unknown knight, even though she might like to think that she can. That recognition essentially depends for its occurrence on the hero's establishment of his own identity and his own prowess as he seeks to defend his lady or to win her. Without the one narrative sequence, the other cannot be brought to a satisfactory end.

5 Speculations and conclusions

Formulaic structures and narrative codes

The structure of the Middle English romances is, as we have seen, very highly formulaic; the evidence brought together here suggests that all of these narratives, so long thought to be heterogeneous, are constructed according to a common model. The basic double patterns of the two major linking structures (*separation-restoration, love-marriage*) provide the foundation for the story, with required (and to some degree ordered) episodic slots that may be filled by some scenes but not by others. These scene-patterns, in turn, possess a formulaic slot structure which may be filled by certain typical motif-patterns. Finally, the motifs are made up of structured sequences of syntagms, or formulaic language structures, which constitute the stylistic texture of the work. In constructing the story the poet chooses from a pool of structurally homologous variants and inserts this choice into the appropriate position in the linear plot sequence.

This procedure is analogous to the selection-combination procedure of speech production outlined by both Saussure and Jakobson and extended as a model to disciplines other than structural linguistics. The pool of variants is similar in many respects to those paradigmatic sets from which the speaker chooses linguistic items; the choice of any item is the product of one or more determining factors: the demands of the narrative context (the earlier selection of certain narrative items may either require or prohibit the later selection of certain other items, so that the poet's freedom of choice becomes much more restricted as the narrative proceeds and the poet becomes more thoroughly bound by its necessities); the audience's expectations about the story; and the poet's own intentions other than that of simple storytelling (to persuade, to praise, to make a didactic point, and so on). Having made the selection, the poet combines this choice with the other choices made in the story-syntagm; this combination may take place in a simple linear fashion, end-to-end, or the new unit may be embedded into an existing complex of units, or separable components of the narrative unit may be interlaced with preceding and succeeding units in the linear chain of the story.

To complement this phrase-structure grammar of traditional narrative, it is useful to postulate the existence of a series of processes which operate, prior to the final selection-combination procedure, upon the deeper structures of the narrative, creating the items that the poets select already formed—and which also account for changes that the storymaker may produce in the received formulaic unit. While these transformational processes (analogous to the processes proposed in transformational-generative grammar) have not been studied in detail here, some of the more obvious ones should be mentioned: chronological transformations (the presentation of certain elements outside of the order in which they ordinarily occur: flashbacks, foreshadowings, etc.); recursive transformations (the repetition of certain events or certain character functions); deletions and contractions; negations (the use of negative or reversed components); and the passive transformation (the hero is acted upon rather than acting). Some of these transformations work at a deeper level than others. That is, they would seem to be ordered to some degree in their occurrence, just as grammatical transformations are ordered: some seem to predicate others, some exclude others, and so forth.

The theory of textual transformations in narrative is new, and its development has been unfortunately hindered by the level of abstraction at which most of these theorists work—and by the kind of mathematical representations that are used to convey the theory.[1] But some very obvious remarks can be made here about narrative transformations in the tales we have studied. First, we have observed that formular structures can be found at all levels: the surface-level syntagms, motifs, scenes, and episodes; the intermediate structures of motifeme, type-scene, and type-episode; and the deep-structural linking-patterns. These formulaic surface and intermediate structures seem to be the result of a formulaic series of transformations, none of which the poet is free to change to any great degree,[2] and none of which the poet is aware of or consciously exercises, except in a minor way. That is, the poet is not a deliberately creative artist in the sense of wishing to produce a new and unique thing; the poet's only purpose is to reproduce the story as it should be told. The transformations, which are the heart of the creative process in literary narrative, belong to the code. The whole process, from the choice of the story plan (the deep structure) to the final production of the individual text (the surface structure), is determined in certain specific ways by the laws of the genre to which it belongs; the patterns, as we noted earlier, are at all levels built into the code, and the individual user has very little control over them.

There are, of course, poets who are able to subvert the laws of the genre and to alter the transformational series in such a way as to exploit the formulas to certain specific esthetic or didactic ends. Almost none of the tales in our study, however, demonstrates any conscious awareness of this possibility (the best example of an exception to this rule is *Amis and Amiloun*, where the poet combines story parts in certain unorthodox ways)—probably because the stories themselves seem to have been a necessary part of community ritual and somehow important to the preservation of community beliefs and expectations. The poets, therefore, made a great effort to preserve the patterns whole and complete. It was only when the community system of belief had begun to change that this popular art form began to change with it.

Community acceptance, as Jakobson and Bogatyrev have argued,[3] is the major factor in deciding whether a piece of oral folk literature or popular literature will survive to the point where it may be recorded and brought into the realm of written literature. In the case of the Middle English romances, which derive from a fairly lengthy period of oral composition, it is apparent that the community was determined to perpetuate these stories and to insure their survival. The reasons for this determination are multiple and complex and of interest to us in this study only insofar as they explain certain compositional problems of the tales themselves—most importantly, the problem of redundance.

It has been argued by proponents of the oral-formulaic school that the surface-level redundance of textural and narrative features is primarily a function of the method of composition. But in addition to these compositional functions, which are undeniably important, narrative redundance has other equally important functions. Because neither the style nor the narrative patterns generally convey a great deal of *new* information to its audience (the audience already knows what will happen—how the story will turn out—and probably even anticipates certain scenes, motifs, and even language formulas), they are free to serve as vehicles for other, perhaps more vital kinds of information. This information (which may be obscured, especially for observers from another culture, by the complexities of the narrative process) is encoded within the deeper structure of the stories and exemplified in the repetition of certain narrative components; it quite clearly has to do with the reinforcement and perpetuation of certain social and political beliefs held by the community. Because of the immense amount of psychological energy which must be invested in these beliefs in order to make them appear viable to all segments of the culture, any formula (either political, social, or artistic) which contains these codes will itself be preserved by the community, often past the time when it ceases to hold importance for the whole group (the general community is almost always extremely conservative and resists change). Any phenomenon which violates community standards will be ignored, and significant violations may be explicitly disallowed.[4] I would like to suggest here that the Middle English romances contain within them certain kinds of encoded information essential in some way to the preservation of the community, that these codes inform the structure of all of the poems, and that they can be used to account for events and attitudes and for compositional habits which have so far seemed to us illogical and incoherent.

Some speculations about sources and codes

Having remarked that a thorough understanding of the linear development of any story must precede deep-structural analysis, I have primarily confined my attention in this study to the syntagmatic arrangement of narrative materials and to an attempt to develop a more complete grasp of the processes involved in the composition of formulaic narratives, specifically of the Middle English romance.[5] However, in the course of this study it has been necessary to isolate and discuss a number of intermediate and deeper generative structures, and some speculations are in order at this point about the possible sources of the energy and force of those structures.

As we move deeper into the structural patterns of the romances and find larger and larger kinds of organizing forces, it becomes much easier to understand and to appreciate the structural coherence produced by these elemental forces. We are able finally to separate out a double story as the fundamental structural basis for the narrative form: the *separation-restoration* sequence and the *love-marriage* sequence. The combination of these two stories is arranged in such a way that one of the sequences provides the necessary means for resolving difficulties and restoring imbalances found in the other. This reciprocating pattern serves as a structural framework for all of the Middle English romances and can be taken as a working definition of the genre itself. But as Claude Lévi-Strauss has suggested in his discussions of the structure of myth,[6] these generative patterns may be precipitated from several different sources and may be encoded on at least four levels: economic, geographic, sociological, and cosmological. While all of these codes may not serve in all kinds of narrative, at least three of them (sociological, cosmological, and economical) can be used as the basis for a brief discussion of the possible origins of the narrative forms and formulas we have studied here.

The *separation-restoration* (or *exile-and-return*) formula is an ancient one, indigenous to many cultures. According to Alfred Nutt and J. G. Von Hahn, whose nineteenth-century studies of the formula still hold interest and value,[7] its origins in Aryan cultures may be found in the annual cycle of the solar myth (Lévi-Strauss's cosmological explanation). R. S. Loomis, investigating the relationship of Celtic mythology to stories in the Arthurian tradition, finds many traces of the solar myth in the narratives of Chrétien;[8] Jessie Weston sees it as the basis for the Grail legend.[9] And Northrop Frye, in his remarks on the theory of myth, notes that the "three-fold structure" of romance (from "struggle" to "ritual death" to a "recognition scene") is shown in the "three-day rhythm of death, disappearance and revival" which he believes serves as a more or less explicit framework for the hero's activity in all manifestations of the romance.[10]

These interpretations of certain structural patterns and links between romance and primitive nature mythology illustrate very clearly the cosmological level of the narrative structure. But it is more important to recognize that the Middle English poets have pieced together these mythic elements (of which only confused and rationalized fragments remain) with other elements within a different kind of structure, a historical chronicle of people who look and act like the people of the late Middle Ages. This new structure bears a close relationship to a culture more deeply concerned with problems of human relationships in the social world (problems of kinship and marriage, political alliances formed by betrothal, and the possession of land as an indication of power) than with the problem of the individual's relationship to either the spiritual or the natural world. While the mythic structures of solar regeneration are certainly present, they appear to have been restructured into a more practical myth of greater immediate energy and relevance which aims at describing an ideal social order and ideal social relationships rather than natural or spiritual phenomena: the myth of power gained through the marriage alliance, and the reconciliation of the contradictory notions of love for power's sake and love for love's sake.

Some other attempts to decipher sociological structures beneath certain folktale patterns have led in a direction which seems closer to a solution of this problem. Murray Potter, surveying the vast amount of folklore and literary materials collected around the epic theme of father-and-son combat, suggests that the origin of such formulaic stories has to do with kinship systems:[11] the stories originally arose, he argues, in exogamous communities which were in a transition phase between a matriarchal and a patriarchal society. The Persian *Shah Nameh* episode of the Sohrab and Rustem story best exhibits the characteristics of the pattern Potter has isolated, and since the *separation-return* sequence in the romances is to some extent parallel, it is worth looking at in full here:

> Rustem, hunting wild asses, falls asleep, and his horse is stolen by Turks. When he awakes, he goes on foot to Semengan, where he is received by the king as an honored guest. The king's daughter, Tehmineh, offers herself to him that night; they are betrothed, and Rustem gives her an onyx for the son she says she will bear him. He leaves her and returns to Zabulistan, and later the boy is born. His strength is so great that at ten years of age no one in the land can contend with him. In order to learn his lineage, he threatens his mother with death, and finally she tells him that Rustem is his father, but warns him not to let Afrasiab know of the relationship. Determined to put his father on the throne of Iran, Sohrab raises an army. Afrasiab, learning his secret, plots to prevent father and son from recognizing one another, in order that one or another of them might be killed. In a battle with his father (whom he does not recognize) Sohrab is unwilling to reveal his true identity as the son of Rustem, and they meet in single combat for three days. At their last meeting Sohrab is mortally wounded and laments his failure to find his father. Rustem, hearing the lament, finds the onyx under Sohrab's armor and covers his head with dust, weeping. "There is no remedy; weep not!" Sohrab says. "I saw the signs which my mother pointed out to me, but I did not believe my eyes. My lot was written above, and I was to die by the hand of my father. I came like the thunderbolt; I pass away like the wind" (pp. 8–11).

As we can see from a brief comparison of this story to the plot of the Middle English romances, there are a number of striking parallels—all of which tend toward the representation of matrilineal, matrilocal practices. The separation of father and son, the continuance of the maternal affiliation, the attempt to learn the father's identity and to restore the filial connection—at least some of these elements appear in almost all of the narratives we have examined. Potter's argument about the kinship patterns manifested in the tales he has studied makes very good sense, and it is useful to apply it to the romances as well. In the Sohrab and Rustem pattern, a man must leave his home to find a bride (his society is exogamous); the hero of our romances is also forced to leave home, and in the course of his journey he finds a wife. Bound up with that phenomenon, Potter believes, is the custom of bride-capturing, not apparent in the tale quoted above, but a major feature of many of the Eastern narratives;[12] we see the same custom (rationalized, perhaps, but still visible) in the numerous threatened marriages of the Middle English romances. The "forth-putting lady" (who is found in "Sohrab and Rustem," in many of Potter's stories, and in several Middle English romances) is also a feature of matriarchal society, Potter says. In addition, the avuncular relationship, evidence of matrilineal practices, is an important part of his stories; if it is absent or rationalized almost past recognition in ours, it is certainly present in a very closely related genre, the French *chanson de geste*. And the hostility between father-in-law and son-in-law, unremarked by Potter but apparent in many of his tales, illustrates matrilocal marriage, according to Lévi-Strauss;[13] often the antagonism is so strong that the father-in-law sends the potential son-in-law off to perform a series of impossible tasks.[14]

But in all of the tales studied by Potter, the hero's stay with the wife in her country and with her people (matrilocal residence) is of short duration; the wife does not leave her family, nor does she fall completely under the power of her husband, and eventually the husband returns alone to his own people, leaving behind his wife and family (a return to patrilocal society). There is no reunion (as there almost always is in the romances), and the quest for the father by the abandoned son almost always ends in the tragic encounter of the two, unable to recognize one another, a representation of the hostility between father and son which exists in a matrilineal society. In Lévi-Straussian terms, the hero's failure to achieve the reconciliation he hopes for is an indication of a given culture's inability to resolve the two contradictory tendencies framed in their myth: matrilineal and patrilineal, matrilocal and patrilocal. The hero is the unhappy man trapped between dual allegiances, tragically attempting to come to terms with both: in "Sohrab and Rustem," the hero tries to establish his own identity as the son of his father, and to force recognition of his father's (and his own) right by marriage to the throne of Iran; because he is unable to accomplish the first, he is unable to achieve the second, and must die as a result of his failure.[15]

The Middle English romances, on the other hand, occupied at one level with this very problem, are able to achieve a final equilibrium within a patrilineal structure and to provide for the hero's successful mediation between the abandoned or wronged mother and the lost or absent father. The reunion at the end of the story (which replaces the tragic combat of Sohrab and Rustem and the unsuccessful mediation of the hero) is a representation of the balancing of forces that comes about in the romance.

This restoration of balance is brought about by the use of a double rather than a single structure: the *separation-restoration* sequence combines with the *love-marriage* sequence, and each one serves as a reciprocating structure to redress the imbalances which occur in the other. The Sohrab and Rustem story does not possess this reciprocal structure—a fact which seems to suggest that it is the association of the two patterns which makes possible the successful mediation of the hero and the dissolution of the tensions brought about by the conflicting patterns of familial relationships. As an escape from the inevitable dilemma (the one that awaits Sohrab), the culture envisages a solution of a related order: the establishment of a marriage which will make possible the restoration.

If we were to apply the sociological arguments of Potter and Lévi-Strauss to these narratives, the following set of conjectures might be made: the fact that the hero of many Middle English romances is adopted by a neighboring king might be seen as a rationalized representation of the nephew's fosterage by the maternal uncle (as so often occurs in the Old French *chansons de geste* and in such Middle English narratives as *Libeaus* and *Perceval*);[16] and the marriage of the hero and the daughter of this uncle figure (or a woman approved by him)[17] might be viewed as a rationalization or fragmented recollection of matrilineal cross-cousin marriage. Such a marriage insures the continued protection of the family holdings, on both patrilineal and matrilineal sides, for the hero inherits both his father's property and the property of his mother's brother.[18] In addition, it overcomes the serious conflicts between patrilineal and matrilineal tendencies and establishes an equilibrium which brings with it a very desirable long-term social stability.[19]

The fact of the matter is, of course, that marriage within certain specified degrees of kinship was prohibited by the Church in the Middle Ages,[20] and while cousin-marriage may both have offered a very attractive solution to the thorny problem of the consolidation and protection of the family inheritances, and have provided a more or less symmetrical system of exchanges which allowed no single family or group of families always to profit, it also offered, in real life, difficulties which only a papal dispensation might relieve. Such difficulties were not impossible to surmount, of course, and many ruling houses, during the time these narratives were popular, apparently contracted such marriages for reasons of stability, self-protection, and self-aggrandizement. Charles Smith, surveying the incidence of papal dispensations, finds them a common occurrence:

Beginning with Innocent IV (1243–54) it is found that the papal
court issued a large number of dispensations as matters of routine,
and the reason which was given for these relaxations of the law
was that the interests of peace were served. A set formula was used
with but few deviations, and it is quite unlikely that the popes
personally interested themselves in these cases. For the most part
these dispensations were disseminated by the Friars, and there apparently was no legatine examination of the facts alleged as jus-
tification for the exercise of papal clemency. Geographically, the
dispensations were granted to individuals all over Christian
Europe. A number of persons with no titles of nobility were the
recipients of such dispensations.[21]

But this argument, while it is interesting and in many ways appeal-
ing—and will doubtless eventually be supported by more complete and
acceptable historical testimony than I can muster here—rests on con-
jecture and will not be pursued here further. These questions, however,
although the likelihood of their immediate answer is in doubt, point
the way toward a related area of investigation, and it will be interesting
and perhaps fruitful to uncover these connections here.

Two mythic levels (in Lévi-Strauss's analysis, the levels of sociology
and economics) come together at this point. Marriage, a sociological
phenomenon, has generally been an economic matter as well, and the
Middle English romances provide no exceptions to this rule. Let me
make several brief observations. First, in terms of the surface structure,
the financial and social status of the hero is very much a matter of
concern. In most stories he has lost his identity and, with that, his
inheritance, his goods, and his property; in many cases, he has spent
his youth as a member of a lower or middle class, working and living as
his foster family does, and learning all the customs and trades of the
lower classes. When he does come to court to be adopted as a squire or
knight into the service of a nobleman, he comes as a foundling; he is, as
far as anyone knows, penniless and landless, undistinguished by either
deed or title, and he is understandably reluctant to contract any un-
equal union. Horn speaks for many unpropertied heroes when he re-
monstrates with Rimenhild, who has offered herself to him:

Ich am hyborn to lowe
Such a wyf to owe
Ich am born thralle
And fundlynge am bi falle.
Ich am nawt of kende
The to spouse welde.

Hit were no fayr wedding
Bituene a thral and the king. (*Horn* Laud 447–454)

The fact of the hero's poverty does not daunt the heroine, however, and in every case she willingly accepts him as a suitable husband, rejecting candidates much better qualified socially and economically. The remainder of the story is concerned with the hero's establishment of his own worth, either in service or by defending her from other suitors, and with their marriage.

This portion of the story (the *love-marriage* sequence) echoes the *swayamvara* marriage (prevalent, according to Lévi-Strauss, in epic poetry and folklore from Assam to western Europe, and in one entire section of the *Mahabharata*). *Swayamvara*, or the marriage of chance, merit, or choice, "consists for a person occupying a high social rank, in the privilege of giving his daughter in marriage to a man of any status, who has performed some extraordinary feat, or better still, has been chosen by the girl herself."[22] The practice, Lévi-Strauss argues, is designed to answer this urgent question: wherever the rule prescribes marriage with a woman of immediately inferior status (or marriage with a man of immediately superior status), how do women of the highest class get married? Lévi-Strauss observes that *swayamvara*

> gives a girl from a superior class to a man from an inferior class, guaranteeing at least symbolically that the distance between the statuses has not irremediably compromised the solidarity of the group. . . . This is why the lower classes have a major interest in the *swayamvara*, because for them it represents a pledge of confidence. Thus they become the jealous guardians of the rules of the game and right up to contemporary folklore, the drama—or the comedy—of *swayamvara* marriage will lie alternatively, according to the viewpoint of the narrator, either in the opportunity offered to natural gifts, or in the adroitness of the great in getting around the law.[23]

Lévi-Strauss describes the major characteristics of such a marriage practice, which have been introduced into the modern European marriage: "These characteristics are: freedom to choose the spouse within the limit of the prohibited degrees; equality of the sexes in the matter of marriage vows; and finally, emancipation from relatives and the individualization of the contract" (p. 477). From the descriptions given by Lévi-Strauss and by Potter, it would seem that the Middle English romances represent a Westernization of a form of the *swayamvara*, and that their popularity is due in part to the fact that they lessen the gap between the classes. But the matter is not so simple as this, for the romance is characterized, as we say, by the addition of another episode sequence (*separation-restoration*) which violates the resolution proposed in the *swayamvara* myth—that is, the marriage of the lady into a lower class (or the marriage of a lower-class man into an upper class)—and substitutes another, much more conservative resolution: marriage of the lady within her own class. For in the romance, the hero never remains unpropertied for long; the truth about his birth and lineage (a part of the *separation-restoration* sequence) is ultimately revealed through his attempts to prove himself worthy of the lady's love, and at the end of the tale, his natural-born aristocracy, newly rediscovered, relieves any embarrassment either the lady or her kinsmen might have felt about marriage to a member of the lower class.

If this analysis is correct—and if it can be extended to other versions of the *swayamvara*—it would seem that more is being offered than is actually being given. For the singular pervasiveness of this male-Cinderella pattern suggests, perhaps, an important fact about the romance: that it serves as a means by which the culture can resolve certain conflicts it feels about the restrictiveness of its class system. In one sense, the romance serves as an apparent vehicle for upward mobility; it offers the hope to the lower class that even a princess can be won by a worthy man, whatever his economic and social status. But at the same time, it endorses the upper-class belief that worth and birth are synonymous, that only a nobleman can be a noble man, fit by nature to gain the princess and the kingdom and to rule over both. Perhaps this ability to bridge two distinctly different classes within the culture, implicit in the two linking structures of the narrative, is one of the most important aspects of the Middle English romance and accounts in large measure for its importance as a community ritual and for the culture's determination to preserve it. This double structure can be viewed as a problem-solving structure, enabling the culture (the producers and audiences of the tales) to mediate certain important contradictions within its social, economic, and mythic structures and to provide a set of categories in terms of which a coherent reality could be constituted. Having once established the romance as one vehicle of this mediation, the community insisted upon its preservation, whole and complete, and used the narratives as a conceptual scheme, a kind of mythic mirror in which a version of reality was created, enabling them to view the world as they wanted—and needed—to view it. The Middle English romances reflect this world view and provide a consistent and coherent pattern that served as an experiential screen which would permit the ordering of reality.

Our own view of the world is very different, and what was coherent and ordered to a time long past is undecipherable confusion to us now. It is not so strange, then, that we find it difficult to see through the multiple intricacies of narrative structures to the simplicity of pattern that lies beneath. But our understanding of this simplicity and coherence is basic to an understanding of the narratives and their functions, both as literary and as social phenomena, and offers a key to the meaningful rediscovery of the complexities themselves.

Notes

Introduction

1. John Lipski, "From Text to Narrative: Spanning the Gap," *Poetics* 5 (1976), 192.
2. Teun A. Van Dijk, "Some Problems of Generative Poetics," *Poetics* 2 (1971), 25.
3. There are, of course, exceptions to this general rule. Richard Ohmann's *Shaw: The Style and the Man* is one example; Tzvetan Todorov's *Grammaire du Décaméron* is another.
4. A. C. Gibbs, *Middle English Romances*, p. 2. Donald Sands asserts that "no really pat and satisfying delimitation of the genre can be made" (*Middle English Verse Romances*, p. 1). And Ojars Kratins says that the term *romance* has a "diminishing usefulness," serving as a "commodious bottom drawer" ("The Middle English *Amis and Amiloun*: Chivalric Romance or Secular Hagiography?" *PMLA* 81 [1966], 347).
5. Northrop Frye, *The Anatomy of Criticism*, p. 247. "The purpose of criticism by genres," Frye says, "is not so much to classify as to clarify such traditions and affinities, thereby bringing out a large number of literary relationships that would not be noticed so long as there were no context established for them."
6. See Kenneth Pike, *Language in Relation to a Unified Theory of the Structure of Human Behavior*.
7. Of Claude Lévi-Strauss's work, see especially "The Story of Asdiwal," in *The Structural Study of Myth and Totemism*, ed. Edmund Leach, and *The Raw and the Cooked: An Introduction to a Science of Mythology*.
8. John Lyons, *Introduction to Theoretical Linguistics*, p. 50.
9. The level of focus, according to Pike, is the span of attention which we devote to any system. "Focus can shift up [to include a larger amount of material] or down [to include less material], and the 'whole' shifts with it" (*Language*, p. 80).
10. Pike coined the words *etic* and *emic* from the words *phonetic* and *phonemic*. His discussion of the characteristics of these two concepts is complex (see *Language*, pp. 37–72).
11. The corresponding linguistic model is the construction of a phrase-structure grammar, in which the sentence is broken down to its constituent elements by labeled brackets which assign the elements to specific categories; these categories are further decomposed until the ultimate constituents are reached, the "terminal strings," or more generally, kernel sentences. The internal rules that govern this arrangement are conceived to be a set of rewriting rules which alter the terminal strings in such a way that the sentence is produced. For a more elaborate description, see Noam Chomsky, *Syntactic Structures*.

1. Problems of stylistic analysis in Middle English romances

1.   Laura Hibbard Loomis, "The Auchinleck Manuscript and a Possible London Bookshop of 1330–1340," *PMLA* 57 (1942), 607. Loomis comments: ". . . most people would agree that these English romances are thoroughly conventionalized and pedestrian in style. They must be put down to the authorship of men of generally humble literary attainments, of no literary ambition, and nearly all of whom were possessed of the same 'patter' of well-worn cliches, the same stereotyped formulas of expression, the same stock phrases, the same stock rimes, which Chaucer was to parody in such masterly fashion in *Sir Thopas*" (pp. 607–608).

2.   Richard Ohmann adopts this view in *Shaw: The Style and the Man*, where he sees style as a reflection of "the writer's organization of experience, his sense of life"; it is his "epistemic stance" (p. 13).

3.   Gibbs, *Middle English Romances*, p. 25. Maldwyn Mills, in the introduction to his edition of *Libeaus Desconus*, comments that Thomas Chestre, the assumed author of the poem, was a "hack writer who had a borrowing acquaintance with a number of other Middle English romances" (p. 21). Clark Slover adopts the same attitude in "*Sir Degare*, a Study of a Medieval Hack Writer's Methods," *University of Texas Bulletin, Studies in English* 11 (1931), 5–23.

4.   Gibbs, *Middle English Romances*, p. 28. The view that these narratives were meant for a reading audience has been used by H. J. Chaytor (*From Script to Print: An Introduction to Medieval Literature*, p. 107) to support his contention that the fourteenth century saw a dramatic rise in the level of literacy in England.

5.   Ruth Crosby, "Oral Delivery in the Middle Ages," *Speculum* 11 (1936), 110.

6.   A. C. Baugh, "The Middle English Romances: Some Questions of Creation, Presentation, and Preservation," *Speculum* 42 (1967), 10. Also see idem, "The Authorship of the Middle English Romances," *Annual Bulletin of the Modern Humanities Research Association* 22 (1950), 13–28; and "Convention and Individuality in the Middle English Romance," in *Medieval Literature and Folklore Studies: Essays in Honor of Francis Lee Utley*, ed. Jerome Mandel and Bruce A. Rosenberg, pp. 123–146.

7.   Chaytor (*From Script to Print*, pp. 67–74) offers several examples from poems which are obviously intended for oral presentation, yet which are intentionally stylistically obscure.

8.   Milman Parry, "Studies in the Epic Technique of Oral Verse-Making, I: Homer and Homeric Style," *Harvard Studies in Classical Philology* 41 (1930), 80.

9.   Albert B. Lord, *The Singer of Tales*. A useful bibliography of Parry's work can be found in this study.

10. Larry D. Benson, "The Literary Character of Anglo-Saxon Formulaic Poetry," *PMLA* 81 (1966), 334–341.

11. Ronald A. Waldron, "Oral-Formulaic Technique and Middle English Alliterative Poetry," *Speculum* 32 (1957), 792–804. Only one of the poems Waldron surveys (*William of Palerne*) is included in this study. The alliterative poems, for the most part, do not belong to the group we are studying here. John Spiers also discusses the problem in "'Wynnere and Wastoure' and 'The Parlement of the Thre Ages,'" *Scrutiny* 17, no. 3 (1950), 221–252.

12. While work on the formulaic nature of Anglo-Saxon poetry continues, the romances have largely been neglected. See Michael Curschmann, "Oral Poetry in Medieval English, French, and German Literature: Some Notes on Recent Research," *Speculum* 42 (1967), 36–52. For a discussion of formulaic repetitions in the alliterative tradition, see Merle Fifield, "Thirteenth-Century Lyrics and the Alliterative Tradition," *JEGP* 62

(1963), 111–118. See also Katharyn Hume, "The Formal Nature of Middle English Romance," *PQ* 53 (1974), 158–180.

13. For a discussion of the problems of sampling, see Joseph Duggan, *The Song of Roland: Formulaic Style and Poetic Craft*, pp. 19–20.

14. Duggan, *The Song of Roland*, pp. 108–109.

15. James Russo, "A Closer Look at Homeric Formulas," *Transactions and Proceedings of the American Philological Association* 94 (1963), 236.

16. Parry, "Studies in the Epic Technique," p. 118.

17. Michael N. Nagler, "Towards a Generative View of the Oral Formula," *Transactions and Proceedings of the American Philological Association* 98 (1967), 270. For a fuller review of the problems of oral-formulaic theory, see my "Theories of Formulaic Narrative," in *Oral Tradition and Old Testament Studies*, ed. Robert Colley, in *Semeia* (in press), and "Formulaic Style and the Problem of Redundancy: A Rhetorical Approach to the Study of Formulaic Functions," *Centrum* 1 (Fall 1973), pp. 123–236.

18. 1: 404, 1067, 1355; 2: 385, 553, 778, 805, 1715; 3: 144, 157, 2448, 2449, 27, 409, 447, 1917.

19. *Degare* 329; *Isumbras* 560, 655, 770; *Degare* 522; *Earl of Toulous* 661, 1057.

20. Waldron, "Oral-Formulaic Technique," p. 798, note 14.

21. Ferdinand de Saussure, *Course in General Linguistics*, trans. Wade Baskin, p. 113.

22. Nagler, "Towards a Generative View," pp. 282, 285.

23. Lord, *Singer of Tales*, p. 35.

24. See especially Pike, *Language*.

25. Lord, *Singer of Tales*, pp. 35–36.

26. The terms have been coined by Pike, using the distinction between phonetic systems (systems of overt phonological distinctions among various human languages) and phonemic systems (significant phonological distinctions in a particular language). For a complete discussion of the words, see Alan Dundes, "From Etic to Emic Units in the Structural Study of Folktales," *Journal of American Folklore* 75 (1966), 95—105.

27. For the hierarchical nature of *emic* systems within a language structure, see Pike, *Language*, p. 79 and passim. See also Robert E. Longacre, *Grammar Discovery Procedures: A Field Manual*, pp. 16–17.

28. On slot-class arrangement see Benjamin Elson and Velma Pickett, *An Introduction to Morphology and Syntax*; Pike, *Language*, pp. 30–32; Zellig S. Harris, "Co-occurrence and Transformation in Linguistic Structure," *Language* 33 (1957), 285–286.

29. According to Pike (*Language*, pp. 84–85) language is trimodally structured; that is, it consists of three simultaneous and complex kinds of organizations, or modes. In terms of the formulaic material we are presently studying, when we look at the contrastive features which distinguish one unit from another we are working in the *feature mode*; when we look at the range of the possible variant forms which have appeared in a particular slot, we are working in the *manifestation mode*; and when we study the distribution of the unit either linearly (in the text) or in a matrix of similar units (as a member of a class), we are working in the *distributive mode*. The feature mode and the manifestation mode have the most importance for us at the moment; we will be working in the distribution mode in Chapters 4 and 5. For an application of this concept to folklore materials, see Dundes, *The Morphology of North American Indian Folktales*, and idem, "From Etic to Emic Units."

30. All of the members of a paradigm, because they may substitute for one another, are homologous. Pike recognizes homology as one of the most important language structures, and offers several tests by which the analyst can check his initial guess about structural identity. The most important of these is the substitution test. See *Language*, pp. 218–224.

31. Rhyme is perhaps the single most prominent feature of the paradigm. With some study of individual romances, rhyming paradigms could be constructed which would demonstrate the particular poet's affinity for certain kinds of rhyming patterns. For a discussion of the perseverance of certain rhyming syntagmemes, see Elizabeth S. Sklar, "'The Battle of Maldon' and the Popular Tradition: Some Rhymed Formulas," PQ 54 (1975), 409–418. Sklar traces out the occurrence of the "brother/other" and "stunde/grunde/wounde" rhymes in five Middle English romances.

32. I am proposing here that the poet receives or develops a number of fixed patterns that can be further transformed. Creativity is limited, however, by the fact that the poet is not free to alter the syntagmemes of the deep structure. Lubomír Doležel ("From Motifemes to Motifs," Poetics 4 [1972], 74) observes that when we move from surface to deep structure "we proceed in the direction of reducing variety." He adds, "At every step we arrive at a more limited number of repetitive invariants. While proceeding in the opposite direction [from deep to surface structure] we observe the generation of variability and singular manifestations."

33. F. G. Cassidy ("How Free Was the Anglo-Saxon Scop?" in Franciplegius: Medieval and Linguistic Studies in Honor of Francis Peabody Magoun, Jr., 75–85) states that there are only twenty-five syntactic patterns, or "syntactic frames," in Old English, six noun-centered, nine verb-centered, five adjective-centered, five adverb-centered, and five other minor types. In Beowulf and the elegiac poems, he says, three-quarters of the verses examined can be accounted for by only ten frames, or syntagmemes. In the romances there is the same kind of structural limitation of types; it is possible that as few as twenty syntagmemes account for the verse features.

34. Saussure, Course in General Linguistics, p. 124.

35. Roland Barthes, Elements of Semiology, p. 19.

36. On the question of information, probability, and redundant features, see Ronald H. Carpenter, "Stylistic Redundancy and Function in Discourse," Language and Style 3 (1970), 62–68, and Colin Cherry, On Human Communication. I have taken up the question at greater length in "Formulaic Style and the Problem of Redundancy."

37. Carpenter, "Stylistic Redundancy," p. 64.

38. Cecil M. Bowra, Heroic Poetry, p. 231.

39. In this technical sense, redundance is a measure of the freedom of choice in selecting a message from its alternatives. The greater the freedom of choice exercised in the selection of a unit, the more information it contains. See Bertil Malmberg, Structural Linguistics and Human Communication, pp. 35, 113, 143; George Miller, Language and Communication, pp. 41, 100–106; Wendell R. Garner, Uncertainty and Structure as Psychological Concepts, Chapters 1, 5, 7, and 8; and Cherry, On Human Communication.

40. When change occurs in the Middle English romance (that is, change in the medium, from oral to written presentation), the narratives themselves undergo a change from poetry to prose. The formulaic phrases are fragmented by the prose line, although the rhythms are frequently maintained.

41. Morris J. Croll, "The Baroque Style in Prose," in Studies in English Philology: A Miscellany in Honor of Frederick Klaeber, p. 456.

2. Larger structural units: the motifeme

1. Evidence: 181a, that riche douke (97, 110, 169, 202); 183b, of grete bounte (969); 184, Sir Amiloun & Sir Amis (178, 251); 187a, Sir Amis (394, 439, 799, etc.); 187b, as ye may here (24, 157, 517, 1917); 189, For he was hend and fre (1875); hend & fre (327, 531,

563, 740, 997, etc.); 190, & *Sir Amiloun* (219, 232, 308, etc.). (I have counted names as formulaic units when they have identical metrical and stress characteristics.)

2.   Evidence: 51, *curtaise hende & good* (423); 52, *when they were* (55, 58, 1636, etc.); 60, *boon & blood* (142, 344, 1420).

3.   Evidence: 421, *that riche douke* (97, 110, 169, 202, etc.); 421b, *that y of told* (691, 2005); 422, *fair & bold* (1633); 423, *curtaise hend & fre* (51); 425, *in al that lond* (62, 1706); 426, *so semely on to se* (534); 429, *as ye may lithe at me* (1881); 430, *bright in bour* (334, 1518); 431, *with honour* (335); 432, *& gret solemptnite* (336).

4.   Evidence: 1633, *so fair & bold* (422); *when he was* (52, 55, 58); 1637, *Amoraunt* (1813, 1837, 1765); 1638, *wel curteys hende & good* (51, 423).

5.   This rhetorical unit of narrative introduction is similar in part to the classical *exordium*.

6.   As Elson and Pickett (*Introduction to Morphology and Syntax*, p. 57) point out, the term *slot* is commonly misunderstood to refer exclusively to the linear position in which linguistic components are found; in fact, however, it refers primarily to function and only secondarily to linear position. Slots may occur simultaneously (as when two functions are satisfied by the same component) or discontinuously, separated by other function slots. For a fuller discussion, see Zellig Harris, "Discourse Analysis," *Language* 28 (1952), 1–30.

7.   The criteria for closure are not easily described. Some self-contained narrative units (like the *exhortation* pattern) function as wholes with definable beginnings and endings; other narrative units have much less definable boundaries, and it is more difficult to speak of them as demonstrating closure.

8.   I would like to insist again on the necessity of seeing the individual manifestation of the pattern as a unit of both form and content. Dundes (*Morphology of North American Indian Folktales*, p. 51) would rather view the type-pattern as a formal unit and the manifestation as a unit of content, and he remarks that Propp's work is organized in this way. But Propp does not discuss the problem in these terms (although later critics appear to believe that he did), and the formalists, within whose sphere of influence Propp moved, were impatient with what they believed to be the naïve notion of the separability of form and content. (See Victor Zirmunskii, *Voprosy teorii literatury*, pp. 20–22.) As I have already observed, too many studies have provided (sometimes apparently without realizing it) a sharp distinction between the constant frame and the changeable filler.

9.   Here I am describing the type-pattern in Pike's *feature mode*, where the unit is seen as being composed of simultaneously occurring identificational-contrastive components. See note 29 of Chapter 1.

10.   Pike, *Language*, p. 150.

11.   As Dundes shows, a motif is a diachronic unit that is not a measure of a single quantity ("From Etic to Emic Units"). He adds: "Perhaps the most important theoretical consequence of the use of the motif as a minimal unit has been the tendency to regard motifs as totally free entities which are independent of contextual environments" (p. 97). As a result, emphasis is placed on isolated units, and their interest is found to lie in their frequency rather than in their function. Stith Thompson's *Motif-Index of Folk Literature* and Gerald Bordman's *Motif-Index of the English Metrical Romances* both catalogue a large number of motifs; their usefulness as analytical tools in a study of the romances, however, is severely limited, because they tend to treat the motif unit itself as a whole.

12.   Dundes, *Morphology of North American Indian Folktales*, p. 35.

13.   Obviously, the motifeme is not a minimal narrative unit; it can be further decomposed into various components. But as we have already seen, a unit may be useful in analysis without being posited as a minimal unit. We may then profitably speak of motifeme components (smaller subunits of the motifeme) and of a motifeme complex

(clusters of traditionally related motifemes on a level beneath that of the scene). Doležel ("From Motifemes to Motifs," p. 79) speaks of motif enjambment or clustering.

14. Dundes, "From Etic to Emic Units," p. 101. Doležel, for example, continues to use the term *motif*, which he defines as the "verbalization" of the motifeme ("From Motifemes to Motifs," p. 67). The major advantage of the term *allomotif* is the fact that it calls attention to its nature as a *variant* of an *emic* unit, while *motif* runs the risk of continuing to be understood without reference to its *emic* qualities.

15. See note 29, Chapter 1, and Pike, *Language*, p. 85. In the feature mode, the emphasis is placed upon the identificational features of the unit under examination. That is, if we have fifteen manifestations (allomotifs) of a single motifeme, we will focus our attention on the features which serve to identify them as members of a single class and which contrast that motifeme class to other motifeme classes.

16. Tzvetan Todorov ("Les Catégories au récit littéraire," *Communications* 8 [1966], 125–151) distinguishes between the chronological ordering of the events of the story (the *histoire*) and the literary reordering of those events (the *discours*). All components which are part of the surface alterations, such as narrative commentary, belong to the *discours*. The terms are translations and reworkings of the formalist terms *fabula* ("story line") and *suzet* ("finished work").

17. This distinction is built on the concept of free and conditioned morphemes. See Pike, *Language*, pp. 164–166.

18. The omission of one narrative component favored in a similar narrative belonging to another people is a "culturally relative phenomenon," to use Alan Dundes's phrase. Dundes considers this phenomenon in terms of Von Sydow's *oicotype*, a "locally preferred special form of tale or other tradition" which may "correlate with a linguistic stock, with a culture area, or with any geographical, political or social unit" (Dundes, "The Making and Breaking of Friendship as a Structural Frame in African Folk Tales," in *Structural Analysis of Oral Tradition*, ed. Elli Maranda and Pierre Maranda, p. 178).

19. Claude Bremond ("Le Message narratif," *Communications* 4 [1964], 4–32) argues that an elementary sequence may be combined in one of two ways: "s'enchainant bout à bout" or in "une succession d'emboitements."

20. There are very few metaphors in the romances, which commonly tend to be quite bare of imagistic patterns. Those that do occur are apt to be shared by many poets and generally belong to quite specific narrative components. In addition to the one just pointed out, there are the common patterns "wolde as a lion," "breme as a bear" (which occur in descriptions of anger), "whyte as lily-flower," "whyte as swan," "whyte as foam" (used to describe a woman), and so forth.

21. Probably the most famous development of this particular pattern is the almost parodic allomotif in Book I of *Troilus and Criseyde*, where Pandarus, the helpful friend, entreats Troilus to tell him his sorrow.

22. This approach requires a "sharp-cut segmentation," as Pike points out (*Language*, p. 551), even though that often must be achieved at the cost of serious distortion of the segmented materials.

23. For these two terms, see Charles Hockett, "Two Models of Grammatical Description," *Word* 10 (1954), 210–234.

24. This motifeme is common to nearly all genres of poetry which include extensive battle scenes. C. M. Bowra observes: "Heroic poetry naturally abounds in accounts of warriors arming themselves. Such are necessary to keep up the reality of a world at war and to show with what weapons a hero fights. The audience knows about weapons and will listen attentively to any mention of them" (*Heroic Poetry*, p. 191).

25. A similar expansion is found in *Guy of Warwick* Caius 8090 ff.

26. Mortimer J. Donovan ("Middle English *Emare* and the Cloth Worthily Wrought," in

The Learned and the Lewed: Studies in Chaucer and Medieval Literature, ed. Larry Benson, pp. 337–342) provides a full discussion of the use of such expansion techniques. 27. *Havelok* is also interesting in this respect. When Havelok (another aristocratic foundling) comes to Lincoln, he has no armor, neither "hosen ne shon," but walks barefoot and wears a cloak made out of a sail. Instead of participating in a courtly tournament, he competes with other bearers for the task of running errands for the earl's cook. The juxtaposition of expectation and actual performance is nowhere so explicit as it is in the lines where Havelok shoves away the others and runs to earn a "ferthing wastel":

> Two dayes ther fastinde he yede,
> That non for his werk wolde him fede;
> The thridde day herde he calle:
> "Bermen, bermen, hider forth alle!"
> Poure that on fote yede
> Sprongen forth so sparke on glede.
> Hauelok shof dun nyne or ten,
> Rith amidewarde the fen,
> And stirte forth to the kok,
> There the herles mete he tok,
> That he bouthe at the brigge:
> The bermen let he alle ligge,
> And bar the mete to the castel,
> And gat him there a ferthing wastel. (865–878)

The substitution pervades this part of the narrative: Havelok excels at stone-putting, wins the grudging praise of his competitors, gains fame in the banquet halls, and finally wins the reluctant Goldborough. Havelok, too, is unwilling to marry, observing plaintively that he has nothing to offer a royal bride—or any bride, for that matter:

> "Hwat sholde ich with wif do?
> I ne may hire fede, ne clothe, ne sho.
> Wider sholde ich wimman bringe?
> I ne haue none kines thinge.
> I ne haue hws, y ne haue cote,
> Ne i ne haue stikke, y ne haue sprote,
> I ne haue neyther bred ne sowel,
> Ne cloth, but of an hold with couel." (1136–1143)

28. The three-day tournament, as a special case of the single-combat scene, is found in a large number of folktales: Chrétien's *Cligès*, *Robert le Diable* and its Middle English analogue, *Sir Gowther*, Zatzihoven's *Lanzelot*, Hue's *Ipomedon*, and the Middle English *Ipomedon*. See Jessie L. Weston, *The Three Days' Tournament: A Study in Romance and Folk-lore*, and entries H331.2 and R222 of Bordman's *Motif-Index*. See also Laura Hibbard Loomis, *Medieval Romance in England*, pp. 226–227.
29. A number of drawings in Roger Sherman Loomis's *Arthurian Legends in Medieval Art* illustrate this point. See, for example, plates 154, 189, 292, 306, 311, and 407.
30. For the rules of the tournament, widely recognized both on the Continent and in England (where tournaments seem to have been alternately encouraged and suppressed according to the wishes of the king), see F. H. Cripps-Day, *The History of the Tournament in England and in France* and R. C. Clephan, *The Tournament: Its Periods and*

Phases. For other useful accounts of the tournament, consult Edouard Sandoz, "Tourneys in the Arthurian Tradition," *Speculum* 19 (1944), 389–420; and Ruth Huff Cline, "The Influence of Romances on Tournaments of the Middle Ages," *Speculum* 20 (1945), 204–211. According to Cline, combatants in tournaments often actually sought to imitate romance features. One of the instances she describes shows how clearly life reflects and pinpoints our difficulties in deciding, from our twentieth-century perspective, which is the primary semiotic system—literature or game: "In 1225 at Freisach after a day of jousting, Usrich [von Lichtenstein] decided that he would mystify the knights next day by disappearing from the jousts, going to the city, and returning in entirely different apparel. This he did. In the city, he had himself and eleven boys, who were to accompany him, and his horse all clothed in green."

31. There are a few cases of single combat, outside of tourneys, where no spectators are present. In *Ywayn* and *Eger* the battle is reported to an audience by the defeated knight. The other instances (in *Torrent* and *Eglamour*) are perhaps special cases of the fight with the giant. Combat in the Middle English romances is always a social activity.

32. It seems best to retain a certain amount of flexibility in the definition of these components. Since a necessary criterion seems to be that of relative size (a motifeme is smaller than a scene), expansions and contractions of the component (in comparison to other occurrences of the same component) should be given some attention. In purely structural terms, of course, it does not matter whether the poet handles the element in a single line or expands it to a hundred lines; but, in a study of narrative technique, such surface-structure manipulations are of very great interest. Here, I am making some attempt to synthesize the two approaches.

33. The *prohibition* motifeme occurs in the romances only in rationalized form. For instance, the knight is forbidden to cross a bridge (*Libeaus Desconus*), to go through a pass (*Sir Triamour*), to cross to a forbidden island (*Eger*). When such a prohibition does occur, it almost always denies the hero passage or prohibits his entry—that is, it has to do with the limitation of movement. There are also a few prohibitions in scene- and episode-patterns: Launfal's fairy lady forbids him to talk about her (*Launfal*); Partonope's fairy mistress forbids him to look at her, even in bed (*Partonope*); and Laudine's command that Ywayn return in a year's time may be seen as a reversal of the prohibition that he stay away for no more than a year (*Ywayn and Gawayn*).

These prohibitions are not really taboos (only those in *Partonope*, *Launfal*, and *Eger* are listed as prohibitions in Bordman's *Motif-Index*), but they do function as commands which must be disobeyed in order to keep the narrative moving. The fact that the romance does not consistently utilize this particular structural component, which is an essential and definitive feature of the European and American folktale, indicates one of the structural differences between the two kinds of narrative. The common pattern in many folktales and fairy stories, according to Dundes (*Morphology of North American Indian Folktales*, pp. 66–72) is the sequence *interdiction, violation, consequences,* and *attempted escape,* and central to this "transcultural form" is the disobedience of the prohibition.

34. Margaret Gist (*Love and War in the Middle English Romances*) says: "Romance upon romance has as a part of its plot-mechanism the joust or tournament in which a strange knight or a knight in disguise wins the hand of a lady" (p. 141). In addition to *Ipomedon,* which she describes in detail, she cites *Degrevant, Eglamour, Degare, Isumbras, Roswall, Torrent,* and several narratives not in this study. Whether this practice reflects medieval reality is still unclear. Cline ("Influence of the Romances on Tournaments," p. 209) cites an instance in Magedburg in 1281, where an old merchant of Goslere won the lady's hand but, instead of keeping it, gave her a dowry and married her off.

35. See T412 ("mother-son incest") of Bordman's *Motif-Index.* Bordman cites as exam-

ples of this motif *Degare, King Alisaunder*, Lydgate's *Siege of Thebes*, and *Eglamour*. He does not cite *Torrent*, presumably because the corrupt text is unclear about whether Desonell is indeed the prize of the tournament in which her betrothed lover and two sons compete. However, by analogy to *Eglamour*, to which *Torrent* is structurally related, we can suggest that the patterns are identical—or perhaps that a moralistic scribe, uncomfortable with the suggestion of threatened incest, simply took it out. For a discussion of the mother-son relationship elsewhere, see F. Xavier Baron, "Mother and Son in *Sir Perceval of Galles*," *Papers on Language and Literature* 8 (1974), 3–14.

3. Larger structural units: the type-scene

1. Lord, *Singer of Tales*, p. 68.
2. Ibid., p. 96.
3. Walter Arend, *Die Typischen Scenen bei Homer*.
4. Milman Parry, Review of Walter Arend, *Classical Philology* 31 (1936), 357–360.
5. Parry, Review of Arend, p. 358.
6. F. P. Magoun, Jr., "The Theme of the Beasts of Battle in Anglo-Saxon Poetry," *Neuphilologische Mitteilungen* 69 (1968), 81–90.
7. J. Rychner, *La Chanson de Geste*. Eugene Dorfman, discussing narrative structure in the *Chanson de Roland*, has also used the term *narreme* (*The Narreme in the Medieval Epic and Romance*). For a discussion of his use of the term, see my review, *Language and Style* 5 (1972), 228–235.
8. David K. Crowne, "The Hero on the Beach: An Example of Composition by Theme in Anglo-Saxon Poetry," *Neuphilologische Mitteilungen* 61 (1960), 362–372. Other examples of this kind of analysis are presented by Alain Renoir, "Oral-Formulaic Theme Survival: A Possible Instance in the 'Niebelungenlied,'" *Neuphilologische Mitteilungen* 65 (1964), 70–75; and Stanley Greenfield, "The Formulaic Expression of the Theme of Exile in Anglo-Saxon Poetry," *Speculum* 30 (1955), 200–206.
9. Donald K. Fry, "Themes and Type-Scenes in 'Elene' ll.1–113," *Speculum* 44 (1969), 35–45; idem, "Old English Oral-Formulaic Scenes and Type-Scenes," *Neophilologus* 52 (1968), 516–522; idem, "The Heroine on the Beach in 'Judith,'" *Neuphilologische Mitteilungen* 68 (1967), 168–184.
10. Fry, "Themes and Type-Scenes," p. 45.
11. Dundes ("From Etic to Emic Units," p. 102) notes that the same motif may be used in different motifemes, and that different motifs may be used in the same motifeme.
12. Fry, "Themes and Type-Scenes," p. 37.
13. In the Proppian scheme this opening move would be called *lack* and its reversal *lack liquidated* (Vladimir Propp, *Morphology of the Folktale*). In my view, however, the Proppian terminology is much too broad and admits far too many possible fillers into its function-slots. Almost all stories, in one way or another, can be seen to begin with a *lack*. It would seem important to be able to describe much more specifically and completely what kind of scenes manifest the pattern in any group of narratives. For the application of Proppian methods and terminology to a study of the romances, see Bruce Rosenberg's "The Morphology of the Middle English Metrical Romances," *Journal of Popular Culture* 1, no. 1 (Summer 1967), 63–77; and Leslie C. Puryear's unpublished dissertation, "A Structural Approach to the Middle English Non-Cyclic Metrical Romance," Vanderbilt University, 1968.
14. There are obvious affinities between this passage and the Anglo-Saxon *hero-on-the-beach* unit that Crowne describes. Of the four components of the *hero on the beach*, three are present here: (1) a hero on the beach, (2) with his retainers, (3) as a journey is

completed or begun. The missing element is the flashing light. Although this narrative unit is not present elsewhere in Middle English romance, so far as I have been able to discover, the *Horn* passage may well represent a survival of it. If so, it acts as a minor pattern and is conflated with the more prominent, functional type-scene pattern here, *death of the father*. It is common, of course, for one narrative pattern to overlie and partially obscure another.

15. H. Creek, in "Character in the 'Matter of England' Romances," *JEGP* 10 (1911), 429–453, recognized the strict limitation of functions which one or another character may perform. This is perhaps the first recognition of what I have called character-event configurations. In Propp's role-oriented analysis, each character is defined by a "sphere of action"; these actions and only these are appropriate to a particular character. A. J. Greimas, in *Sémantique structurale*, extends the notion of grammatical structure to the whole tale; his *modèle actantiel* establishes the character categories of *sujet* and *objet*, with the addition of *destinateur, destinataire, adjuvant, opposant*. He sees the work as a *sentence* in which these elements function in semantic and syntactic systems; his reinterpretation of Propp emphasizes the grammatical possibilities of Propp's scheme. Doležel ("From Motifemes to Motifs," p. 63) finds Greimas's system too limited and proposes instead a much more open system of character-action configurations.

16. *Bevis of Hampton* was perhaps the most popular Middle English romance. It has three principal versions (Anglo-French, Continental French, and Italian), of which over twenty-five texts are extant; it also exists in Dutch, Russian, Jewish, Middle-High German, and Rumanian versions and has a large number of more remotely related descendants. The structural patterns remain the same in almost all of these tales, so that we can say that these are all variants of a single narrative form.

17. The *January-May* motif, so far as I know, occurs in the metrical romances only in the versions of *Bevis*. It is, however, present in a large number of medieval tales including *The Merchant's Tale* and *The Seven Sages of Rome*. See J445.2 ("foolish marriage of old man and young girl") in Bordman's *Motif-Index*.

18. In *Generides*, King Aufreus, Generides' father, is the object of a plot between his wife and his false steward Sir Amalek (1995 ff.), who plan "treason to shape for the king/For to gete him foul ending" (2019–2020). While Aufreus is out hunting, Sir Amalek enters the city and is welcomed by Aufreus's queen:

> She seid, "myn ovn loue, welcome to me;"
> Anoon she yeld him vp the Citie,
> Castel, and toure, with all the tresoure,
> And hir bodie; what might she more? (2049–2052)

19. The head of the victim sent as proof of the slaying is a motifeme manifested in various ways depending upon its narrative context: in *Octavian*, the head of the giant, the princess's would-be paramour, is sent to her as proof that he is dead; Torrent, Eglamour, and Bevis return the heads of their victims as witness to accomplished tasks. *Bevis* is the only narrative, however, in which a husband's head is sent to his widow.

20. It may be that character development, when applied to the romances, is a narrative technique designed to deal with the problems posed by action. Robert Stevick has remarked that even when a character in Middle English narrative "thinks or talks to himself, it is more to inform us of his strategy of action than to interest us in his psyche" (*Five Middle English Narratives*, p. xiv).

21. See Thorlac Turville-Petre, "Humphrey de Bohun and *William of Palerne*," *Neuphilologische Mitteilungen* 75 (1974), 250–252.

22. *Havelok* departs noticeably from the pattern I have laid out in Table 6 and in the

text, but it is similar enough to be noted here. Rather than dying a violent death, the father dies of natural causes, and the surrounding allomotifs reflect this change. In this poem, the *death-of-the-father* scene appears twice: King Athelwold of England, the father of Goldborough, dies of "an evel strong"; Birkabein of Denmark, the father of Havelok, also falls ill and dies. The stewards appointed as guardians over the minor children maliciously violate their trust and attempt in one way or another to get rid of them.

23. "Exposure in a boat" is listed in Bordman's *Motif-Index* of the romances (S141) as occurring in *Generides* (90 ff., W. A. Wright's edition, EETS 55, 70 [ms. Trinity Cambridge 1283]), *Emare* (265 ff.), and *Titus and Vespacian* (4528 ff.). It also occurs in *Eglamour* and *Torrent*, although Bordman does not include these.

24. The *incestuous father* appears in a number of medieval tales, many of which are versions of the *Constance* story (see Thompson, *Motif-Index*, Tale-Type 706). Laura Loomis notes: "In *Manekine* the king has promised to wed no one save a woman like his dead wife; he is reluctant when his nobles wish to make him marry his daughter. In the Catalan tale, *Historia del rey de Hungrie*, the father loves the daughter because of the beauty of her white hands, and for this reason she cuts them off" (*Medieval Romance in England*, pp. 25–26). It is likely that the fathers in *Torrent* and in *Eglamour*, and perhaps as well in *Degare*, are rationalizations of this more primitive motifeme.

25. Eugene Dorfman (*The Narreme*) asserts that the narrative sequence is based on causality; Propp's thesis has also been interpreted as causalistic (see Bremond, "Le Message narratif").

26. Dorfman, *The Narreme*, pp. 6–7. A more specific criticism of this approach appears in my review in *Language and Style* 5 (1972), 228–235.

27. The hero born irregularly is a feature common to most folktale cycles. J. G. von Hahn (*Sagwissenschaftliche Studien*), in surveying the basic occidental folktale cycles, found four kinds of irregular birth: the hero born (1) out of wedlock; (2) posthumously; (3) supernaturally; (4) as one of twins. Alfred Nutt ("The Aryan Expulsion-and-Return Formula," *Folk-Lore Record* 4 [1881], 1–44) applied von Hahn's formula to Gaelic and Celtic tales and discovered the same patterning in the birth of the hero, but also found a decided preference for the hero born out of wedlock or posthumously—and almost no preference for twin heroes. That the Middle English romances are cut from the same traditional cloth cannot be doubted.

28. L. Loomis, *Medieval Romance in England*, p. 279 ff.

29. See Bordman's *Motif-Index*, T548.1 ("child born in answer to prayer") and T548.5 ("childless couple build abbey that they might conceive").

30. This motif also appears in *Earl of Toulous*, where two false stewards, left in charge of the lady in her husband's absence, trick a young boy into the lady's bed, kill him, and report to the king (709 ff.). It is interesting to note that the husband in this case has a prophetic dream during her betrayal:

Hym thoght ther come two wylde berys
And hys wyfe al to-terys,
    And rofe hur body in twoo;
Hymselfe was a wytty man,
And be that dreme he hopyd than
    Hys lady was in woo. (808–813)

31. Bowra, *Heroic Poetry*, p. 193.

32. Edmund Leach, *Genesis as Myth and Other Essays*, p. 9.

33. The treacherous steward (see Bordman's *Motif-Index*, K2242) appears in many ro-

mances; through his agency the hero and heroine are often betrayed. The act is usually motivated by envy of the hero's position or a desire to possess the princess and/or her wealth and lands. Quite often the act is unmotivated in the text, and it seems that the motivation (like that of the heathen Saracens) is simply understood. The variant motif which occurs in *Triamour* (the steward tells the wife that his temptation was only a test) appears as well in *Toulous*, where the function of betrayer is doubled.

34. See Bordman's *Motif-Index*, B301.2 ("faithful animal at master's grave, avenges his murder").

35. For a complete account of the tale's analogues, see L. Loomis, *Medieval Romance in England*, pp. 295–296.

36. This apparent expendability of the father is structurally demonstrated in the fact that the first two type-scenes (*death of the father* and *irregular birth*) in fact obliterate the father's influence in the son's life. If any familial influence lingers, it is the mother's.

37. L. Loomis, *Medieval Romance in England*, p. 302. The term *rationalization* describes a fairy-tale motif that has been altered in the direction of realism.

38. For example, throughout the poem the *Degare* poet exhibits a marked sympathy for women. Before the proposed marriage between the mother and her lost and unidentified son, the poet pauses to add a few remarks on the hapless lot of women who have to take potluck in marriage:

> Than was the damaisele sori;
> For hi wiste wel, forwhi:
> That hi scholde ispoused ben
> To a knight, sche neuer had sen,
> And lede here lif with swich a man,
> That sche ne wiste, who him wan
> No in what londe he was ibore.
> The leuedi was carful therfore. (585–592)

39. This variant is related to the tale of Robert the Devil, known in at least 106 texts—French, Spanish, Portuguese, English, Dutch, and German. (For a complete listing of the analogues, see K. Breul's edition of *Sir Gowther*, pp. 198–207.) All of these tales exhibit the same initial pattern, although the Middle English version includes Gowther's marriage to a princess whom he has rescued; this rescue is the heavenly sanction which frees him from his penitential exile and returns him to human society. For related motifs, see Bordman's *Motif-Index*, T548.1 ("child born in answer to prayer"), C758.1 ("monster born because of hasty wish of parents"), and T556 ("woman gives birth to demon"). Also see Thompson's *Motif-Index*, Tale-Type 307 (I), "The Princess in the Shroud" ("The Parents' Hasty Wish").

40. The motifeme almost surely is a remnant of Nutt's "Incident VIII: the hero is of passionate and violent disposition." This component is present in all of the Gaelic and Celtic tales that Nutt examines ("Aryan Expulsion-and-Return Formula") and is, as he shows, a prominent feature of *Peredur*, a recognized analogue of *Perceval of Galles*. *Libeaus Desconus* and *Gowther*, which both retain this motifeme, are also structurally related, as we have noted, through the motif of self-exile. In addition, see Thompson's Tale-Type 650A (I) "The Strong Youth." For another view of the *Perceval* type, see Caroline D. Eckhardt, "Arthurian Comedy: The Simpleton-Hero in *Sir Perceval of Galles*," *Chaucer Review* 8 (1974), 205–220.

41. See above, note 24; also S51 ("cruel mother-in-law") in Thompson's *Motif-Index*.

42. See Bremond, "Le Message narratif," pp. 14–15.

43. One of the basic tenets of structural analysis is that an element has significance only

in relation to other items in the same whole. The relationship we have defined here cannot be perceived by looking at either of these type-scenes individually; they must be seen as members of a linking pattern, syntagmatically related to one another, and associated both syntagmatically and paradigmatically with other linking patterns in the same narrative and with other patterns in the same system of narratives, the romances as a group.

44. Since, as von Hahn (*Sagwissenschaftliche Studien*) and Nutt ("Aryan Expulsion-and-Return Formula") have both pointed out, the expulsion of the hero born in some irregular way is a fundamental opening scene in many Aryan tales, it must be considered archetypal and therefore not peculiar to the culture which produced the particular narrative. I have noted some cultural preferences of patterns which are used to fill this particular *expulsion* slot: the hero born out of wedlock or under the suspicion of bastardy. Later on, we shall see that other cultural preferences make themselves apparent in certain variant narrative forms.

4. Larger structural units: the type-episode

1. The treatment of time is usually very simple in these narratives. The tale is almost always executed in a straightforward chronological fashion, and not even the simple device of the flashback is available to the poets. To put it in structuralist terms, the *histoire* and the *discours* are almost identical as far as the manipulation of chronology is concerned.

2. Betrothal was considered a legal form of marriage through the mid-sixteenth century. See George Elliott Howard, *A History of Matrimonial Institutions*, vol. 2, 340–349.

3. See Bordman, *Motif-Index*, H172.1 ("recognition by a horse who will permit only a certain man to ride him").

4. The abduction of the lady by the fairy king (and *Floris* almost certainly represents a rationalized version of the same story) seems to have been a favorite story type among the Celts. (See L. Loomis, *Medieval Romance in England*, p. 198.) This structure may be associated in similar traditions of *marriage-by-capture*, as I will indicate below.

5. Both of these tales represent a special case, however; in *Emare* the one who performs the service is a woman and hence cannot be expected to perform the alternative rescue; in *Amis* the performance of the task is altered in the direction of the Amiloun *loss of property* structure that is added to the romance.

6. Propp designates one typical task as a "test of strength," which fits the pattern of these two narratives (*Morphology of the Folktale*, pp. 60–61).

7. Bordman, *Motif-Index*, K.3 ("substitution in contest").

8. M. A. Potter (*Sohrab and Rustem: The Epic Theme of a Combat between Father and Son*, pp. 152–180), surveys the widespread appearance of this particular type-scene in Persian, Old French, Russian, and Irish oral literatures. See also Alfred Nutt (*The Legends of the Holy Grail*, p. 241), who attributes this type-scene in the twelfth-century narratives to *minnedienst*. In Potter's stories, however, the scene does not occur with *betrayal* as it does in the Middle English romances.

9. In *Squyr of Lowe Degre* the father, learning that a pledge has been exchanged between his daughter and a squire, first imprisons the squire and then sends him out of the land for seven years. Then, on the following grounds, he grants the princess freedom to marry the squire if she chooses:

And yf she wyll assent him tyll,
The squyer is worthy to have none yll;

For I haue seen that many a page
Haue become men by maryage;
Than it is semly to that squyer
To haue my doughter by this manere,
And eche man in his degre
Become a lorde of ryaltye,
By fortune and by other grace,
By herytage and by purchace. (371–380)

Such a statement in the mouth of a mid-fifteenth-century father is without parallel in the romances.

10. See Chomsky, *Syntactic Structures*.

11. The Proppian sequence *interdiction-violation-villainy* does not completely correspond to this particular three-part sequence. In the poems cited above, *villainy* follows *violation* only once (in *Eger*, where Graysteele appears and does battle with the disobedient knight), and even that is a marginal case.

12. The structural similarities between *Launfal, Ywayn and Gawayn, Partonope,* and *Eger and Grime* are marked. *Eger* is interesting from the standpoint of its rationalizations of the fairy-tale structure in the retelling, as L. Loomis (*Medieval Romance in England,* p. 314) indicates, by a poet "more interested in personality and in scenes of fact rather than of fancy." The frame story of *Eger* (Eger returns to tell Grime about his battle with Graysteele, just as Colgrevance tells the story of his encounter with the knight of the fountain) bears a definite structural resemblance to that of *Ywayn*. The prohibition lies in the fact that Graysteele's land is a "forbidden countrye" (102, 108) that can only be reached by crossing a river.

13. Dundes, *Morphology of North American Indian Folktales*, pp. 66–67.

14. In *Amis and Amiloun* this produces a strange situation, for Amis knows very well that he is high-born, and so do the members of the court, and yet, when Belisant woos him, he offers the standard protest that he is a "poor man" and his lineage is not of a quality suitable to marry her.

15. In addition to the similarity of the opening scene the two narratives also share another important structural feature: in *Toulous* the hero marries his opponent's widow; in *Degrevant* the hero marries his opponent's daughter—and any future quarrels over the disputed land are ended before they are begun.

16. In both these tales the hero's generosity is repaid by a supernatural donor who tests the hero's fidelity. In *Launfal* the test is one of secrecy, which Launfal fails (he is later forgiven); in *Amadace* the donor tests the hero's ability to keep his promise, and Amadace succeeds. *Sir Cleges,* a narrative not in our study, begins with the same component—loss of property because of excessive generosity—but ends with a *fabliau*-like joke.

17. In *Amis* and *Isumbras* the loss of identity is literal, and identification is provided through the agency of a token—a gold cup in *Amis* and a mantle and money in *Isumbras*.

18. See Theodore Andersson, *The Icelandic Family Saga*.

19. Ojars Kratins ("Treason in the Middle English Metrical Romances," *PQ* 45 [1966], 668–688) cites a number of specific treasons—petty treason, high treason, unlawful carnal knowledge, and so forth—with their appropriate punishments.

20. See Bordman, *Motif-Index*, H13.5 ff.

21. The pattern is also characteristic of the Greek romances that became so popular in translation in England in the 1500s. It seems likely that public taste simply shifted from the indigenous form to the imported form.

5. Speculations and conclusions

1. On transformational theory and applications to narrative analysis, see Julia Kristeva, "Narration et transformation," *Semiotica* 1 (1969), 422–448; Tzvetan Todorov, "Les Transformations narratives," *Poétique* 3 (1970), 322–333; and William O. Hendricks, "Linguistics and Folkloristics," in *Essays on Semiolinguistics and Verbal Art*. For a discussion of text structure similar to the one developed here, see Siegfried Schmidt, "Théorie et pratique d'une étude scientifique de la narrativité littéraire, à propos de Plume au restaurant de Henri Michaux," in *Sémiotique narrative et textuelle*, ed. Claude Chabrol. Schmidt proposes a model which moves from an underlying *genotext* to a surface *phenotext* through a series of transformational procedures. However, the actual transformational process itself is never fully described. See also Teun A. Van Dijk, "Grammaires textuelles et structures narratives," in *Sémiotique narrative et textuelle*, ed. Chabrol.

2. For another view, see Baugh, "Convention and Individuality in the Middle English Romance."

3. R. Jakobson and P. Bogatyrev, "Die Folklore als eine besondere Form des Schaffens," in *Donum Natalicium Schrijnen*, pp. 900–913.

4. Pornography, for example, is censored in American society, according to a highly structured system of rules whose purpose is to define community standards with regard to moral standards in literature and to enforce them upon the community at large.

5. If the model presented here is to be of any use, however, it must be capable of extension (with modification, of course) to all forms of traditional narratives.

6. Lévi-Strauss, "The Story of Asdiwal."

7. Nutt, "Aryan Expulsion-and-Return Formula"; von Hahn, *Sagwissenschaftliche Studien*.

8. Roger Sherman Loomis, *Arthurian Tradition and Chrétien de Troyes*.

9. Jessie L. Weston, *From Ritual to Romance*.

10. Frye, *Anatomy of Criticism*, p. 187.

11. Potter, *Sohrab and Rustem*.

12. Potter, *Sohrab and Rustem*, p. 182. "Naturally," he says, "[the capturing of brides] has left its impress on literature. The theft of Subhadra in the *Mahabharata*, the rape of Helen, and the carrying off of Gudrun, are instances of it." Edward Westermarck (*The History of Human Marriage*, vol. 2) cites a large number of the customs which are supposed to be survivals of marriage by capture. Some of these examples have parallels in the *threatened-marriage* sequences of the romances: "Among the Vonums of Formosa the custom of pretending to seize a bride by force is in existence. . . . With a company of friends the bridegroom goes to the house of his intended, and in the face of pretended opposition seizes his bride and carries her off to his own habitation" (pp. 257–258). Among European peoples, according to Westermarck, there is a common marriage custom of stopping the bridal procession, sometimes by a barricade of logs or weapons, sometimes by a rope of flowers. In eighteenth-century Wales, however, the resistance was more serious: "On the morning of the wedding day the groom with his friends demanded the bride. Her friends gave a positive refusal, upon which a mock scuffle ensued. The bride, mounted behind her nearest kinsman, is carried off and is pursued by the groom and his friends with loud shouts. When they have fatigued themselves and their horses, he is suffered to overtake his bride, and leads her away in triumph" (p. 261).

13. Matrilocal marriage in the tale of Asdiwal is "accompanied by antagonism between the husband and his in-laws . . . the father-in-law shows so much hostility toward his son-in-law that he sets him trials which are deemed to be fatal" (Lévi-Strauss, "The Story of Asdiwal," p. 12).

14. In the Middle English romances this takes place in the *service* episodes of *Torrent* and *Eglamour* and possibly in *Degare*; in all three narratives the tasks are so dangerous that it is clear that the father is out to dispose of any prospective son-in-law. Westermarck (*History of Human Marriage*, p. 369) cites a large number of examples of marriage after a period of service (often seven years), and notes that in many cases it is a substitute for marriage-by-purchase.

15. As Lévi-Strauss says about the Tmishian myth of Asdiwal, the society's failure is admitted in the failure of the hero, and therein lies the function of the myth ("The Story of Asdiwal," p. 16). Edmund Leach, examining various Old Testament stories, comes to a similar conclusion: that the Solomon story is a "myth which 'mediates' a major contradiction"—in this case, concerning endogamous and exogamous marriage (*Genesis as Myth and Other Essays*, p. 31).

16. The close relationship between uncle and nephew and the observance of the "nephew-right" in such poems as *Boeve de Haumtone*, *La Naissance du Chevalier au Cygne*, and *Fierabras* (many of which made their way into Middle English narratives) includes William Farnsworth (*Uncle and Nephew in the Chansons de Geste: A Study of the Survival of Matriarchy*) to postulate that these traditions are based on the survival of matrilineal descent. He views the common practice in the Old French *chansons* of marrying outside the clan, either by elopement, capture, or consent, as an indication of exogamy. Because historical evidence does not support the theory that matriarchy existed during the time the *chansons* were composed, Farnsworth is inclined to believe that the kinship structure represented in these poems is a matter of tradition. But these underlying traditions, while they are certainly conservative and often maintained in legend long past the time of their viability in real life (which may in fact be why Lévi-Strauss finds myth a "dialectical reversion" of reality), are maintained for some reasons which are considered immediately important to the culture. A similar argument about matriarchy is set forth by William A. Nitze ("The Sister's Son and the Conte del Graäl," *MP* 9 [1912], 291–322), who asserts that the many remnants of matriarchal practices in those cultures influenced the Grail legend and other romance narratives. Among the evidence he cites is the fact that Irish law provided for the avenging of the death of a sister's son by a maternal uncle; the fact that in old Welsh law, an orphaned child under twelve is placed in the care of the maternal uncle; and the fact that the Pict royal succession did not go from father to son but to the son of the sister. Francis B. Gummere ("The Sister's Son in the English and Scottish Popular Ballads," in *An English Miscellany for Dr. Furnivall*, ed. Walter P. Ker, A. S. Napier, and W. W. Skeat) makes a similar proposal supported with additional evidence.

17. For example, the Lady of Synadowne refuses to marry Libeaus until their union can be approved by the king. The right of the lord to arrange marriage in the Middle Ages was one of the most jealously guarded of feudal rights. It is guaranteed against the king's encroachment in the Magna Carta (see C. Petit-Dutaillis, *Feudal Monarchy in France and England*, pp. 331–333), a sure indication that the king did exercise quite frequently the right to marry his subjects where he pleased.

According to Robert Briffault (*The Mothers: A Study of the Origins of Sentiments and Institutions*, vol. 1), in a patrilineal society the father invariably has the right to dispose of his daughters in marriage; in a matrilineal society, however, the marriage arrangements are given over to the maternal uncle. The reservation to the feudal lord of the right to dispose of his vassals' daughters provides us with a specific instance in which the rights which normally belong to a family and kinship system are given over to a political institution. In fact, discussions of kinship and clan in the Middle Ages are severely complicated by the political institution of feudalism, which usurps rights and loyalties that were once due only to the kindred. It may be that within these narratives we find an attempt to bring to the solution of political problems some recollected answers that have their source in kinship resolutions.

18. F. J. Richards ("Cross Cousin Marriage in South India," *Man* 14 [1914], 194–198) asserts that the earlier matrilineal society in Southern India, replaced by the patrilineal Brahmanic culture, was still evident in the eighteenth century in the favored cousin marriages. This cross-cousin system, he says, is largely economic. He adds: ". . . in a matrilineal community one of the main advantages of patrilineal transmission of property, viz., the gratification of the natural desire of a father to provide for his offspring, may be effectively secured by insisting that a man should marry the daughter of either his maternal uncle, his paternal aunt, or his sister; . . . the same rule would enable a matrilineal community to conform to a patrilineal system of inheritance without fear of dissipating the family property, the integrity of which is dependent on the continuance of inheritance on matrilineal lines." Westermarck observes that such marriages "may serve the object of keeping together related families" and also "prevents dispersion of the family property" (*History of Human Marriage*, p. 76). It is interesting to note that the heroine of the romance is invariably (I know of no exceptions to this rule) the only heir to her family's lands; she has no brothers to hold the land under the control of the family, and her marriage threatens to disrupt the family's holdings.

19. Westermarck (*History of Human Marriage*, p. 76) believes that cousin marriages were often sought for the purpose of "strengthening the bonds" between families. However, Lévi-Strauss ("The Story of Asdiwahl," p. 27) remarks that the equilibrium established by a cross-cousin system is only an "apparent stability." In a discussion of some Pacific Northwest societies which practice cousin marriages, he says that one way to establish stability is to stipulate that one of the positions (wife-giver or wife-taker) is by definition superior to the other. The groups he studied, however, did not achieve a permanent stability, because they refused to stipulate such positions and—as in the system of medieval marriages—used each marriage as an occasion to redistribute the power: ". . . the respective superiority or inferiority of the groups involved was openly contested on the occasion of each marriage. Each marriage, along with the potlatches which accompanied and preceded it, and the transfers of titles and property occasioned by it, provided the means by which the groups concerned might gain an advantage over each other while at the same time putting an end to former disputes. It was necessary to make peace but only on the best possible terms. French medieval society offers, in terms of patrilineal institutions, a symmetrical picture of a situation which had much in common with the one just described" (p. 27).

20. For an excellent discussion of the impediment of consanguinity and the various calculations of the degrees of relationship, see Charles Edward Smith, *Papal Enforcement of Some Medieval Marriage Laws*. Generally speaking, in the period with which we are concerned, marriage through the fourth degree was prohibited. However, the great concern over the question would indicate that marriage within the prohibited degrees was much more widespread than it has been believed to be. Smith lists fifty-one synods and councils which acted on the matter between 506 and 1215, along with a number of additional papal decretals. In 874 the synod of Douci plaintively confessed that "it is to our humiliation that it was reported by no uncertain relation and consultation how many go to ruin in deadly pestilence in incestuous marriages, especially the nobles by blood and those exalted in temporal honor" (Smith, *Papal Enforcement*, p. 14). In 1002 Henry II of Germany declared to the synod held under his direction that "among the many things which are to be corrected in our kingdom and in your parishes is that relatives, very close to each other, are joined in marriage; so that, not fearing God and not revering men, they do not shrink from associating in marriage a relative even of the third degree, which is horrible to say" (Smith, *Papal Enforcement*, p. 15). It was clearly in the

interests of the church and the state to prohibit the intermarriage of the more powerful families, for by so doing, both the ecclesiastical and temporal lords could limit the wealth and influence of those under them. Here we have the interesting situation of two kinds of systems, both aimed at establishing overlapping spheres of control: the church and state by limiting marriage within certain groups, the nobles and, later, the rising middle class, by marrying within these groups.

21. Smith, *Papal Enforcement*, p. 194.
22. Claude Lévi-Strauss, *The Elementary Structures of Kinship*, p. 475.
23. Lévi-Strauss, *Elementary Structures of Kinship*, p. 476.

Bibliography

EDITIONS OF ROMANCES

The editions listed below provide the sources for all quotations in the text, unless otherwise indicated in the notes.

Amis and Amiloun. Ed. M. Leach. EETSOS 203. London, 1937.
Bevis of Hampton. Ed. E. Kölbing. EETSES 46, 48, 65. London, 1886–1888.
Le Bone Florence of Rome. Ed. J. O. Halliwell-Phillipps. In *Thornton Romances.* London:
    Camden Society, 1844.
Chevalere Assigne. Ed. H. H. Gibbs. EETSES 6. London, 1868.
Earl of Toulous. Ed. G. Ludtke. Berlin: Weimar, Hof-buchdrukerei, 1881.
Eger and Grime. Ed. J. R. Caldwell. In *Harvard Studies in Comparative Literature.* Cam-
    bridge, Mass.: Harvard University Press, 1933.
Emare. Ed. Edith Rickert. EETSES 99. London, 1906.
Floris and Blancheflur. Ed. A. B. Taylor. Oxford: Clarendon Press, 1929.
Generides. Ed. F. J. Furnivall. Roxbury Club 85. London, 1865.
Guillaume de Palerne. Ed. H. Michelant. Paris: Firmin Didot et Cie, 1876.
Guy of Warwick. Ed. J. Zupitza. EETSES 42, 49, 59. London, 1883, 1887, 1891.
Havelok. Ed. W. W. Skeat. EETSES 4. London, 1868.
Horn Child and Maiden Rimenhild. Ed. J. Ritson. In *Ancient English Metrical Ro-
    mances*, vol. 2. Edinburgh: E. & G. Goodrich, 1884.
Ipomedon. Ed. Henry Weber. In *Metrical Romances of the 13th, 14th, and 15th Cen-
    turies*, vol. 2. Edinburgh: A. Constable and Company, 1810.
King Horn. Ed. George McKnight. EETSOS 14. London, 1901.
The Knight of Curtesy and The Fair Lady of Faguell. Ed. E. McCausland. *Smith College
    Studies in Modern Language*, vol. 4, no. 1. 1922.
Lai le freine. Ed. M. Wattie. *Smith College Studies in Modern Language*, vol. 10, no. 3.
    1929.
Libeaus Desconus. Ed. M. Mills. EETSOS 261. London, 1969.
Le Morte Arthur. Ed. J. D. Bruce. EETSES 88. London, 1903.
Octavian. Ed. G. Sarrazin. *Altenglische Bibliothek* 3. Heilbronn, 1885.
Partonope of Blois. Ed. A. T. Bodtker. EETSES 109. London, 1912.
Reinbroun. In *Guy of Warwick* (see above).
Roswall and Lillian. Ed. O. Lengert. *Englische Studien* 16. 1934.

Sir Amadace. Ed. J. Robson. In *Three Early English Metrical Romances*. London: J. B. Nichols and Son, 1842.

Sir Degare. Ed. G. Schleich. *Englische Textbibliothek* 19. Heidelberg, 1929.

Sir Degrevant. Ed. L. F. Casson. EETSOS 221. London, 1943.

Sir Eger, Sir Grahme, and Sir Gray-Steele. In *Eger and Grime* (see above).

Sir Eglamour of Artois. Ed. F. E. Richardson. EETSOS 256. London, 1965.

Sir Gowther. Ed. K. Breul. Oppeln, 1886.

Sir Isumbras. Ed. G. Schleich. *Palaestra* 15. Berlin, 1901.

Sir Landeval. Ed. R. Zimmermann. Königsberg: Hartung, 1900.

Sir Launfal. Ed. A. Bliss. In *Thomas Chestre: Sir Launfal*. London: T. Nelson, 1960.

Sir Orfeo. Ed. J. Ritson. In *Ancient English Metrical Romances*, vol. 2. Edinburgh: E. & G. Goodrich, 1884.

Sir Perceval of Galles. Ed. J. Campion and F. Holthausen. Heidelberg and New York: Carl Winter's Universitätsbuchhandlung and G. E. Stechert & Co., 1913.

Sir Torrent of Portyngale. Ed. A. Aman. EETSES 51. London, 1887.

Sir Triamour. Ed. J. O. Halliwell. Percy Society 16. London, 1846.

Squyr of Lowe Degre. Ed. W. E. Mead. Boston: Ginn & Co., 1904.

William of Palerne. Ed. F. Madden. In *The Ancient English Romance of William and the Werewolf*. London: Roxbury Club, 1832.

Ywayn and Gawayn. Ed. Friedman and Harrington. EETSOS 254. London, 1964.

CRITICISM AND REFERENCE WORKS

Romances, Formulaic Poetry, Folklore, Medieval History

Aarne, Antii. *The Types of the Folk-Tale*. Trans. and enl. Stith Thompson. FF Communications 184. Helsinki, 1961.

Andersson, Theodore. *The Icelandic Family Saga*. Cambridge, Mass.: Harvard University Press, 1967.

Arend, Walter. *Die Typischen Scenen bei Homer*. Berlin: Weidmann, 1933.

Baron, F. Xavier. "Mother and Son in *Sir Perceval of Galles*." *Papers on Language and Literature* 8 (1974), 3–14.

Barrow, Sarah F. *The Medieval Society Romances*. New York: Columbia University Press, 1924.

Baugh, Albert C. "The Authorship of the Middle English Romances." *Annual Bulletin of the Modern Humanities Research Association* 22 (1950), 13–28.

———. "Convention and Individuality in the Middle English Romance." In *Medieval Literature and Folklore Studies: Essays in Honor of Francis Lee Utley*, ed. Jerome Mandel and Bruce A. Rosenberg, pp. 123–146. New Brunswick, N.J.: Rutgers University Press, 1971.

———. "Improvisation in the Middle English Romance." *Proceedings of the American Philological Society* 103 (1959), 418–454.

———. "The Middle English Romances: Some Questions of Creation, Presentation, and Preservation." *Speculum* 42 (1967), 1–31.

Benson, Larry D. "The Literary Character of Anglo-Saxon Formulaic Poetry." *PMLA* 81 (1966), 334–341.

Billings, Anna H. *A Guide to the Middle English Metrical Romance*. Yale Studies in English 9. New York: Henry Holt and Company, 1901.

Bloch, Marc. *La Société féodale: La Formation des liens de dépendance*. Paris: A. Michel, 1939.

Bordman, Gerald. *Motif-Index of the English Metrical Romances*. FF Communications 190. Helsinki, 1963.

Bowra, Cecil M. *Heroic Poetry*. London: Macmillan, 1952.

Briffault, Robert. *The Mothers: A Study of the Origins of Sentiments and Institutions*. Vol. 1. New York: Macmillan, 1927.

Bruce, James D. *The Evolution of Arthurian Romance*. Baltimore: Johns Hopkins Press, 1923.

Cassidy, F. G. "How Free was the Anglo-Saxon Scop?" In *Franciplegius: Medieval and Linguistic Studies in Honor of Francis Peabody Magoun, Jr.*, ed. J. B. Bessinger and R. P. Creed, pp. 75–85. New York: New York University Press, 1965.

Chaytor, H. J. *From Script to Print: An Introduction to Medieval Literature*. Cambridge: W. Heffer and Sons, 1950.

Clephan, Robert C. *The Tournament: Its Periods and Phases*. New York: F. Ungar, 1967.

Cline, Ruth Huff. "The Influence of Romances on Tournaments of the Middle Ages." *Speculum* 20 (1945), 204–211.

Creek, H. "Character in the 'Matter of England' Romance." *JEGP* 10 (1911), 429–453.

Cripps-Day, F. H. *The History of the Tournament in England and in France*. London: B. Quaritch, 1918.

Croll, Morris J. "The Baroque Style in Prose." In *Studies in English Philology: A Miscellany in Honor of Frederick Klaeber*, ed. Kemp Malone and Martin B. Ruud, pp. 427–456. Minneapolis: University of Minnesota Press, 1929.

Crosby, Ruth. "Oral Delivery in the Middle Ages." *Speculum* 11 (1936), 88–110.

Crowne, David K. "The Hero on the Beach: An Example of Composition by Theme in Anglo-Saxon Poetry." *Neuphilologische Mitteilungen* 61 (1960), 362–372.

Curschmann, Michael. "Oral Poetry in Medieval English, French, and German Literature: Some Notes on Recent Research." *Speculum* 42 (1967), 36–52.

Donovan, Mortimer J. "Middle English *Emare* and the Cloth Worthily Wrought." In *The Learned and the Lewed: Studies in Chaucer and Medieval Literature*, ed. Larry Benson, pp. 337–342. Cambridge, Mass.: Harvard University Press, 1974.

Duggan, Joseph. "Formulas in the *Couronnement de Louis*." *Romania* 87 (1966), 315–354.

———. *The Song of Roland: Formulaic Style and Poetic Craft*. Berkeley: University of California Press, 1973.

Eckhardt, Caroline D. "Arthurian Comedy: The Simpleton-Hero in *Sir Perceval of Galles*." *Chaucer Review* 8 (1974), 205–220.

Farnsworth, William O. *Uncle and Nephew in the Chansons de Geste: A Study of the Survival of Matriarchy*. New York: AMS Press, 1966.

Fifield, Merle. "Thirteenth-Century Lyrics and the Alliterative Tradition." *JEGP* 62 (1963), 111–118.

Fry, Donald K. "The Heroine on the Beach in 'Judith.'" *Neuphilologische Mitteilungen* 68 (1967), 168–184.

———. "Old English Oral-Formulaic Scenes and Type-Scenes." *Neophilologus* 52 (1968), 516–522.

———. "Some Esthetic Implications of a New Definition of the Formula." *Neuphilologische Mitteilungen* 69 (1968), 516–522.

———. "Themes and Type-Scenes in 'Elene' ll. 1–113." *Speculum* 44 (1969), 35–45.

Frye, Northrop. *The Anatomy of Criticism*. New York: Atheneum, 1969.

Gibbs, A. C. *Middle English Romances*. Evanston, Ill.: Northwestern University Press, 1966.

Gist, Margaret A. *Love and War in the Middle English Romances*. Philadelphia: University of Pennsylvania Press, 1947.

Greenfield, Stanley. "The Formulaic Expression of the Theme of Exile in Anglo-Saxon Poetry." *Speculum* 30 (1955), 200–206.

Gummere, Francis B. "The Sister's Son in the English and Scottish Popular Ballads." In *An English Miscellany for Dr. Furnivall*, ed. Walter P. Ker, A. S. Napier, and W. W. Skeat, pp. 133–149. Oxford: Clarendon Press, 1901.

Hainsworth, J. B. "Structure and Content in Epic Formula: The Question of the Unique Expression." *Classical Quarterly* 14 (1964), 155–164.

Howard, George Elliott. *A History of Matrimonial Institutions*. 3 vols. Chicago: University of Chicago Press, 1904.

Hume, Katharyn. "The Formal Nature of Middle English Romance." *PQ* 53 (1974), 158–180.

Jakobson, R., and P. Bogatyrev. "Die Folklore als eine besondere Form des Schaffens." In *Donum Natalicium Schrijnen*, pp. 900–931. Nijmegan-Utrecht, 1929.

Ker, W. P. *Epic and Romance: Essays on Medieval Literature*. New York: Dover, 1957.

Kilgour, R. L. *Decline of Chivalry, as Shown in the French Literature of the Late Middle Ages*. Cambridge, Mass.: Harvard University Press, 1937.

Kratins, Ojars. "The Middle English *Amis and Amiloun*: Chivalric Romance or Secular Hagiography?" *PMLA* 81 (1966), 347–354.

———. "Treason in the Middle English Metrical Romances." *PQ* 45 (1966), 668–688.

Loomis, Laura Hibbard. "The Auchinleck Manuscript and a Possible London Bookshop of 1330–1340." *PMLA* 57 (1942), 595–627.

———. *Medieval Romance in England: A Study of the Sources and Analogues of the Non-Cyclic Metrical Romances*. New York: B. Franklin, 1960.

Loomis, Roger Sherman. *Arthurian Legends in Medieval Art*. London: Oxford University Press, 1938.

———. *Arthurian Tradition and Chrétien de Troyes*. New York: Columbia University Press, 1949.

———. "Chivalric and Dramatic Imitations of Arthurian Romance." In *Medieval Studies in Memory of A. K. Porter*, pp. 79–97. Cambridge, Mass.: Harvard University Press, 1960.

Lord, Albert B. *The Singer of Tales*. Cambridge, Mass.: Harvard University Press, 1960.

Magoun, F. P., Jr. "Oral Formulaic Character of Anglo-Saxon Poetry." *Speculum* 28 (1953), 446–467.

———. "The Theme of the Beasts of Battle in Anglo-Saxon Poetry." *Neuphilologische Mitteilungen* 69 (1968), 81–90.

Mehl, Dieter. *The Middle English Romance of the Thirteenth and Fourteenth Centuries*. London: Barnes and Noble, 1969.

Nagler, Michael N. *Spontaneity and Tradition: A Study in the Oral Art of Homer*. Berkeley: University of California Press, 1974.

———. "Towards a Generative View of the Oral Formula." *Transactions and Proceedings of the American Philological Association* 98 (1967), 269–311.

Nitze, William A. "The Sister's Son and the Conte del Graäl." *MP* 9 (1912), 291–322.

Nutt, Alfred. "The Aryan Expulsion-and-Return Formula in the Folk and Hero Tales of the Celts." *Folk-Lore Record* 4 (1881), 1–44.

———. *The Legends of the Holy Grail*. London: D. Nutt, 1902.

Ohmann, Richard. *Shaw: The Style and the Man*. Middletown, Conn.: Wesleyan University Press, 1962.

O'Neil, W. "Oral-Formulaic Structure in Old English Elegiac Poetry." Ph.D. dissertation, University of Wisconsin, 1960.

Ong, Walter J. "Oral Residue in Tudor Prose Style." *PMLA* 80 (1965), 145–154.

Parry, Milman. Review of Walter Arend, *Die Typischen Scenen bei Homer*. *Classical Philology* 31 (1936), 357–360.

———. "Studies in the Epic Technique of Oral Verse-Making, I: Homer and Homeric Style." *Harvard Studies in Classical Philology* 41 (1930), 73–197.

———. "Studies in the Epic Technique of Oral Verse-Making, 2: The Homeric Language as the Language of an Oral Poetry." *Harvard Studies in Classical Philology* 43 (1932), 1–50.

Petit-Dutaillis, C. *Feudal Monarchy in France and England*. New York: Barnes and Noble, 1964.

Phillpotts, Bertha. *Kindred and Clan in the Middle Ages*. Cambridge: The University Press, 1913.

Potter, M. A. *Sohrab and Rustem: The Epic Theme of a Combat between Father and Son*. London: D. Nutt, 1902.

Puryear, Leslie. "A Structural Approach to the Middle English Non-cyclic Metrical Romance." Ph.D. dissertation, Vanderbilt University, 1968.

Renoir, Alain. "Oral-Formulaic Theme Survival: A Possible Instance in the 'Niebelungenlied.'" *Neuphilologische Mitteilungen* 65 (1964), 70–75.

———. "Oral Theme and Written Text." *Neuphilologische Mitteilungen* 77 (1976), 337–346.

Richards, F. J. "Cross Cousin Marriage in South India." *Man* 14 (1914), 194–198.

Russo, James A. "A Closer Look at Homeric Formulas." *Transactions and Proceedings of the American Philological Association* 94 (1963), 235–247.

Rychner, J. *La Chanson de Geste*. Société de Publications Romanes et Francaises 53. Geneva: Librairie E. Droz, 1955.

Sandoz, Edouard. "Tourneys in the Arthurian Tradition." *Speculum* 19 (1944), 389–420.

Sands, Donald. *Middle English Verse Romances*. New York: Holt, Rinehart and Winston, 1966.

Severs, J., ed. *A Manual of the Writings in Middle English, 1050–1500*. New Haven: Yale University Press, 1967.

Sklar, Elizabeth S. "'The Battle of Maldon' and the Popular Tradition: Some Rhymed Formulas." *PQ* 54 (Spring 1975), 409–418.

Slover, Clark. "*Sir Degare*, a Study of a Medieval Hack Writer's Methods." *University of Texas Bulletin, Studies in English* 11 (1931), 5–23.

Smith, Charles Edward. *Papal Enforcement of Some Medieval Marriage Laws*. New Orleans: Louisiana State University Press, 1940.

Spiers, John. "'Wynnere and Wastoure' and 'The Parlement of the Thre Ages.'" *Scrutiny* 17, no. 3 (1950), 221–252.

Stevick, Robert D. *Five Middle English Narratives*. Indianapolis and New York: Bobbs-Merrill, 1967.

———. "The Oral-Formulaic Analysis of Old English Verse." *Speculum* 37 (1962), 382–389.

Thompson, Stith. *Motif-Index of Folk Literature*. Bloomington: Indiana University Press, 1955–1958.

Turville-Petre, Thorlac. "Humphrey de Bohun and *William of Palerne*." *Neuphilologische Mitteilungen* 75 (1974), 250–252.

von Hahn, J. G. *Sagwissenschaftliche Studien*. Jena: F. Mauke, 1871.

Waldron, R. A. "Oral-Formulaic Technique and Middle English Alliterative Poetry." *Speculum* 32 (1957), 792–804.

Westermarck, Edward. *The History of Human Marriage*, vol. 2. London: Macmillan, 1903.

Weston, Jessie L. *From Ritual to Romance*. Garden City, N.Y.: Doubleday, 1957.
———. *The Three Days' Tournament: A Study in Romance and Folk-lore*. London: D. Nutt, 1902.
Wittig, Susan. "Formulaic Style and the Problem of Redundancy: A Rhetorical Approach to the Study of Formulaic Functions." *Centrum* 1 (Fall 1973), 123–236.

STRUCTURAL AND LINGUISTIC THEORY

Barthes, Roland. "Introduction à l'analyse structurale des récits." *Communications* 8 (1966), 1–27.
———. "Rhétorique de l'image." *Communications* 4 (1964), 40–51.
———. *Writing Degree Zero and Elements of Semiology*. Trans. Annette Lavers and Colin Smith. Boston: Beacon Press, 1970.
Bremond, Claude. "La Logique des possibles narratifs." *Communications* 8 (1966), 60–76.
———. "Le Message narratif." *Communications* 4 (1964), 4–32.
Carpenter, Ronald H. "Stylistic Redundancy and Function in Discourse." *Language and Style* 3 (1970), 62–68.
Chabrol, Claude. *Sémiotique narrative et textuelle*. Paris: Larousse, 1973.
Chatman, Seymour. "New Ways of Analyzing Narrative Structures with an Example from Joyce's *Dubliners*." *Language and Style* 2 (1969), 3–36.
———. "On Defining Form." *New Literary History* 3 (1971), 217–228.
Cherry, Colin. *On Human Communication*. Cambridge, Mass.: MIT Press, 1957.
Chomsky, Noam. *Syntactic Structures*. The Hague: Mouton, 1969.
Doležel, Lubomír. "From Motifemes to Motifs." *Poetics* 4 (1972), 55–90.
———. "Toward a Structural Theory of Content in Prose Fiction." In *Literary Style*, ed. Seymour Chatman. London and New York: Oxford University Press, 1971.
Dorfman, Eugene. *The Nareme in the Medieval Epic and Romance: An Introduction to Narrative Structure*. University of Toronto Romance Series, No. 13. Toronto: University of Toronto, 1969.
Dundes, Alan. "From Etic to Emic Units in the Structural Study of Folktales." *Journal of American Folklore* 75 (1966), 95–105.
———. *The Morphology of North American Indian Folktales*. FF Communications 195. Helsinki, 1964.
Elson, Benjamin, and Velma Pickett. *An Introduction to Morphology and Syntax*. Huntington Beach, Calif.: Summer Institute of Linguistics, 1967.
Garner, Wendell R. *Uncertainty and Structure as Psychological Concepts*. New York: Wiley, 1962.
Greimas, A. J. "Eléments pour une théorie de l'interprétation du récit mythique." *Communications* 8 (1966), 28–59.
———. *Sémantique structurale*. Paris: Larousse, 1966.
Harris, Zellig S. "Co-occurrence and Transformation in Linguistic Structure." *Language* 33 (1957).
———. "Discourse Analysis." *Language* 28 (1952), 1–30.
Hendricks, William O. "Linguistics and Folkloristics." In *Essays on Semiolinguistics and Verbal Art*. The Hague: Mouton, 1973.
Hockett, Charles. "Two Models of Grammatical Description." *Word* 10 (1954), 210–234.
Jakobson, R. "Linguistics and Poetics." In *Style in Language*, ed. T. A. Sebeok, pp. 350–377. Cambridge, Mass.: MIT Press, 1960.

Kristeva, Julia. "Narration et transformation." *Semiotica* 1 (1969), 422–448.
Leach, Edmund R. *Genesis as Myth and Other Essays*. London: Jonathan Cape, 1969.
———, ed. *The Structural Study of Myth and Totemism*. London: Jonathan Cape, 1967.
Lévi-Strauss, Claude. "Analyse morphologique des contes russe." *International Journal of Slavic Linguistics and Poetics* 3 (1960), 122–149.
———. *The Elementary Structures of Kinship*. Trans. J. H. Bell and J. R. von Sturmer. Boston: Beacon Press, 1969.
———. *The Raw and the Cooked: An Introduction to a Science of Mythology*. Trans. John and Doreen Weightman. New York: Harper and Row, 1969.
———. "The Story of Asdiwal." In *The Structural Study of Myth and Totemism*, ed. Edmund Leach. London: Jonathan Cape, 1967.
Lipski, John. "From Text to Narrative: Spanning the Gap." *Poetics* 5 (1976), 192–205.
Longacre, Robert. *Grammar Discovery Procedures: A Field Manual*. The Hague: Mouton, 1964.
Lyons, John. *Introduction to Theoretical Linguistics*. Cambridge: Cambridge University Press, 1968.
Malmberg, Bertil. *Structural Linguistics and Human Communication*. New York: Academic Press, 1963.
Maranda, Elli, and Pierre Maranda. *Structural Analysis of Oral Tradition*. Philadelphia: University of Pennsylvania Press, 1971.
Miller, George. *Language and Communication*. New York: McGraw-Hill, 1951.
Pike, Kenneth. *Language in Relation to a Unified Theory of the Structure of Human Behavior*. The Hague: Mouton, 1967.
Propp, Vladimir. *Morphology of the Folktale*. Trans. Laurence Scott. Austin: University of Texas Press, 1968.
Rosenberg, Bruce. "The Morphology of the Middle English Metrical Romances." *Journal of Popular Culture* 1, no. 1 (Summer 1967), 63–77.
Saussure, Ferdinand de. *Course in General Linguistics*. Trans. Wade Baskin. Ed. Charles Bally and Albert Sechehaye. New York: Philosophical Library, 1959.
Schmidt, Siegfried. "Théorie et pratique d'une étude scientifique de la narrativité littéraire, à propos de 'Plume au restaurant' de Henri Michaux." In *Sémiotique narrative et textuelle*, ed. Claude Chabrol, pp. 137–160. Paris: Larousse, 1973.
Todorov, Tzvetan. "Les Catégories du récit littéraire." *Communications* 8 (1966), 125–151.
———. "La Description de la signification en littérature." *Communications* 4 (1964), 33–39.
———. *Grammaire du Décaméron*. The Hague: Mouton, 1969.
———. "Les Transformations narratives," *Poétique* 3 (1970), 322–333.
van Dijk, Teun A. "Grammaries textuelles et structures narratives." In *Sémiotique narrative et textuelle*, ed. Claude Chabrol, pp. 177–206. Paris: Larousse, 1973.
———. "Some Problems of Generative Poetics." *Poetics* 3 (1971), 5–35.
Wittig, Susan. "The Historical Development of Structuralism." *Soundings* 58, no. 2 (Summer 1975), 145–156.
———. Review of Dorfman (1969). *Language and Style* 5 (1972), 228–235.
———. "Theories of Formulaic Narrative." In *Oral Tradition and Old Testament Studies*, ed. Robert Colley, in *Semeia* (in press).
Zirmunskii, Victor. *Voprosy teorii literatury*. s'-Gravenhage: Mouton, 1962.

Index

Alliterative poetry, 16, 192
Allomotif: conditioned, 64, 68, 87; as *emic* unit, 60, 79, 196; examples of, 60, 64–65; free, 64, 68, 87. *See also* Motif
Alloscene. *See* Scene
Amis and Amiloun: construction of, 181; descriptive formulas in, 26–28; substituted heroes in, 155; substitution systems in, 130; syntagmemes in, 47–51
—*emic* units in: burning, 124; exhortation, 55, 57–58; loss of identity, 204; loss of property, 168–169, 203; love-betrayal-separation, 157–159; recognition, 174; revenge, 155, 171–173; separation-adoption, 164, 167–168; separation-restoration, 177; service, 155, 203; service-marriage, 155, 157; trial by combat, 155
Anglo-Saxon poetry, 6, 104
Asdiwal, tale of, 205, 206
Assimilation, 153

Barthes, Roland, 3, 42, 46
Bevis of Hampton: characterization in, 111; formula count in, 18; predicate formulas in, 19–20, 23–26; versions of, 200
—*emic* units in: bargaining, 110, 200; battle, 66; betrayal-rescue, 162; burning, 124; challenge, 110; combat, 91–92; death of the father, 109–111; death of the father–expulsion, 119, 121; description of the battlefield (carnage), 69–70; expulsion, 119; January-May, 109–110, 200; kidnapping, 117–118; love-betrayal-separation, 158–159; marriage, 153;

procession, 63; recognition, 174; rescue, 145; revenge, 170–173; scene-setting, 110; separation-adoption, 163–164, 166; separation-adoption-recognition-restoration, 176; service-marriage, 155–157; single-combat, 81–83; spectator, 88; threatened marriage–rescue, 162; threatened marriage–rescue–marriage, 145, 146–147
Bone Florence of Rome, Le, 124
Bookshop theory of composition, 13–14

Chanson de geste, 68, 185–186, 206
Chanson de Roland, 16
Chaucer, Geoffrey, 11, 15
—works by: *Man of Law's Tale*, 133; *Merchant's Tale*, 200; *Sir Thopas*, 192; *Troilus and Criseyde*, 196
Chevelere Assigne, 124
Chomsky, Noam, 191
Cline, Ruth Huff, 198
Closure, 195. *See also* Segmentation
Computer counts, 16–17

Discours, 61, 196
Dundes, Alan, 59, 104, 162, 195, 196

Earl of Toulous: descriptive formulas in, 27; formula count in, 18; syntagmemes in, 32–36, 39–40, 51
—*emic* units in: adultery, 124, 201; battle, 66; combat, 96; confession-promise-plan, 72–73, 77; exhortation, 56, 58; loss of property, 168, 204; loss of property–restoration, 177; prophetic dream, 201; recognition, 174; revenge, 155, 172–173;

service-marriage, 155, 157; treacherous steward, 202; trial by combat, 155
Eger and Grime: descriptive formulas in, 28; formula count in, 18; predicate formulas in, 24; substitution systems in, 31
—emic units in: arming, 85; combat, 95; prohibition, 198, 204; single combat, 198
Emare: descriptive formulas in, 27–28; formula count in, 18; predicate formulas in, 22–23, 26; transitional motifeme in, 61
—emic units in: adultery, 124; arming, 85; exile, 115, 120, 132–133, 201; incest, 130; irregular birth, 132–133; irregular birth–expulsion, 120–121, 130; recognition, 174; separation-adoption, 163, 165–166; separation-adoption-recognition-restoration, 176; service, 155, 203; service-marriage, 156–157; threatened marriage, 162
Emic units: concept of, 8, 40, 191, 193, 195; and the episode, 135; and the motif, 104; and the motifeme, 59; and the scene, 136
Episode. See Type-episode
Etic units, 8, 60, 191, 193

Floris and Blancheflur: descriptive formulas in, 27–28; formula count in, 18; predicate formulas in, 21–23, 26
—emic units in: arming, 85; confession-promise-plan, 72–75, 76, 77–78; recognition, 174; threatened marriage–rescue, 154–155; threatened marriage–rescue–marriage, 150–151
Formalists, Russian, 3, 195–196
Formula: definitions of, 15, 17–18, 29, 36; descriptive, 19, 26–28; and meter, 29–32; predicate, 19–26; and redundance, 19; in statistical counts, 17, 19; and syntax, 32–36. See also Syntagmeme
Formulaic action. See Formula, predicate
Formulaic language: composition of, 15–16, 37–41, 65, 106; and cultural beliefs, 45–46, 65, 160; function of, 41–46, 125–126. See also Oral-formulaic theory; Redundance
Fry, Donald, 104–105
Frye, Northrop, 5, 183

Generides
—emic units in: arming, 84–85, 87–88, 91; bargaining, 200; combat, 93–94, 96; confession-promise-plan, 71, 72–73, 74, 77–78; council, 67–68; death of the father, 112; exile, 120, 200; expulsion, 131; irregular birth, 131; irregular birth–expulsion, 120–121, 131; love-betrayal-separation, 158–159; marriage, 153; procession, 63; recognition, 174; rescue, 152; separation-adoption, 164, 166; separation-adoption-recognition-restoration, 176; spectator, 89–90; threatened marriage–rescue–marriage, 144, 145, 146–147
Gower, John, 11
Grammar: generative, 180; phrase-structure, 191; transformational, 180, 204–205
—tagmemic: definition of, 7–8, 37–38; and emic units, 38, 40, 59–60; methods of, 6–7; and poetic composition, 37–41; and slots, 38, 106; and variants, 114
Guillaume de Palerne, 20–21, 111
Guy of Warwick: predicate formulas in, 23; substituted heroes in, 155
—emic units in: arming, 84; combat, 92, 95–97; council, 67–68; disguise, 152; kidnapping, 118, 120; love-marriage, 176; procession, 62–63; recognition, 174; reward, 97; separation-adoption, 163–164; separation-adoption-recognition-restoration, 176; service-marriage, 155–156; threatened marriage–rescue–marriage, 145, 150–151, 155

Havelok: descriptive formulas in, 28; formula count in, 18; predicate formulas in, 24; stanzaic development in, 52–63
—emic units in: arming, 197; battle, 66–67; council, 68; death of the father, 200–201; death of the father–expulsion, 119, 121; description of the battlefield (carnage), 69; exhortation, 55–56, 58; kidnapping, 117, 118, 119; recognition, 174; revenge, 170–173; separation-adoption, 165–167; separation-adoption-recognition-restoration, 176; threat, 68
Histoire, 62, 196
Homeric narrative, 6, 103–104
Horn Child and Maiden Rimenhild, 18, 66

Ipomedon: predicate formulas in, 24; slot patterns in, 38–39; substitution system in, 31; three-day tournament in, 197; transitional motifeme in, 61
—*emic* units in: arming, 87; combat, 91–92; disguise, 152; reward, 98; service-marriage, 156–157; spectator, 89; threatened marriage–rescue–marriage, 150–151

Jakobson, Roman, 7, 179, 181

King Alisaunder, 199
King Horn: characterization in, 109; formula count in, 18; slots in, 142–143; structure of, 137–143; versions of, 137
—*emic* units in: arrival-disguise, 142; battle, 109; betrayal, 141; betrayal-separation, 162; birth of the child, 109; challenge, 109; combat, 106–109; death of the father, 106–109, 112–113, 200; death of the father–expulsion, 119, 121; exile, 113–114, 119; hero on the beach, 200; loss of property, 187–188; love, 141; love-betrayal-separation, 157–159; love-marriage, 162; prophetic dream, 137, 143; recognition, 174–175; rescue, 157; restoration, 141; revelation of identity, 142; revenge, 141, 169–173; scene-setting, 109; separation, 141; separation-adoption, 163–164; separation-adoption-love, 141; separation-adoption-recognition-restoration, 176; service, 170; service-marriage, 155–157; slaying, 142; threatened marriage, 141, 142; threatened marriage–rescue, 139–140, 141–143, 162; threatened marriage–rescue–marriage, 143–145, 146–147; warning, 142
Knight of Curtesy, The, 124

Lai le freine: analogues of, 129; formula count in, 18
—*emic* units in: adultery, 128–129; exile, 120, 129; irregular birth–expulsion, 120–121, 127–129; recognition, 174; separation-adoption, 165–166; separation-adoption-recognition-restoration, 176; twins, 128
Langue, 41–42
Leach, Edmund, 8, 125–126, 134

Lévi-Strauss, Claude, 3, 6–8, 182–183, 185–188, 206
Libeaus Desconus: author of, 192; formula count in, 18; predicate formulas in, 24–25
—*emic* units in: adoption, 186; combat, 94–97; exile, 120, 132, 202; irregular birth, 120, 122–123; irregular birth–expulsion, 120–122; marriage, 206; procession, 62; prohibition, 198; recognition, 174; reward, 98–99; separation-adoption, 164; separation-adoption-recognition-restoration, 176; spectator, 89; threatened marriage–rescue–marriage, 144, 145, 150–151
Linguistics, 3–9. *See also* Grammar, tagmemic
Linking: of episodes, 141, 143–144, 157, 162; of scenes, 131, 133–135
Linking patterns: 179, 183–184, 186, 188–189, 203
Loomis, Laura Hibbard, 12–14, 130, 192
Lord, Albert B.: formula defined by, 15; motif defined by, 19, 104; and oral-formulaic studies, 7, 16; substitution system of, 37, 106; theme defined by, 19, 103
Lydgate, John, 199

Marriage: by capture, 205; of choice (*swayamvara*), 188–189; and kinship, 186–187, 206; and matriarchy, 205–206; in the Middle Ages, 186–187; and patrimony, 134; and property, 207; by purchase, 205
Matriarchy, 184–186, 206
Middle Ages: and feudalism, 206; literacy in, 192; marriage customs in, 203, 206–207; social classes in, 189; tournaments in, 91, 197–198
Mode: distributive, 193; feature, 60, 193, 195; manifestation, 193
Morte Arthur, Le, 124
Motif: definitions of, 19, 59–60, 104, 195, 196, 199. *See also* Motifeme
—examples of: adultery, 126, 128–129; beasts of battle, 104; exile, 125; exile-return, 183; expulsion, 202; hero on the beach, 104, 199–200; incest, 154, 198–199, 201; incest–death of the father, 133; interdiction-violation-villainy,

204; irregular birth, 201, 203; January-May, 200; loss of identity, 187; loss of property, 187; marriage by capture, 203, 205; prophetic dream, 137, 141; recognition by token, 174; supernatural strength of child, 132; task, 155; treacherous steward, 201; twins, 124–125, 128

Motifeme: conditioned, 105, 115; definition of, 59–60, 80, 196, 198–199; of the *discours*, 61–62; free, 105, 115; of the *histoire*, 62; ordering, 64–65, 101, 105; and slots, 100–101, 120; transitional, 61; variants of (allomotifs), 80. *See also* Motif

—examples of: arming, 88, 90, 196; battle, 65, 109; birth of the child, 109; carnage, 69–70; challenge, 97, 109; combat, 91–97; confession, 70–76, 78; council, 67–68; death of the father, 106–113; description of the battlefield, 69–70; exhortation, 58–61; expulsion, 133; incestuous father, 133; innocent persecuted wife, 133; irregular birth, 133; knight in disguise, 173; plan, 70, 75, 77, 78, 79; prayer, 58, 60; procession, 62, 64; prohibition, 97, 198; promise, 70, 73, 75, 77, 78, 79; reward, 97–101; scene-setting, 107, 109; substituted letters, 133; synopsis, 58, 60

Myth: of Asdiwal, 206; and cultural beliefs, 181–182; function of, 125–126, 206; levels of, 182, 187–188; and marriage of choice (*swayamvara*), 188–189; and patrimony, 134; primitive, 183; and the romance, 183

Narrative, Middle English. *See* Romance, Middle English
Narrative units. *See* Motif; Motifeme; Scene; Type-episode; Type-scene

Octavian: descriptive formulas in, 27–28; formula count in, 18; predicate formulas in, 22, 25
—*emic* units in: arming, 85–86, 88; bargaining, 200; burning, 124; combat, 94–97; confession-promise-plan, 70–71, 72–73, 77; description of the battlefield, 69–70; exhortation, 56–58; exile, 132; irregular birth, 119, 121, 123–125; ir-

regular birth–expulsion, 119, 121, 123–125; kidnapping, 116, 118, 119; recognition, 174–175; revenge, 170–172; separation-adoption, 165–167; separation-adoption-recognition-restoration, 176; spectator, 90; twins, 124–125

Oral-formulaic theory, 6, 15, 181, 193
Oral poetry: composition of, 16, 43, 181; origins of, 16; performance of, 14–15, 42, 192; techniques of, 37, 53–54, 125–126; transmission of, 15; and written texts, 54, 141

Parole, 41–42
Parry, Milman: formula defined by, 15, 17–18, 25, 29; and oral-formulaic studies, 7, 16; and substitution system, 30, 37; theme defined by, 19; and type-scene analysis, 104
Partonope of Blois
—*emic* units in: council, 68; disguise, 152; prohibition, 198, 204; prohibition-violation-restitution, 161; recognition, 174; threatened marriage–rescue–marriage, 150–151
Patriarchy, 184–186, 206
Pike, Kenneth, 6, 8, 37
Potter, Murray, 183–186, 188
Propp, Vladimir, 6, 153, 195, 199–200, 204

Rationalization: definition of, 202; of fairy-tale characters, 162; of motifs, 130, 154, 185–186, 198; of myth, 183; of narrative structures, 144, 177
Redundance: and formulaic structures, 15, 18, 41–43, 126; function of, 13–15, 43–45, 160, 181; in Middle English romance, 5, 12, 16, 18; of myth, 125–126, 134; as oral technique, 14, 43, 125–126; and theories of poetic composition, 13–15, 194
Reinbroun. See Guy of Warwick
Rewriting rules, 160–161, 191
Romance, Greek, 204
Romance, Middle English: and authorial collaboration, 13–15; character development in, 28, 200; composition of, 13–15, 42–46; construction of, 179–180; and cultural beliefs, 7, 65, 133–134, 182, 189–190; dialogue in, 20–21; and folktales, 201; formulaic quality of,

18–19, 179–180; hero's identity in, 87; hero's patrimony in, 134; imagery in, 12, 70, 196; loss of identity in, 173; marriage in, 134, 186–188, 207; and matriarchy, 186; metrical forms of, 5, 29–36, 53; and oral tradition, 13–16, 20, 181, 192, 194; and patriarchy, 185; plot structure of, 162–163, 177–178, 182, 184; and primitive myth, 183; prohibition in, 198; ritualistic action in, 24–26; ritualistic language in, 22–24, 43–46; and social order, 183; syntax of, 32–36; tournaments in, 198; treason in, 204; treatment of time in, 203; treatment of villains in, 173; as written product, 13, 192

Roman courtois, 20–21

Roswall and Lillian: formula count in, 18
—*emic* units in: arming, 87; disguise, 152; recognition, 174; reward, 198; separation-adoption, 164–166; separation-adoption-recognition-restoration, 176; service-marriage, 156–157; threatened marriage–rescue–marriage, 145, 146–147

Saga, Icelandic, 169

Saussure, Ferdinand de, 36, 41–42

Scene: analysis of, 103–105; construction of, 103, 109–110, 115–116; definitions of, 81, 103–106; as *emic* unit, 103–105. *See also* Type-scene

Segmentation, 79–80, 131, 136–137, 196

Siege of Thebes, 199

Sir Amadace: formula count in, 18
—*emic* unit in: loss of property, 168, 177, 204

Sir Cleges, 204

Sir Degare: assimilation in, 153–154; descriptive formulas in, 27; formula count in, 18; predicate formulas in, 26; sympathy for women in, 202
—*emic* units in: arming, 54; combat, 93, 96; exile, 120; incest, 129–131, 154, 199, 201; irregular birth, 129–131; irregular birth–expulsion, 120, 121; rape, 129–131; recognition, 131, 154, 174–175; rescue, 152, 154; reward, 97, 100, 198; separation-adoption, 165–166; separation-adoption-recognition-restoration, 176; service, 206; spectator, 89; threat-

ened marriage, 162; threatened marriage–rescue–marriage, 145, 148–149

Sir Degrevant: formula count in, 18
—*emic* units in: arming, 83, 85; confession-promise-plan, 72–73, 74–75, 76, 77, 78; exhortation, 54–55, 58; loss of property, 168, 177, 204; rescue, 152; reward, 97, 198; threatened marriage–rescue–marriage, 145, 148–149

Sir Eger, Sir Grahme, and Sir Gray-steele, 96

Sir Eglamour of Artois: assimilation in, 153–154; descriptive formulas in, 28; formula count in, 18, 22; predicate formulas in, 22; slot patterns in, 39; substitution system in, 81
—*emic* units in: arming, 87–88; bargaining, 200; combat, 97, 198; confession-promise-plan, 72–73, 75–76, 77; exhortation, 54, 58, 62; exile, 119, 201; incest, 199, 201; irregular birth, 119, 121, 123; irregular birth–expulsion, 119, 121; kidnapping, 118, 119; procession, 63; recognition, 87–88, 154, 174; rescue, 154; revenge, 171–172; reward, 98, 100, 198; separation-adoption, 163, 165; separation-restoration, 176; service, 162, 206; service-marriage, 155–156; spectator, 89; task, 155; threatened marriage–rescue–marriage, 148–149

Sir Gawain and the Green Knight, 85

Sir Gowther: three-day tournament in, 197; versions of, 212
—*emic* units in: arming, 87; disguise, 152; exile, 120, 131–132, 202; irregular birth, 131–132, 202; irregular birth–expulsion, 120–121; recognition, 174; separation-adoption-recognition-restoration, 176; threatened marriage–rescue–marriage, 145, 150–151

Sir Isumbras: formula count in, 18; predicate formulas in, 23–25; slots in, 33
—*emic* units in: exhortation, 55, 58; loss of identity, 204; loss of property, 168–169, 177; prayer (exhortation), 60; recognition, 174; reward, 198

Sir Landeval, 18

Sir Launfal: formula count in, 18
—*emic* units in: arming, 83; loss of property, 168, 204; prohibition, 198, 204;

prohibition-violation-restitution, 161–162; recognition, 175

Sir Orfeo, 150–151

Sir Perceval of Galles: analogues of, 202; descriptive formulas in, 28; formula count in, 18

—*emic* units in: adoption, 186; death of the father, 109, 112–113; death of the father–expulsion, 119, 121; exile, 114–115, 119, 132, 202; rescue, 152; revenge, 171–172; separation-adoption, 164; separation-adoption-recognition-restoration, 176; single combat, 108–109; threatened marriage–rescue–marriage, 145, 148–149

Sir Torrent of Portyngale: assimilation in, 153–154; descriptive formulas in, 26–28; formula count in, 18; predicate formulas in, 24

—*emic* units in: bargaining, 200; exile, 119, 201; incest, 199, 201; irregular birth, 119, 121–123; irregular birth-expulsion, 119, 121–123; kidnapping, 118, 119; love-marriage, 176; recognition, 154, 174; rescue, 152, 154; revenge, 171; reward, 99–100, 198; separation-adoption, 163, 165–166; separation-restoration, 176; service, 162, 206; service-marriage, 155–156; single combat, 198; task, 155; threatened marriage–rescue–marriage, 144, 145, 148–149

Sir Triamour: descriptive formulas in, 28; formula count in, 18; predicate formulas in, 25–26; transitional motifemes in, 61

—*emic* units in: adultery, 126–127; arming, 85, 87; combat, 91, 93; disguise, 152; exhortation, 57–58, 60; irregular birth-expulsion, 120–121, 126–128; prayer (exhortation), 60; prohibition, 198; recognition, 174; rescue, 152; revenge, 171–172; reward, 98; separation-adoption, 165–167; separation-adoption-recognition-restoration, 176; spectator, 88, 90; threatened marriage–rescue–marriage, 145, 146–149; treacherous steward, 202

Slot: definition of, 38, 195; optional or obligatory, 58, 60–79, 106

Slot-class theory, 118–120, 193, 199

Slot patterns, 38–42, 47–51, 53

Slot sequence, 58–59, 116

Sohrab and Rustem, story of, 184–186

Squyr of Lowe Degre: formula count in, 18; predicate formulas in, 24

—*emic* units in: exile, 203–204; love-betrayal-separation, 158–159; revenge, 172; service-marriage, 155–156

Stanza, 9, 47–54

Structuralism, 7–8, 9, 115, 202–203

Structuralists, French, 3, 7, 61

Substitution system: concept of, 17, 29–30, 36–37, 106; examples of, 30–32

Swayamvara (marriage by choice), 188–189

Syntagm, 41, 163

Syntagmeme, 40–42, 47–54. *See also* Formula; Slot

Theme, 19, 103–105. *See also* Motif

Tournament, three-day, 87, 152, 197

Type-episode: definition of, 106, 135–137; organization of, 135

—examples of: adoption, 138–139, 141, 163, 168, 176; betrayal, 138, 141; betrayal-separation, 162; loss of property, 168–169; loss of property-restoration, 177; love, 138–139, 141, 144; love-betrayal-separation, 157–161; love-marriage, 162–163, 175–179, 182; marriage, 140, 145, 153, 155, 175; prohibition-violation-restitution, 161–162; recognition, 140, 173–176; recognition-restoration-marriage, 173–175; rescue, 145, 147, 149, 151–153; restoration, 140, 141, 176–177; revenge, 140, 141, 155, 169–173, 176; separation, 106, 138, 139, 141, 159, 163, 167–169, 176–177; separation-adoption, 163; separation-adoption-love, 141; separation-adoption-recognition-restoration, 176; separation-restoration, 175–179, 182; service, 141, 155, 162, 169–170, 206; service-marriage, 155–157; service-revenge, 138, 139, 172; threatened marriage, 145, 162, 205; threatened marriage–rescue, 139–143, 162; threatened marriage–rescue–marriage, 143–155, 161; trail by combat, 155

Type-scene: definitions of, 103–106, 135–136

—examples of: adoption, 166; death of the father, 106, 109, 121, 130, 133, 202; death of the father–expulsion, 112–121, 163; exile, 112–116, 119–120; expulsion, 106, 111–112, 114–116, 119–122, 125, 203; hero on the beach, 199–200; irregular birth, 106, 119, 121–122, 129–131, 133; irregular birth–expulsion, 106, 121–134, 159, 163, 202; kidnapping, 112, 116–120; recognition, 131; tournament, 106; villainy, 171

William of Palerne: as alliterative poem, 192; descriptive formulas in, 27–28; predicate formulas in, 20–21
—emic units in: battle, 67; confession-promise-plan, 71, 72–73, 74, 77; death of the father, 111–112; death of the father–expulsion, 119, 121; disguise, 151–152; exhortation, 58; expulsion, 111; kidnapping, 116, 119; marriage, 153; recognition, 174; rescue, 151–152; separation, 111; separation-adoption, 164, 166; separation-adoption-recognition-restoration, 176; service-marriage, 155–157; threatened marriage, 162; threatened marriage–rescue–marriage, 145, 146–147, 151

Ywayn and Gawayn: formula count in, 18
—emic units in: arming, 87; burning, 124; combat, 94–95; confession-promise-plan, 72–73, 77; procession, 62; prohibition, 198, 204; prohibition-violation-restitution, 161; recognition, 174; reward, 99–100; single combat, 198; spectator, 89; threatened marriage–rescue–marriage, 144, 150–151